THE STORY OF
BRITISH COINAGE

The Tower of London, the site of the London mint until 1810 (*Royal Mint*)

The Royal Mint, Tower Hill, 1810–1975 (*Royal Mint*)

THE
STORY
OF
BRITISH COINAGE

PETER SEABY
FRSA, FRNS

Seaby

LONDON

To MURIEL

and for

MARK, REBECCA, LUCY and KATY

© Peter Seaby
First published 1985

Typeset by Keyspools Ltd, Golborne, Lancs
and Printed in Great Britain by
Butler & Tanner Ltd, Frome, Somerset
for the publishers B. A. Seaby Ltd
8 Cavendish Square, London W1M 0AJ

Distributed by
B. T. Batsford Ltd
P. O. Box 4, Braintree, Essex CM7 7QY

ISBN 0 900 652 74 8

CONTENTS

⇒⟨⟨⟨⟩⟩⟩⇐

LIST OF FIGURES

꿏 ⚜❀ ꞔ

LIST OF MAPS

The majority of the illustrations in this book are reproduced from coins illustrated in Seaby's *Coin and Medal Bulletin* over the past ten years.

Additional illustrations have been provided by courtesy of The Royal Mint; The British Museum; The Ashmolean Museum, Oxford; The Ulster Museum, Belfast; Mr Steve Fenner; Mr David Miller; Mr Richard Lubbock. The maps were drawn by Alan Miles. References to illustrations in the text appear in bold numbers.

PREFACE

⤙❧❦❧⤚

This book is a revision and extension of a small volume, *The Story of the English Coinage*, which had begun as a series of articles published in Seaby's *Coin and Medal Bulletin* (1949–52) and which was then reprinted in book form in 1952. It has been out of print for many years. My excuse for compiling this new book is that I have repeatedly been asked for an updated version and, having recently retired from company management, I have at last had an opportunity to do something about it.

During the years immediately following the Second World War virtually the only book generally available on English coinage was George C. Brooke's *English Coins* (1932). It had been my aim to provide a short guide at a modest price which was intended primarily for the younger collector and for those relatively new to coin collecting. As such it was hoped to follow the tradition set by earlier writers such as Henry Henfrey in *A Guide to the Study and Arrangement of English Coins* (1870) and Colonel W. Stewart Thorburn in *A Guide to the Coins of Great Britain and Ireland* (1884) and by those two small but excellently written volumes, *The Story of the British Coinage* (1898) by Gertrude Rawling and *The Pleasures of English Coin Collecting* (1934) by John Shirley-Fox.

In this present volume I have substantially revised the chapters on the period prior to 1300 and on post-war coinage, I have added chapters on Scottish and Irish coinage and on the coins of the Isle of Man and the Channel Islands. In part this book will serve to supplement the information contained in Seaby's *Standard Catalogue of British Coins*, originally compiled by my father, H. ('Bert') A. Seaby, continued under my editorship and currently edited by Mr Stephen Mitchell. Though it might have been numismatically more logical to have divided the book into chapters dealing with the age of the stater, the denarius and follis, the silver penny, the groat and the shilling, etc., I have thought it preferable to retain the more traditional division into dynasties and reigns.

It is not pretended that this book supersedes Brooke's *English Coins*, mentioned above, for long considered the ideal handbook on the earlier English coinage, nor the more recent publication by Dr C. H. V. Sutherland, *English Coinage 600–1900*, and the more detailed *English Hammered Coinage* by J. J. North, the last two of which incorporate the results of recent numismatic research. However, I have endeavoured to present information gleaned from a variety of sources within a modest compass and in easily readable form.

I must acknowledge with grateful thanks the unfailing help and advice from members of the coin cabinets at the British Museum and the Ashmolean Museum, Oxford, given over many years, the helpful suggestions made by my colleagues on the staff of B. A. Seaby Ltd, information kindly supplied by Mr Graham Dyer, Librarian at the Royal Mint, and by a number of my friends and fellow members of the British Numismatic Society, though any errors are my sole responsibility. Mark Cox, my grandson, has kindly assisted in the compilation of the index. Finally I would like to thank my wife for her encouragement and patient help.

Peter Seaby
York
July 1985

INTRODUCTION

⤜⥾⥾⥾⤛

NUMISMATICS

Numismatics, the scientific study of coinage, has done much to provide evidence, often unobtainable from other sources, for building up our knowledge of the past. However, numismatics must not be looked upon as just a dry science dealing with one particular class of inanimate objects. The collecting and study of coins has developed into a most fascinating and exciting recreation for a growing number of people. There is probably no easier way of acquiring a collection of genuine antiques than by collecting coins. Coins are almost indestructible objects and even ancient coins exist in such quantities that a really interesting collection can be assembled for a moderate outlay. As the schoolboy said, when asked what he knew of the Romans, 'the Romans went about making roads and dropping coins all over the place'.

Questions regarding the period of issue of a coin which bears no date, the authority responsible for its issue, the place of issue and its area of circulation, its denominational value, the standards of weight and metal quality (fineness), and the factors governing its design and inscriptions can all be relevant subjects of research. An interesting and concise account of the techniques of numismatic research has been given by Dr Philip Grierson in *Numismatics* (OUP, 1975) in chapters on coin finds and hoards and on numismatic techniques.

Coins can be a valuable visual aid in the teaching of history. They help to bring history to life by providing us with portraits in miniature of many famous (and infamous) men and women, some of whom, for all we know, may have actually handled some of the coins in our collections. Coin collecting is an education in itself. It stimulates our curiosity, urging us to seek further information on such subjects as economic, political and social history, geography, art, heraldry, theology, lettering, architecture, metallurgy and many other things. A collector cannot begin to call himself a numismatist until he takes the trouble to study his coins and find out all that he can about them. If his sole aim is merely to increase the number of his specimens then he is only an accumulator. This book is devoted to only one section of numismatics – British coinage – although this section cannot be considered as a watertight compartment entirely cut off from outside influences. The collector of British coins would find it useful to acquire at least a rudimentary knowledge of the coins of the Ancient World and an acquaintance with the coinage of our medieval neighbours.

Before dealing with the earliest British coins it may be desirable to discuss briefly the origins of coinage and the methods of coinage manufacture.

THE ORIGINS OF COINAGE

We are so used to handling coins every day of our lives that it is difficult to imagine how we could manage without them. Yet there are still people in the more remote parts of the world who have no common unit as a medium of exchange and who rely on barter for trading with their neighbours. A system of barter can supply the needs of a primitive society quite well, but with the development of commercial contacts with other communities such a system has definite drawbacks. Someone wishing to obtain a particular commodity might find that they had nothing to offer in exchange which was of comparable value or was wanted at that time by the seller. The solution to that kind of problem was the adoption of some medium of exchange. These mediums of exchange had to be things that were fairly durable, easily portable and widely recognized as having a stable value. Many nomadic and agrarian people have used cattle as a form of currency, indeed, the Latin word for money, *pecunia*, is derived from *pecus*, meaning cattle. A variety of other objects have also been used, such as cowrie-shells, wampum, blocks of tea, beaver skins, sharks' teeth, rolls of tobacco and even large stones.

Peoples with access to metals and a knowledge of metal-working usually found that metal objects of one sort or another made the most satisfactory form of money. Before 200 BC bronze objects made in the form of miniature bridges, spades and knives were in use in China. In Sparta spits of iron were being used long after true coinage had been introduced into other parts of Greece; in Britain rings of gold and bronze may have been used as a medium of exchange before the first century BC, and until relatively recent times some of the West African tribes used metal spade-shaped objects as a form of currency. We know that gold was used in Sumer before 3000 BC, and that in Egypt, Babylonia and Assyria bars or pellets of gold, silver and copper were passed by weight as objects of value. We also know that the 'shekels' of gold and silver mentioned in the Old Testament were not coins but merely weights of bullion. It is strange that the earlier civilizations of Mesopotamia and the Nile Valley should have been unaware of the benefits of coinage, for the necessity of weighing quantities of precious metal must have made commercial dealings far more tedious than they need have been, but they did have detailed accounting systems supported by papyrus accounts and baked clay receipt tablets or tallies. It was not until the early seventh century BC that true coins made their first appearance.

Herodotus, who died in 425 BC , ascribed the introduction of gold and silver coins to the Lydians of Asia Minor. It is believed that early in the first millennium BC the Lydians and the Ionian Greeks of Western Turkey were using small lumps of 'electrum' as a form of currency. This was a natural 'white gold' alloy of roughly 75% gold and 25% silver. The first true coins were not struck until after 650 BC, probably at Sardis, the capital city of the kings of Lydia. What are probably the earliest coins were bean-shaped *staters* of electrum of standard weight and they are only distinguishable from the earlier electrum lumps by having two to three incuse depressions hammered into one side with rough punches. A further development was the use of an engraved lower 'die' which impressed a design, or type, into the underside of the coin at the same time that the upper side received the impression of the moneyer's puncheon, these marks being a guarantee of the correct quality.

The art of coining soon spread to the Aegean Islands and the mainland of Greece. The majority of types chosen were either the heads of local deities or of animals that had been adopted as the badges of the city or state. Some of the types commonly met with are the head of Pallas Athene and the little owl of Athens (**1**), the winged horse (Pegasos) of Corinth, the turtle of Aegina (**2**), the shield of the Thebans, the rose of Rhodes and the bee or stag of Ephesos. These emblems served to distinguish the coins of one city state from another and they provided a guarantee that the coins were of the proper quality or 'fineness'.

1 Athens, mid 5th cent. BC Æ tetradrachm   2 Aegina, 6th – 5th cent. BC Æ triobol

From the city states of the Greek mainland the art of coining spread westward to the Greek colonies in the Adriatic, southern Italy, Sicily and beyond, eastward to Cyprus, Phoenicia and Persia, northward to the Black Sea and southward to Egypt and the Greek settlements along the North African coast. By the beginning of the fifth century BC most coins were being made with a type impressed on both sides and this was done by engraving a design on the moneyer's punch, or upper die, as well as on his lower die. At the end of the fifth century BC, when Greek art was approaching its zenith, superb examples of the art of die-engraving were being produced by some of the finer artists of the time. Fifteen hundred years later Norman moneyers were still striking coins by the same simple method.

By the end of the fourth century BC Greek coins had reached India, taken there by Alexander the Great's conquering armies, though crude punch-marked pieces of silver, *karshapana*, had developed independently throughout northern India. To the north and west were the Celtic tribes of central and western Europe who were continually exerting pressure on their more sophisticated Mediterranean neighbours. These Celtic peoples became familiar with and soon copied the coins of the northern Greeks. Philip II of Macedon (366-359), the father of Alexander, had had vast quantities of gold staters (**3**) and silver tetradrachms minted from the rich mines of Philippi and other places in eastern Macedonia, and it was these Macedonian staters, or 'Philippi' as they came to be called, which were most frequently copied by the Celts of central Europe and northern Gaul. In the Danube basin, northern Italy and southern Gaul it was primarily silver coins that were imitated. It was from Gaul that traders and migrating tribes brought coins to Britain some time during the second century BC.

3 Macedon, Philip II, 359–336 BC, *N* stater

DIES AND DIE-MAKING

The operations of minting, whether of ancient, medieval or modern coins, can be separated into three main processes: the making of the dies, the preparation of the coinage 'blanks' and the actual striking of the coins.

It has already been explained how punches or dies were used to mark ancient coins. The pair of dies illustrated (Figure 1) were made for striking thin twelfth-century English silver pennies. They consist of two bars of

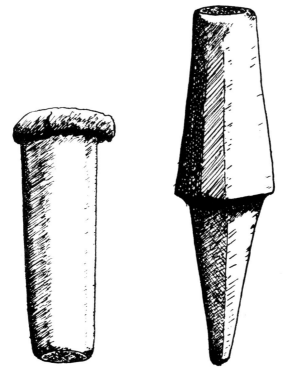

Figure 1 A pair of medieval dies

wrought iron several inches long and tapering slightly towards their working surfaces. The lower die, known as the 'pile', was given a spike at the bottom so that it could be fixed into a heavy block of wood when in use. The upper die, called the 'trussel', has a flattened head for taking the shock of the hammer blows. The working surfaces of the dies were filed flat and a design was then cut into them by the engraver or die-sinker. In ancient times, when coins were thick and made from rounded lumps of metal, the lower die was often made slightly concave to prevent the metal blank from rolling off before it was struck and to ease the flow of metal under pressure. In medieval and later periods this was not necessary as coins were thinner and were struck from flat blanks. Not all coin dies were of the simple type illustrated here: it is known that some ancient dies were hinged to ensure that both trussel and pile were in alignment when the coin was struck, while others, for the same reason, had a raised rim around the head of the pile into which the trussel fitted or else had pegs and sockets which fitted into each other.

When a moneyer was supplied with dies it was usually in the proportion of two or even three trussels to each pile as it was estimated that, on average, the pile lasted over twice as long as the trussel which received the main shock of the hammer blows. It was because the lower die normally had a longer life that the obverse design was usually engraved on that side, the 'head' side of the coin tending to require the more skilled and careful engraving. It has been estimated that a set of early dies could strike something between 10,000 and 20,000 coins before being worn out, unless a flaw in the metal resulted in an early fracture.

Though we normally speak of dies being 'engraved', designs could also be punched into the dies with punches of various shapes; when designs and lettering were somewhat crude only a few punches were needed. On some Celtic, Anglo-Saxon and Norman coins most of the design and lettering could be made from punches shaped to a pellet, wedge, crescent and short line, any other marks being made with a gouge or graving tool. By the end of the thirteenth century larger and more intricate punches were being used, one punch making a complete letter and other punches providing the king's crown, his face, his side locks of hair and his drapery. Later still, in the reign of Henry VII, the complete portrait of the king was sunk into the die with a single punch. By the latter half of the sixteenth century die-making had become a more complex and accurate craft.

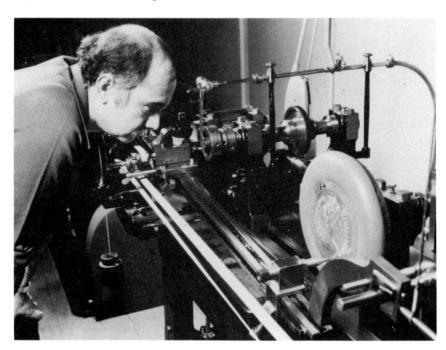

Figure 2 A reducing machine in the die-making department of the Royal Mint (*Royal Mint*)

Today new designs are no longer cut into metal dies by the engraver. The artist now has to prepare an enlarged plaster model of his design, six to ten inches (15–25 cm) in diameter, and from this a metal reproduction is made. A reducing machine (Figure 2) operating on a beam-and-fulcrum principle, with a tracer at one end of the beam which can move all over the large model and a revolving metal cutter at the short end, transfers the design onto a 'reduction punch' of the correct size. If the die is a very small one the reduction can be completed in two stages. From the reduction punch an incuse master matrix is struck, from this come working puncheons, which in turn will produce the coinage dies. This may seem a complicated process, but it is necessary owing to the vast quantities of coins produced every year and the large number of dies that are required. At the end of the year, assuming that the design is to remain the same, the last numeral of the date is removed from one of the working punches. A new matrix is then made into which the final figure of the new date is sunk, and from this new working puncheons and dies are struck. This ensures the continuity of the design. Modern coinage dies of medium size will strike on average 200,000 to 300,000 coins before they have to be replaced.

EARLY COIN MANUFACTURE

It has been explained briefly above how ancient coins were minted. To all intents and purposes the method of manufacture remained unaltered until the sixteenth century. Until 1816 the intrinsic metal value of English gold and silver coins was roughly equal to their face value. It is true that there were one or two attempts at debasement, but, generally speaking, the quality (fineness) of the English coinage, from Anglo-Saxon times until the present century, was of a particularly high standard and the envy of many of our continental neighbours. One of the first essentials, therefore, was the testing and, if neccessary, the refining of precious metal before it was made into coin. At one time gold was checked by a touchstone with trial plates of gold of a known standard to see if the colour was the same, but fairly accurate methods of quantitative analysis, or assay, had been introduced by the thirteenth century and the touchstone was therefore abandoned.

Blanks for coins were occasionally cast in moulds. Usually metal was either hammered into thin plates out of which round blanks were punched or cut or made into bars of roughly the same diameter as the coins, the bars then being sliced into blanks which were trimmed to roughly the correct weight. The sixteenth-century mint workshop illustrated (Figure 3) depicts the furnace in which the coinage metal is melted down; one workman is marking circles on a thin sheet of metal on an anvil, to the left another workman is cutting out and trimming the blanks with a pair of shears, whilst on the right the minter is striking coins from blanks which the apprentice places on the lower die. In the foreground is a chest, or pyx, into which there had to be placed a fixed proportion of coins from each batch to be minted. These were to be assayed before a jury of worthy citizens at a latter date. Supervising the operations is the mintmaster.

Figure 3 A sixteenth-century mint workshop (from an old French print)

It is not certain when the screw-press was first applied to the minting of coins, but it is known that in 1550 the French secretly acquired the inventions of a German engineer in Augsburg and that in 1551 a mechanical mint was installed at Paris on the Ile du Palais. Water power from the Seine actuated rolling mills for rolling out bars of metal to a uniform thickness and also machines for punching out blanks and for stamping the blanks with the impressions from the dies. Though handsome and precisely struck gold and silver coins were produced these proved to be more expensive to mint than hand-hammered coins and there was considerable opposition to the new techniques from the guild of moneyers.

It was early in the reign of Elizabeth I that coins were first struck by machinery in England, though rolling mills may have been in use before that time. Although a better shaped coin could be produced, the machines were found to be defective, or so they were reported to be by the officers of the mint who were prejudiced against them. The new method of manufacture was therefore temporarily abandoned. Machine-made coins were minted again for a time during the reign of Charles I but it was not until 1662 that machine manufacture finally superseded the hand-hammering method.

The early rolling mills were driven either by horse or water power and the term 'milled money' came to be applied to any coins produced by machinery, coins made by the older method being known as 'hammered money'. After bars of metal had been dragged through the rolling mills, being reduced in the process to thin strips of nearly the thickness of the finished coin, they were passed through the blank-cutting machine where a sharp punch with an inclined face forced out the circular blanks. As the blanks became curved in the cutting-process they were flattened again by a heavy drop hammer. Blanks were weighed individually before being struck. If they were much under weight they were rejected and if too heavy they were filed across their surface until they came within the prescribed limits. Remains of the file marks can sometimes be seen on the milled gold and silver coins of the seventeenth and eighteenth centuries. Another common flaw in coins of this period is 'flecking' of the flan which was caused by small air bubbles that were trapped in the ingots of coinage metal. If the upper part of the ingots was not cut off and rejected before going through the rolling mill the bubbles would be elongated and cause a slight but unsightly roughening of the surface of the coin.

So long as coins were made by the hand-hammering method they were always liable to suffer from clipping, particularly as they were seldom circular in shape. With the introduction of machine-made blanks and coining presses coins could be produced that were perfectly circular. The clippers were not finally defeated, however, until coins were made with graining or lettering around the edge. There were two methods employed for marking the edges of coins during the seventeenth century. The first method was to mark the edge at the moment of striking. This was done by using a solid collar around the lower die inside of which there fitted a detachable inner collar made up of one or more steel strips engraved with an inscription. On being struck the metal of the blank spread out and flowed into all the hollows in both dies and collar. Every time a coin was

struck the inner collar had to be removed to release the coin and it then had
to be re-assembled which cut down the speed of production. The other
method employed for marking the edge was to use a special edge-marking
machine, the 'castaing' machine, which formed the edge of the blanks
before they went into the minting press. In this machine one or more blanks
were placed edgeways between steel bars engraved in intaglio with an
inscription or graining. One bar was fixed and the other, which was forced
against the blanks with strong springs, was moved forward for the length
of the inscription, thus impressing the edge of the blanks with the required
markings. After 1816 the graining on the edge was formed at the moment
of striking by means of a steel collar with a grained wall or, if raised
lettering had to be put on the edge, a split collar of three segments was used
which opened after the coin had been struck.

We do not know what the earliest screw-press used in this country was
like, but the eighteenth-century minting press had the lower die fixed to its
base whilst the upper die moved up and down in guide plates at the lower
end of the screw shaft (Figure 4). Two arms with heavy weights at the ends
were fixed to the top of the screw and a team of labourers heaved on the
thongs attached to the ends of the arms, thus spinning the loaded screw and
trussel down on to a coin blank placed on the lower die by an apprentice
crouching in a well in the floor. The screw was taken back to the top of the
press by the force of the rebound, and this gave the boy time to flick the
struck coin away and to centre another blank on the top of the pile – a
somewhat hazardous occupation! The manually operated screw press
could strike between 20 and 25 coins a minute. The exploitation of steam
power towards the end of the eighteenth century made possible great
improvements in minting techniques which will be discussed in the
appropriate chapters.

SOME TECHNICAL TERMS

Like most other subjects numismatics has its own vocabulary of technical
terms, some of which have already been mentioned above but they will
bear repetition. The front of the coin which names and usually portrays the
monarch (the 'heads' side) is called the *obverse* and the other side (the 'tails')
is the *reverse*. The main design is called the *type* and the inscription is
sometimes known as the *legend*. The flat part of the coin between the main
type and the edge is the *field* and the area below the reverse type is the
exergue, which might contain a mint signature on a Roman coin or possibly
a date on a more modern coin. The piece of shaped metal from which the
coin is to be struck is called the *blank* or *flan* (USA, 'planchet') though the
latter term is now more commonly applied to the metal surface of the coin

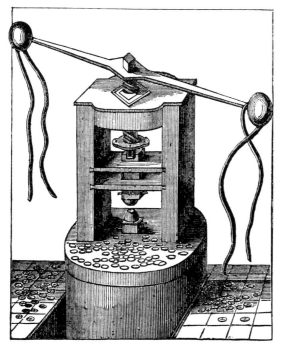

Figure 4 An eighteenth-century screw-press

after it has been struck, for instance, one might speak of 'a flaw in the flan'. The two engraved cylinders of metal with which the designs are impressed on the coin are the *dies*, the upper die being the *trussel* and the lower the *pile*. A *die variety* refers to a coin which differs from another coin of similar type through having been struck from a different die. An *issue* comprises the group of coins of a particular type struck over a certain period of time which are distinct for some reason from coins of earlier or later issues. A *mule* is a coin which has the obverse of one type or issue and a reverse of a type or issue which is not usually associated with that obverse. A *brockage* is a term which was originally applied to any mis-struck or broken coin, but which is now usually restricted to a coin which has one side struck in relief, as normal, but with the same design on the other side *incuse* (sunk in), caused by being struck by a coin lodged in one of the dies instead of by the die itself. A *restrike* is a coin stuck from original dies at some time after its proper period of issue. A *double-striking* results from some movement of a coin between the reception of more than one blow from the dies with a consequent blurring of the design. An *overstrike* occurs when an earlier coin is used as a blank and part of the design of the original coin is still visible. *Obsidional coins* are emergency pieces struck in a besieged town or castle.

Recoinage is the replacement of the coins in circulation, usually by coins of different weight or metal content.

A *mintmark* ('mm.') is some object or symbol used to distinguish coins of one mint from those of another. It is also a term used for marks to distinguish coins struck during one period of issue from those of earlier or later issues, as date marks are used on plate. These marks are more correctly termed *initial marks* as they are usually placed at the beginning of the inscriptions. *Privy marks* are secret marks inserted into the design or inscription of a coin as a security measure or for some other purpose. A *countermark* is a mark punched into a coin at a later date, usually for the purpose of altering its value. A *counterfeit* is a false copy of a genuine coin; a *concoction* is a figment of the maker's imagination.

The condition of a coin usually concerns the state of wear and tear or its lack of wear. Perfect condition is called *mint state* or, more usually, 'FDC' (from the French *fleur-de-coin*). Under modern conditions of manufacture few coins made for general circulation warrant the description 'FDC', so for a modern unused coin the description *Uncirculated* ('unc') is often applied. With virtually no easily visible imperfections, classed as *extremely fine* ('EF'), a coin in circulation will gradually deteriorate through the grades *very fine* ('VF'), *fine* ('F') to *fair* or *mediocre* and ultimately to *poor*, which means that it is practically worn flat. Occasionally one sees the terms *good* and *very good* and one needs to treat them with caution as they can usually be translated as 'bad' and 'not quite so bad'! In any case, the estimation of grading must inevitably be subjective. One really needs to know the person using the grading scale, though amongst collectors and reputable dealers there seems to be a reasonable consensus of opinion on the estimation of condition. These grades of condition are frequently qualified by *good* or *nearly*. A descriptive phrase may also be used to indicate that a coin is cracked, holed, or has had a hole plugged; is scratched or engraved; that the edge has been damaged, perhaps by having had a mount removed; that the surface has been burnished or badly cleaned, or there may be a reference to colour by toning or patination. *Lustre* describes the bright, untarnished colour of new (mainly copper or bronze) coins. When the condition of the obverse of a coin differs from that of the reverse the condition of the obverse of a coin is stated first, followed by that of the reverse, e. g. 'nearly VF/good VF'.

A *proof* is a coin that is struck from specially prepared and usually highly polished dies made as a specimen of the coinage and sold at a premium above the face value if released for public sale. At one time proofs were usually very limited in number but in recent years very large numbers are sometimes made for sale (n.b. in the United States the term 'proof' is sometimes mis-applied to the condition of a coin instead of denoting a coin struck from specially prepared dies). *Patterns* are proposed designs for a new coinage, most of which do not go into production for general circulation. A *piedfort* is a coin struck on an extra thick blank, usually as an unusual specimen for presentation purposes.

The directions *left* and *right* refer to the viewer's left and right, not that of the object being viewed. Quarters of a design are usually not numbered clockwise but in heraldic fashion: (1) top left, (2) top right, (3) bottom left and (4) bottom right. Weights of coins were and sometimes still are given in Troy grains in Great Britain and sometimes in Troy ounces or decimals thereof, though with the progressive decimilization in Britain, grammes/grams are beginning to take the place of grains, particularly in scientific publications. Grammes are, of course, the norm in many other parts of the world. Diameters are normally indicated in millimetres. The abbreviations *AV (aureus)* for gold, *AR (argentus)* for silver and *AE (aureus)* for copper or bronze are normally employed and if followed by a numeral, e.g. *AR* 33, will indicate that the item is made of silver and is 33 millimetres in diameter. The two initial letters are sometimes ligatured. Any other technical terms will be explained in the chapters that follow.

I

CELTIC BRITAIN

⁓⧉⊛⧉⊱

That gold was highly regarded by the Celtic people of the British Isles there is no doubt. Gold neck torques and arm bands have frequently been found in different parts of Britain and Ireland and it is quite possible that smaller gold rings, sometimes described as 'ring money', may have passed as a type of currency. From a number of sites in the West Country there have been found iron bars which, as they appear to have been forged to a related series of sizes and weights, may also have circulated as a form of currency. However, true coins came late to Britain. Gold coins minted in northern Gaul probably arrived in this island during the second half of the second century BC from the Belgic people of the Somme Valley and the Pas-de-Calais regions. Such coins have been found throughout the southern and eastern counties and the Thames basin, probably as a result of both trade and immigration.

The Gallo-Belgic coins found in Britain are typical Celtic adaptations of the gold staters of King Philip II of Macedon whose prolific coinage obviously had a special attraction for the Celts of northern Gaul. The original Macedonian coin had a laureate Apollo head on the obverse and a *biga*, a two-horse chariot, driven by a charioteer flourishing a whip on the reverse. The Celtic copies tended to deviate progressively in style the further they spread in time and space from the original source. In northern Gaul from Brittany to the Rhine there was a degree of disintegration of the design, sometimes exotic, sometimes grotesque, with a symbolism closely linked to religious beliefs, which reflects the artistic vigour of the Belgic and Armorican Celts. Amongst the earlier Gallo-Belgic gold staters are broad flan coins of the Ambiani (from around Amiens) which have a profile head with luxuriant waves of hair (**4**). Later issues of the Ambiani are uniface with a plain convex obverse and a concave reverse depicting a disjointed horse with a large pellet below. The majority of Celtic coins have this concavo-convex form of flan, the result of hollowing the lower die in order to prevent the lump of metal to be struck from rolling off the edge.

4 Gallo-Belgic A Ambiani, 2nd–1st cent. BC, *N* stater

Found principally in Kent and along the Sussex coast is a group of Gallo-Belgic quarter staters of seemingly meaningless design which originated from the Pas-de-Calais and coastal region of Flanders. They have been designated 'geometric' types by reason of their angular lines. Also sometimes found along the South Coast are billon (silver, copper and tin alloy) staters and quarter staters from the Armorican tribes of Brittany and the Cotentin peninsular, known as 'Channel Island' coins owing to the large hoards found in Jersey which were buried there at the time of the Roman conquest of Gaul. These have a horse on the reverse, often with a human head, and with a boar or lyre-shaped object set below.

THE FIRST BRITISH COINS

The earliest coins to be minted in Britain were gold staters and, like their Gallo-Belgic prototypes, these have no inscriptions so a record of their find sites has been essential for an understanding of the areas in which each type circulated. It has been suggested that the earliest of these coins date from the first or second decade of the first century BC.

Many types are named after a particular hoard: for instance, the 'Westerham' type (**5**) is found principally along the West Sussex and

5 'Westerham' type *N* stater, early 1st cent. BC

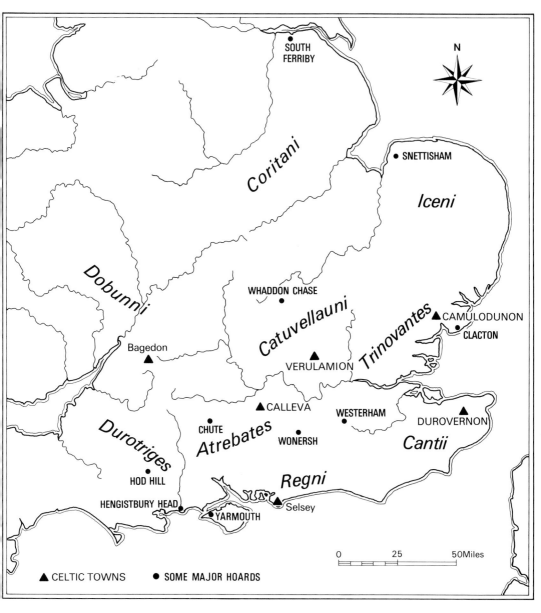

Map 1 Celtic Britain

Hampshire coasts, the North Hampshire and Surrey hills and in the mid-Thames area, that is, the region settled by the Atrebates whose Gaulish territory lay around Arras. The 'Chute' type gold staters are found mostly in West Hampshire, Dorset and Wiltshire; the 'Cheriton' type appears to be restricted to South-East Hampshire, and there are other somewhat similar types concentrated in East Anglia and in the coastal regions of Lincolnshire, Yorkshire and adjacent counties. One interesting variant is the Norfolk 'wolf' type which has a wolf-like animal on the reverse instead of the more normal horse. On most of these uninscribed staters the Apollo wreath appears to be that part of the obverse design which is emphasized, the face degenerating into a few squiggles, whilst on the reverse the horse becomes broken down into groups of lines and pellets.

In East Kent copies and adaptations of the Gallo-Belgic 'geometric' quarter staters were minted. Also copied from Central Gaulish prototypes, themselves derived from bronze coins of the Greek colony at Massilia (Marseilles), are cast 'tin' or 'potin' coins, actually of bronze with a high tin content, with a very crude design representing a profile head on one side and a charging bull on the other (**6**). They are found principally in Kent and the lower Thames area, though some coins come from further afield. As they were cast in groups in moulds they frequently show traces of the 'git' – the connecting channel of metal which was not always carefully snipped off.

6 Cast potin ('tin') coin, 1st cent. BC

The latest of the Belgic migrations into Britain were closely connected with the campaigns of Julius Caesar in Gaul, 59–61 BC, and it is from this time and the decades that followed that the pattern of tribal areas in southern Britain began to assume the form that they occupied at the time of the Roman conquest. The principal Belgic peoples were the Atrebates in Hampshire, Berkshire and Surrey; the Regni in Sussex and eastern Hampshire; the Cantii in Kent; the Trinovantes in Essex and part of Suffolk, and the Catuvellauni centred in Hertfordshire and adjacent counties north of the Thames. In the surrounding counties were the established tribes who had arrived earlier in Britain: the Durotriges in Dorset, West Hampshire and parts of Somerset and Wiltshire; the Dobunni in Gloucestershire and Worcestershire and parts of Somerset,

Wiltshire, Oxfordshire, Monmouth and Herefordshire; the Coritani in Leicestershire, Nottinghamshire and Lincolnshire, and the Iceni in East Anglia and Cambridgeshire. No form of coinage seems to have been adopted by the non-Belgic tribes in those parts of Britain more remote from Belgic influence.

THE ATREBATES AND REGNI

It is possible that by the middle of the first century BC the Regni of Sussex had come under the hegemony of the Atrebates. During the third quarter of the century gold staters were minted by the Atrebates which are distinguished by a horse with a triple tail and a wheel below, copying a prototype of the Gaulish Remi. Some of these staters have an Apollo wreath, others are uniface with a blank obverse. Triple-tailed quarter staters (7) are relatively common, found largely in the territory of the Regni, numbers having been cast up on the beach at Selsey Bill. Silver first appears as a coinage metal about the middle of the first century BC and an interesting Regni coin has recently come to light depicting the horned head of the god Cernunnos.

7 Regni, late 1st cent. BC, *N* quarter stater

About 35 BC there appear triple-tailed staters with the inscription COMMIOS around the horse, the earliest inscribed coins to be minted in Britain. These were issued for Commios who is known to have been king of the Gaulish Atrebates from about 57 BC. Initially he had been an ally of Julius Caesar and had been sent to Britain as an envoy before Caesar's expedition in 55 BC to try to persuade the British tribes to submit to the authority of Rome. Later Commios quarrelled with the Romans and fled to Britain where he founded a dynasty which ruled over both Atrebates and Regni.

Commios appears to have been succeeded by his son Tincommios. His name is recorded on the Ancyra monument as having petitioned the emperor Augustus for aid when he was forced to flee the country. His first coins were close copies of his father's typically Celtic type, but his later issues were based on contemporary Roman types, notably that of the galloping horseman. The legend on his coins is normally TINC and COM.F (*Commii filius*) and he issued staters, quarter staters and silver coins.

Tincommios may have been driven from his throne by his brother Eppillos, and he, in his turn, was probably deposed by Verica, another son of Commios, after only a short reign as his later coins were only found in Kent. The early coins of Eppillos, which are rare, read EPPI CALLEV or EPP REX CALLE, indicating that they were minted at Calleva Atrebatum (Silchester, Hants.) which in Roman times was the tribal centre of the Atrebates.

Verica, the third son of Commios, must be the ruler who, according to Dion Cassius, had been exiled from Britain and who appealed for help to the emperor Claudius in AD 43. He issued staters, quarter staters and silver coins which are inscribed VIRI or VERIC COM F, with sometimes the title REX added. His coins are all of Roman style, one of them being copied from a coin of the emperor Tiberius. His early coins have a horseman similar to that on the coins of Tincommios (**8**), while some of his later coins bear a vine-leaf emblem. It has been suggested that he may have been driven from his kingdom by the expansion of the Catuvellauni under Epaticcus or Caratacus. It is certain that at some time during his reign Epaticcus occupied part of his realm. A ruler whose coins are inscribed CRAB may have succeeded Verica as king of the Regni, his coins, which are rare, having an eagle on the reverse copied from the later coins of Eppillos.

8 Atrebates, Verica, *c.* AD 10–40, *A*/ stater

THE CATUVELLAUNI AND TRINOVANTES

The Catuvellauni, though centred around Verulamio (St Albans) had, by the time of the Roman conquest, extended their dominion over the Trinovantes of Essex and the Cantii of Kent and had pushed their way westward to the borders of the Dobunni and south-west into the territory of Verica. The Trinovantes, though sometimes independent, seem to have been a tributary kingdom of the Catuvellauni. Caesar mentions the Catuvellauni in his account of his British expedition: they were apparently the most powerful tribe in Britain and under Cassivellaunos put up a determined resistance to Caesar's forces. No coins are known with the name of Cassivellaunos, but the uninscribed staters known as the 'Whaddon Chase' type (**9**) have been tentatively attributed to him.

Tasciovanos is the first ruler of this tribe to be named on coins. His

9 Catuvellauni, 'Whaddon Chase' type, *c.* 45–20 BC, *N* stater

earliest issue is derived from the 'Whaddon Chase' coins but later designs
were of Roman style and some of his coins bear a portrait which is very
similar to that of the Emperor Augustus. Amongst the emblems used on his
coins are the horse, horseman, Pegasus, centaur, bull, boar and eagle. His
main mint was at Verulamio and the mint name occurs on many of his
coins, other legends being CAMV (*Camuloduno*, Colchester), DIAS, RICONI
(**10**), RUIIS and SEGO, though it is doubtful if these are all names of towns.
Gold staters and quarter staters, silver coins and two sizes of bronze coins of
Tasciovanos are known.

10 Catuvellauni, Tasciovanos, *c.* 20 BC–10 AD *N* stater

Tasciovanos may have occupied Camuloduno, capital of the Trinovantes for a time, but the first independent ruler of that tribe to be known
from his coins is Addedomaros. He struck gold staters and quarter staters
which are similar in style to the 'Whaddon Chase' coins of the Catuvellauni
and he may also have issued uninscribed bronze. At a later date
Dubnovellaunos, ruler of the Cantii, appears to have acquired the
leadership of the Trinovantes and his gold staters are somewhat similar to
those of his predecessor. Dubnovellaunos was probably ejected from his
territory in Essex by Cunobelin, the son of Tasciovanos. Some time during
the reign of Tasciovanos a ruler named Andoco (Andocommios?),
unknown except from his coins, ruled over the western territory of the
Catuvellauni. His coins are mostly similar in style to the coins of
Tasciovanos.

Cunobelin, the 'Cymbeline' of Shakespeare, succeeded to his father's
kingdom and it is during his reign that the greatest expansion of the
Catuvellauni took place. He is mentioned by several Roman historians
though he died a short time before the Roman conquest. During his reign
the Trinovantes were finally absorbed and Cunobelin transferred his
capital to Camulodunum. He later occupied the whole of Kent and his

brother Epaticcus invaded the territory of Verica, thus extending the dominion of the Catuvellauni over all south-east Britain. The commonest coins of Cunobelin are the gold staters minted at Colchester with the legend CAMV divided by an ear of corn and a galloping horse on the reverse with the name CVNO below (**11**). Some of his other coins bear the legend TASCIOVANTIS, i.e., '(son) of Tasciovanus' as well as his own name. He issued staters and quarter staters and silver and copper coins of a variety of types, most of which show a combination of Roman and Celtic design. The staters of Epaticcus are copies of the coins of his brother Cunobelin which have an ear of corn, but they have a horseman on the reverse instead of just a horse, and they are mostly found south of the Thames.

11   Catuvellauni, Cunobelinos, *c.* AD 10–40, A/ stater of Camulodunon (Colchester)

On the death of Cunobelin his kingdom was divided between his sons Caratacus and Togodumnus. Their armies were defeated by Aulius Plautius on the invasion of Britain in AD 43, but Caratacus was able to escape and organize resistance amongst the Silures of South Wales. Later he was forced to flee to the Brigantes in the north, but he was betrayed to the Romans by their queen Cartimandua. Several of his silver coins have been found (**12**), being copies of the silver coins of Epaticcus which show an eagle seizing a snake but with the inscription CARA. No coins are known of Togodumnus.

12   Catuvellauni, Caratacus, *c.* AD 35–40, silver

THE CANTII

The first king of the Cantii of whom coins are known was Dubnovellaunos, ruling about the end of the first century BC. He was one of the British petitioners to Augustus mentioned on the Ancyra monument. His Kentish gold staters are uniface and the reverses have a leaping horse of the style of the early staters of Tasciovanos, and he also issued silver and copper coins. It seems that he was expelled from Kent as he is later found issuing coins as ruler of the Trinovantes of Essex. Succeeding him in East Kent was a King Vose(*nios?*), unknown to history, whose uniface gold coins have a serpent below the horse on the reverse.

Eppillus, son of Commios, is the next known ruler of the Cantii, having earlier been king of the Atrebates until being removed by his brother Verica. He is usually styled EPPI COM F, and his staters usually show a horseman similar to that on his brother's coins, except for one type which portrays a winged Victory. He also issued silver and bronze coins of various types. There are silver and bronze coins known of a ruler named Amminus who may have been a king or sub-king of the Cantii. This may be the same person as Adminius, son of Cunobelin, who was expelled from Britain by his father in AD 40.

<h3 style="text-align:center">THE DOBUNNI</h3>

The uninscribed gold coins of the Dobunni, who inhabited the upper Thames and lower Severn valleys and parts of Somerset and Worcestershire, are copied from those of the Atrebates and Regni which have a triple-tailed horse. On the obverse, however, is a crude ear of corn somewhat similar to that on the staters of Cunobelin. Later gold coins of similar type are inscribed with the names of Antedrig (**13**), Eisu, Inam (?), Catti, Comux and Corio. Presumably these are all names of rulers, though it has been suggested that CORIO may stand for Corinium (Cirencester, Gloucs.) which in Roman times was the tribal capital of the Dobunni. The uninscribed silver coins (**14**) of the Dobunni bear a strange conglomeration of pellets,

13 Dobunni, Antedrig, *N* stater   14 Dobunni, uninscribed silver

crosses and lines vaguely arranged in the form of a profile head, and similar later coins are known with the names ANTED, EISV and COR. The latest coins of this tribe are probably those of a ruler named Bodvoc, his gold staters having his name set across the obverse field and his silver having a neat profile portrait with his name in front.

<h3 style="text-align:center">THE DUROTRIGES</h3>

Only uninscribed coins are known of the Durotriges who occupied Dorset, South Wiltshire and West Hampshire. Their coinage consisted of base silver and bronze 'staters' which were degenerate copies of uninscribed gold staters that circulated to the east of their territory. The horse on the reverse of the silver is composed of a mass of lines and pellets whilst the copper or bronze coins are of even cruder style and were cast in moulds instead of being struck. Large numbers of these have been found at Hengistbury Head near Bournemouth, and there is some evidence that they continued in use for some time after the Roman occupation.

THE ICENI

The uninscribed gold coins of the Iceni who inhabited Norfolk, Suffolk and Cambridgeshire, usually have a cruciform design with a rosette at the centre of the obverse and a crude horse on the reverse. The uninscribed silver have a somewhat similar horse, the obverses having a crude boar, a profile head, likewise, is sometimes extremely crude (**15**), or a double crescent ornament. Inscribed gold staters are known with the names ECEN and ANTED, the latter being in the form of a monogram. The obverses of the silver inscribed coins of Celtic style are mostly of the double-crescent type and these are known with a variety of names: ANTED, ECEN, AESV and ECEN, amongst others. It is possible that the 'Anted' and 'Aesu' of the Iceni refer to the same persons as the 'Antedrig' and 'Eisu' of the Dobunni and the 'Asu' of the Coritani, in which case this may point to a confederation of the tribes under a single leader, perhaps to contain the expansion of the Catuvellauni. The silver coins of Anted and Ecen are amongst the commonest of Celtic coins.

15 Iceni, *c.* 10 BC–AD 10, uninscribed silver

The latest Icenian coins are of Roman style, having a neat portrait with a torque in front and the inscription PRASTO SVB RI and, on the reverse, a rearing horse with a crescent above and, unusually, the name of a moneyer, ESICO FECIT (Esico made *me*). These have been attributed to Prasutagus who was a vassal king of the Iceni under the Roman emperor Claudius. It was Boudicca, the widow of Prasutagus, who revolted against the Romans in AD 61, but no coins are known in her name.

THE CORITANI

The coins of the Coritani whose territory lay in the East Midlands and Lincolnshire were originally attributed to the Brigantes of Yorkshire as a result of several hoards having been found on Brigantian territory, probably having been deposited at the time of the Roman campaign in the north in AD 69. The earliest Coritanian coins were gold staters copied from Gallo-Belgic coins of the Ambiani during the first century BC. One group, the 'South Ferriby' type, are extremely crude. Later types, with the same kind of disintegrated horse and with a double crescent and annular ornamentation on the obverse, have inscriptions such as AVN COST, ESVP ASV and VEP CORF (**16**), etc., but whether these are names of rulers or of officials responsible for the coinage is uncertain. A later type has a vertical wreath design on the obverse with DVMNO across the field and the inscription TIGIR SENO around the horse on the reverse, and a similar type has the word VOLISIOS in two lines on the obverse and DVMNOCOVEROS or DVMNOVELLAV on the reverse. Uninscribed silver coins have a boar on the obverse and a horse on the reverse (**17**), while later silver follows the pattern of the inscribed gold. There is one silver coin with the inscription VOLISIOS CARTIVEL which at one time had been attributed to Cartimandua, the Brigantian queen, but this is now considered unlikely.

As in Gaul, so in Britain, the local coinages were soon superseded by the coinage of the conquerors following the Roman occupation, but even so the evidence of hoards shows that in some places the transition was not immediate.

16 Coritani, Vep Corf, 1st cent. AD, *Æ* stater

17 Coritani, *c.* 60 BC–AD 10, uninscribed silver

2

ROMAN BRITAIN

For four hundred years southern Britain was a province of the Roman Empire, and it is only right, therefore, that in reviewing the coinage of this country Roman coins should receive some attention. The coinage of the Roman Empire, however, is a study in itself and it is beyond the scope of this book to cover it in any detail. It will only be possible to give a very brief introduction to the series here.

GENERAL CHARACTERISTICS

For the first two centuries of the Roman Empire the main denominations were the gold *aureus*, which was only slightly lighter than the modern British sovereign, and the silver *denarius* (the *d.* of our former £.*s.d.*), twenty-five of which equalled an aureus. A half-denarius, called a *quinarius*, was sometimes issued. The base metal coinage consisted of the copper *as* (**18**), its half the *semis* and its quarter the *quadrans*; two copper *asses* equalled one brass *dupondius*, two *dupondii* equalled one brass *sestertius*, and four *sestertii* made up one silver *denarius*. The *as* and *dupondius* are about the same size and, though they could originally be recognized by the colour of the

18 Nero, AD 54–68, Æ as, Victory holding shield

metal and difference in weight, they can also usually be distinguished by the laureate head on the former and the radiate crown on the latter, at least from the later years of the first century AD. Coins of the later Empire will be mentioned towards the end of this chapter.

Except for some of the early imperial bronze, the Roman coins issued after the reign of Augustus normally have a portrait on the obverse. This is usually that of the emperor, though sometimes he allowed coins to be issued bearing the name and portrait of his wife, his heir or another of his close relatives. The obverse inscription, besides giving the emperor's name or names, also includes some of his ranks or titles, usually in an abbreviated form. On a denarius of Claudius, for instance, the inscription might read TI CLAVD CAESAR AVG P M TR P VIIII IMP XVII (there was no J or U in the Latin alphabet, and where we would now use these letters the Romans used I and V respectively). The inscription can be expanded as follows:

> TI CLAVD is the abbreviation of the emperor's full name which was *Tiberius Claudius Nero Germanicus*: CAESAR was originally a family name and was later used as a title in honour of Julius Caesar: AVG (*Augustus*) was the name given by the Senate to Octavianus, the first Roman Emperor, and was used as an imperial title by all later emperors: PM (*Pontifex maximus*) was the title of High Priest given to the emperor which acknowledged his religious office: TR P (*Tribunicia potestate*) VIIII indicated that Claudius was holding tribunician powers for the ninth year: IMP (*Imperator*) XVII means that he had been invested by the Senate on seventeen occasions with the rank of commander-in-chief of the army. It later came to mean the head of the Empire.

Other abbreviations found on imperial coins are COS (*Consul*), one of the two heads of the executive who were appointed annually (if followed by a numeral, e.g., COS V, this indicated that the emperor was Consul for the fifth time): P F (*Pius et felix*, Righteous and Fortunate): P P (*Pater patriae*, Father of the Country): and DN (*Dominus noster*, Our Lord). A female relative was titled AVGVSTA, and when a coin was struck to commemorate an emperor or relative after death the word DIVVS or DIVA was used to signify that he or she was recognized as a divinity. The S C found on the earlier copper and brass coins stands for *Senatus consulto*, indicating that these were issued by the authority of the Senate and not directly by the emperor.

Reverse types are extremely numerous, many being of great interest as they commemorate important events. The Romans appreciated the value of coinage as a medium for propaganda and the fullest use was made of it for glorifying the Empire and the emperor. Personifications of the various virtues with which the emperor was supposed to be endowed appear with some regularity, such as Aequitas (Equity), Liberalitas (Generosity), Pietas

(Righteousness), Providentia (Forethought), Virtus (Courage), etc. Other types refer to the well-being of the empire under the emperor's beneficent rule, with personifications of Abundance, Concord, Good Fortune, Liberty, Peace, Security and Victory, and other inscriptions such as RESTITVTOR REIPUBLICAE (Restorer of the Republic), GLORIA ROMANORUM (The Glory of the Romans) and GENIO POPVLI ROMANI (The Genius of the Roman People). A type commonly used in the fourth century depicts an altar or standard with an inscription such as VOT X, commemorating the fact that the emperor had taken his vows for the tenth time, and sometimes has the addition of, say, MVLT XX, 'may he live to make them twenty times more'. From the time of Constantine the Great other coins have Christian symbols, notably the *Chi-Rho* monogram, these being the first two letters of the Greek word for Christ (XPICTWC).

Successful military campaigns, particularly those in which the emperor himself took part, frequently received publicity on the coinage, for example, the capture of Jerusalem by Titus in AD 70, which is commemorated by the IVDAEA CAPTA coins, the invasion and conquest of Britain under Claudius, and the other military operations during the reigns of Hadrian, Antoninus, Commodus and Severus. There are gold and silver coins of Claudius which show a triumphal arch inscribed DE BRITANN surmounted by an equestrian statue of the emperor between two trophies of captured arms (**19**). Another of Hadrian has the inscription BRITANNIA and the personification of the province seated with spear and shield and with her foot upon a pile of stones (**20**). It has been suggested that this alludes to the construction of Hadrian's Wall. There is a copper *as* of Antoninus Pius which depicts Britannia seated on a rock in an attitude of

19 Claudius, AD 41–54, AV aureus, triumphal arch, DE BRITANN

20 Hadrian, AD 117–138, Æ as, Britannia seated

dejection, and some of the denarii of Severus have the inscription VICTORIAE BRIT and a figure of Victory holding a laurel wreath and palm branch.

During the first and second centuries AD the majority of Roman coins were struck in Rome, though from time to time imperial coins were struck in the provinces. Also a number of cities were granted the privilege of striking their own coins, particularly in the eastern Greek-speaking areas of the Empire, though apart from a few mints these were limited to issuing bronze coins. In the third and fourth centuries a number of new mints were opened in the central and western parts of the Empire, all issuing coins of uniform style, and these were legal tender throughout the Empire irrespective of which mint they came from. Mint letters are found in the exergue of most of these coins, such as ANT, Antioch, KART, Carthage, L, LN, or LON, London, LVG, Lugdunum (Lyons), TR, Trier, to name only a few. These letters are sometimes preceded by P, M or SM, for *pecunia, moneta* or *sacra moneta*, and if more than one mint workshop was operating at a particular mint then the letters P, S, T or Q were used to denote *prima, secunda, tertia* or *quarta officina*, i.e., first mint workshop, etc., and in the eastern part of the Empire the Greek letters A, B, Γ, Δ etc., were used in numerical order to denote the same thing. Other letters are sometimes found in the reverse field to distinguish various issues.

ROMAN COINS IN BRITAIN

By the end of the second century BC the silver denarius of the Roman Republic had begun to infiltrate into Celtic Europe and at the time of the Roman conquest of Gaul these coins had reached as far as Britain. One of the commonest types of these Republican denarii has a head of Roma on the obverse. Numbers of these denarii, as well as coins of the early Empire have been found deposited in hoards together with native Celtic coins. Following the Roman occupation of Britain, which was begun in AD 43 in the reign of the Emperor Claudius, the native currency was superseded by the coinage of imperial Rome except in some tribal areas where base metal Celtic coin still served the local population for some years. Roman coins as a whole are common and large hoards, sometimes numbering tens of thousands of pieces, have been discovered in many parts of the country.

There was no official mint in Britain before the latter part of the third century and it appears that the amount of coin brought into the country immediately following the Roman invasion was insufficient to meet demand from the Roman forces and their followers. Local copies of the bronze coins of Claudius were made in large quantities, some being of good workmanship while others are extremely crude. It may be that some were produced by semi-official mints set up to supply the army of occupation.

The copper *as* bearing the standing figure of Minerva is the type most commonly met with (**21**).

By AD 80 Britain south of the Cheviots had been subdued, though revolts were to break out from time to time for another hundred years or more. During this period, in fact until the middle of the third century, a plentiful supply of coin reached this country from Rome or mints in Gaul; but when, during the latter half of the third century, the Empire suffered from a deteriorating economic position and from a succession of usurpers, particularly in Gaul, the supply of coin from the continent began to diminish and the currency had to be supplemented by local copies (**22**). These third-century 'barbarous radiates' as they are called are mainly copied from the *antoniniani* of Postumus (259–68), Victorinus (268–70), Tetricus (270–3) and Claudius Gothicus (268–70). The silver *antoninianus* had been introduced by Caracalla (Antoninus) as a double-denarius in AD 214, but these coins soon became so debased that after the reign of Postumus they were nothing more than copper with a silver or tin wash on their surface. As a result of this debasement the issue of large bronze denominations was virtually abandoned. On these antoniniani the emperor wears a radiate crown, the sun rays providing an emblem of his divine status.

21 Claudius, after AD 43, Æ as, local imitation, Minerva standing

22 Romano-British 'barbarous radiate' imitation of antoninianus, *c*. AD 270–285

In 286, during the joint rule of Diocletian and Maximian, the commander of the Channel fleet, the *Classis Britannica*, M. Aurelius Mausaeus Carausius, revolted against the central authority and was declared emperor by his forces. He destroyed a fleet sent by Maximian to reconquer Britain and at one time he extended his control over northern Gaul. He established mints at London and Camulodunum (Colchester) and possibly at Clausentum (Bitterne, near Southampton). He also minted coins at Rotamagus (Rouen) in Gaul. His gold aurei are very rare and his base silver denarii somewhat less so, but his bronze antoniniani were issued in large quantities and they are relatively common. The base silver denarius had been re-introduced by Aurelian but the denomination was not issued for long.

The commonest coins of Carausius are those with Pax on the reverse (**23**). Sometimes AVG on this and other types is spelt AVGGG as an indication that he considered himself to be ruling jointly with two colleagues. He did, in fact, strike coins at London and Colchester in the names of Diocletian and Maximian, and one rare antoninianus even bears the portraits of all three emperors and has the inscription CARAVSIVS ET FRATRES SVI (Carausius and his brothers). Amongst other interesting coins are those which name the various legions that supported him or which might possibly support him in Britain and Gaul. These were the Legion I Minerva, II Augusta, II Parthica, IV Flavia, VII Claudia, VIII Augusta, XX Valeria Victrix, XXII Primigenia and XXX Ulpia Victrix. In addition there is also a coin inscribed COHRT PRAET, which presumably refers to his personal bodyguard of Praetorian guards. Another interesting reverse is that inscribed GENIO BRITANNI and showing the spirit of the Province standing before an altar. The usual mint marks are ML (London) and C (Colchester), and on the antoniniani the value XXI is sometimes added, perhaps indicating a value or the quality of the metal.

23 Carausius, AD 287–293, Æ antoninianus, Colchester mint, Pax standing

In 293 Carausius was murdered by his chief minister Allectus who assumed the title of Emperor in Britain until, in his turn, he was killed by Constantius Chlorus Caesar in 296. Besides rare aurei and denarii Allectus issued a number of types of antoniniani at London and Colchester as well as somewhat smaller quinarii (half-antoniniani) which are denoted by the letter Q before the mint mark.

On the restoration of Britain to the Roman Empire by Constantius the mint of Colchester was closed down but London continued to operate. Diocletian had introduced the *follis*, a new large bronze denomination with a silver wash which was tariffed at 120 to the gold aureus. These folles were issued at London for Diocletian and Maximinian, both of whom abdicated in 305, to be followed by Constantius Chlorus (305–6), Galerius (305–11), Severus II (305–7), Maximinus Daza (309–13), Licinius (308–24) and

Constantine the Great (307–37). During this period two emperors (*Augusti*) reigned jointly and they each appointed an heir (*Caesar*) who also had coins struck in their names. An interesting and unique gold medallion of Constantius Chlorus, equal to ten aurei, was found at Arras in 1922. It was struck at Trier and shows the conquering Caesar being welcomed by a kneeling Britannia before the walls of London.

The Empire was united for a number of years under Constantine the Great, the founder of Constantinople. Folles were struck at London in the early years of his reign, but the bronze coins then began to decrease in size and the names of the smaller pieces are not known. Constantinian bronze was issued from London in large quantities, and perhaps the commonest types are those showing a Roman gateway, an altar, Sol (**24**), Mars, the Genius of the Roman People, winged Victories, and the emperor with one captive or two captives seated below a standard. During the reign of Constantine coins were struck at London with the names and portraits of his mother Helena, his wife Fausta, and of his three sons, Constantine II, Constantius II and Crispus, the last being put to death by his father.

24 Constantine the Great, AD 307–337, Æ follis of London, Sol standing

The mint of London appears to have closed down on the death of Constantine I and after this time any new coin needed in Britain had to be imported from Gaul. Under Constantine the gold aureus had been replaced by a lighter coin, the *solidus*. In the middle of the fourth century two new silver coins appeared, the *siliqua* and its double value the *miliarense*, the latter replacing the *argenteus* of Diocletian's monetary reform. The bronze coins were reduced in size and, due to the troubles that the Romans were having with barbarian invaders from Central Europe, the number of coins finding their way to Britain became increasingly fewer. To supply local needs copies of fourth-century bronze coins were made in Britain, and they are now referred to as 'minimi'. The commonest type copied are those with the inscription FEL TEMP REPARATIO (Happy times restored) the emperor depicted spearing a fallen horseman. These reproduce the laureate head used on late fourth-century Roman coins, but it seems that barbarous 'radiates' were also being made until a late date.

Roman troops were withdrawn from Britain between about AD 380 and the opening years of the fifth century as they were needed for defence elsewhere in the Empire, and by 410 the country had been virtually abandoned by the central imperial government. By this time what gold and silver coin there was in the country had been withdrawn from circulation and even copper was so scarce that older Roman coins were cut up into fragments and restamped. It has been suggested that barbarous coins that appear to bear the name of a second Carausius might have been issued by some local ruler after the departure of the imperial administration. The minimi became smaller and smaller and their legend and design more and more illegible, until the limit seems to have been reached by 'minimissimi' that were discovered in a hoard found at Lydney, Gloucs., some of which measured only 3 mm in diameter (**25**). From about AD 450 until the beginning of Anglo-Saxon coinage, a period of some two hundred years, the economic life of the towns was in such a state of decline that there was probably little need for coin and it appears that none was minted.

25 Late Romano-British 'minimissimi', late 4th early 5th cent.

3

ANGLO-SAXON ENGLAND

⟫❀❀❀⟪

Jutes, Angles and Saxons began to settle in eastern England in the second half of the fifth century, but not until the end of the sixth century did they finally occupy the west of England, with the exception, that is, of Wales, Devon and Cornwall and Strathclyde. The establishment of the mini-kingdoms of the 'Heptarchy' – Kent, Wessex, Mercia, East Anglia, etc. – brought a semblance of order out of the chaos of the preceding two centuries. There was renewed contact with the continent, in particular with the kingdom of the Merovingian Franks, resulting in a revival of Christianity, an increase in commerce and the re-introduction of coinage. Though the craft of striking coins seems to have been lost in Britain owing to the decay of urban life during the fifth and sixth centuries, in France the Franks had assimilated much of the culture and organization of Roman Gaul and their kings had adopted the style of coinage of the Roman emperors, though in the main limiting themselves to the production of gold *tremisses* and silver *denarii* or 'deniers'. A number of Merovingian gold tremisses found their way to this country during the latter half of the sixth century and may have been used as currency to some extent. A purse full of these coins was found in the famous Sutton Hoo ship burial of an East Anglian king believed to have been Raedwald who died before 628. The British sterling pound-shilling-pence (£.s.d.) system appears to have had its origin in the seventh-century Romano-Frankish *libra-solidus* (solidus-tremissis) -*denarius* accounting system, with 12 denarii to the tremissis and 240 denarii to the Frankish pound (*libra*).

At some time after 600, during the reign of King Ethelbert of Kent (560–616), a mint was established at Canterbury and worked by Frankish moneyers, though none of the coins bear the king's name. The earliest Anglo-Saxon gold tremisses or *thrymsas*, as they are usually called, were somewhat similar to the Frankish coins. One type bears a diademed head, copied from that of a long-deceased Roman Emperor, with the legend EVSEBII MONITA, 'money of Eusebius', and DOROVERNIS CIVITAS, 'City of Canterbury,' on the reverse with a cross in the centre. This design soon degenerated in style and legends became meaningless when copied by other Saxon moneyers (**26**). One thrymsa bears the name of Bishop Leudard who was chaplain to Queen Bertha, the wife of Ethelbert and daughter of the Frankish king Charibert, and another bearing the inscription AVDVARLD REGES has been ascribed tentatively to Eadbald of Kent (616–40). Other coins which may be ecclesiastical have what appears to be a tonsured head and the inscription LONDINI, possibly a coinage of one of the bishops of London. A few larger gold solidi are known, copied from earlier Roman models, but they are extremely rare and may only have been made for ornamental purposes. Some coins have inscriptions which are partly in Latin and partly in Runic characters. The Runic script originated in Scandinavia and north Germany and, though it was largely superseded by the Latin alphabet soon after the introduction of Christianity, silver pennies are found with the occasional Runic character up to the middle of the ninth century. There are a number of variations in the form of Runic letters.

26 Early Anglo-Saxon *Æ* thrymsa with 'Two Victories' reverse

Owing to an increasing scarcity of gold, later thrymsas were alloyed with silver, and some time before 700, probably during the reign of Wihtred of Kent (690–725), these were superseded by a silver *sceatta* coinage. These sceattas, the equivalent of the Frankish *denier* and the direct descendant of the Roman *denarius*, are really the first English silver pennies, though the word 'sceatta', which was the Anglo-Saxon term for money, is now used for convenience to distinguish these small coins from the later broader silver pennies. Most of these early sceattas, or 'sceats' as they are sometimes called, were struck to a standard of 20 grains weight and were of relatively good silver, but some of the later coins tended to deteriorate in weight and in quality of metal.

There are a great number of types. Some are copies of Roman types that were current two hundred years earlier, the commonest being the 'standard' type imitating a coin which depicts two captives seated below a Roman standard, though generally only the top part of the standard is shown. The 'wolf and twins' and the 'two standing emperors' types are also reproduced and yet other sceattas are copied from Frankish coins. Some coins with good style portraits were minted in Kent (**27**) and some London coins have the mint name LVNDONIA. Others with rather cruder portraits have the moneyer's name inscribed in Runic letters (*Apa, Epa, Wigraed,* etc.) and these appear to have been minted in East Anglia (**28**). Many coins have animals, birds or fantastic monsters (**29**), interesting examples of Anglo-Saxon art, and others have crude standing human figures. One common group of sceattas degenerates in style until the head takes a 'porcupine' form (**30**). Some types may be South Saxon or Wessex issues, but many are Mercian, struck during the reign of Aethelbald (716–57) who was overlord of the southern English kingdoms, though none of the coins bear his name. Other sceattas occur with the names of Beonna, king of East Anglia (*c.*758), and of an Ealdfrith who may have been sub-king of Lindsey (northern Lincolnshire) about 790.

27　Early Anglo-Saxon Æ sceatta, Kentish, Bird on Cross type

28　East Anglian type, with Runic inscription

29　South Wessex type, whorl of wolves' heads

30　'Porcupine' type, with Standard reverse

In Northumbria an interesting series of regal and ecclesiastical silver sceattas commenced about the middle of the seventh century and then deteriorated to a copper coinage which ends with the conquest of York by the Vikings in 867. King Eadberht (737–58) (**31**) and his successors Alchred, Aethelred I and Alfwald, all issued silver sceattas with their name around a cross on the obverse and a wolf-like animal on the reverse. During Alfwald's reign the animal on the reverse was replaced by the name of the moneyer, and this set the pattern for the coinage during the second reign of Aethelred I and the reigns of Eanred (**32**), Aethelred II, Redwulf and Osberht. One interesting coin of Aethelred I has a small shrine surmounted by a cross on the reverse with the inscription SCT CVD, 'Saint Cuthbert'. During the reign of Eanred copper or brass replaced silver and these base metal coins are sometimes known as 'stycas'. The latest regal stycas, issued during a period of dynastic struggle preceding the Viking conquest, are usually poorly struck and have blundered inscriptions.

31 Northumbria, Eadberht, Æ sceatta, quadruped

32 Eanred, Æ 'styca'

Besides the issue of regal coins sceattas were also minted by the archbishops of York who held minting privileges for many years. Those of Archbishop Ecgberht (734–66) have his name and a figure holding two crosses on one side and the name of one of three kings on the other, i.e., his brother King Eadberht (**33**), Aethelwald Moll (759–65), who does not seem to have issued coins independently, and Alchred. Stycas of the later regal type were issued by Archbishops Eanbald (796–808), Wigmund (837–54) and Wulfhere (854–900). A unique gold solidus of Wigmund shows his facing tonsured bust on one side and on the reverse, around a cross within a laurel wreath, the inscription MVNVS DIVINVM the divine gift), a type imitating a Frankish solidus of Louis the Pius.

33 Archbishop of York, Ecgberht, Æ sceatta, naming King Eadberht

KINGS OF KENT

Pepin, king of the Franks and founder of the dynasty that reached its peak under his son Charlemagne, had reformed the French coinage in the year

755, abandoning the dumpy silver denier of Merovingian type in favour of a broader, thinner coin. That a similar change should be made in Kent, the Anglo-Saxon kingdom nearest to continental influence, is not surprising but it was not until about the last quarter of the eighth century that broad silver pennies were minted in the names of two little known Kentish kings, Heaberht and Ecgberht II. These are not portrait coins; the king's name surrounds a RX monogram, for *rex*, and on the reverse the moneyer's name is set around a central cross or horizontally across the field. Pennies of Eadberht Praen (796–8) (**34**) and the early coins of Cuthred (*c.*801–7) follow the same pattern. The later coins of Cuthred, who was a brother of Coenwulf of Mercia, have the king's name around his head sometimes with the title REX CANT, 'King of Kent'. The moneyer's name appears on the reverse arranged in the angles of a cross or tribrach (a three-limbed cross) or in a circle around some central ornament. In the latter case it is usually followed by the word MONETA, '(*his*) money'. One of the first pennies to give the name of the mint town is a coin of Baldred with the inscription DRVR CI̅ T̅ s in the inner circle of the reverse, an abbreviation of *Dorovernia civitas*, 'City of Canterbury', the sign ‾ indicating a contraction.

Little is known of Cuthred's successor Baldred (**35**), except that in 825, after Ecgberht of Wessex defeated the Mercians at Ellandune and the king of Kent could no longer look to Mercia for protection, he was expelled by Ecgberht's son Aethelwulf. After the expulsion of Baldred, and before coins were minted for Ecgberht, there was an anonymous issue from Canterbury retaining the portrait of Baldred but with the moneyer's name on the obverse instead of that of the king. Kent then ceased to be an independent kingdom, though for some time to come it was governed as a sub-kingdom by the king of Wessex or by one of his sons.

34 Kent, Eadberht Praen, Æ penny, moneyer Ethelnoth

35 Baldred, Æ penny, moneyer Dunun

ARCHBISHOPS OF CANTERBURY

It is probable that some of the thrymsas and sceattas were ecclesiastical issues of Canterbury, but the first coins to bear the name of an archbishop were silver pennies of Jaenberht (766–91). He was succeeded in office by Aethelheard (791–805), Wulfred (805–32), Ceolnoth (833–70), Aethered (870–89) and Plegmund (890–914). These coins have the title 'Archiepiscopus', sometimes abbreviated, after the name of the archbishop, though coins of Aethelheard issued after he was elected but before he was consecrated bear the title PONT, *Pontifex*, instead of ARC.

The pennies of Jaenberht (**36**) and Aethelheard are without portraits and have on one side the names of Offa or Coenwulf of Mercia, their overlords, but Wulfred, who came to office when the power of Mercia was declining, omitted the king's name and issued pennies bearing his own tonsured bust. The coins of Wulfred have the mint name DOROBERNIA, as on the coins of Baldred, though on some the name is arranged in the form of a monogram. Some pennies of Ceolnoth have the sacred *Chi-Rho* monogram (**37**); other coins have the name of the moneyer arranged in the limbs and angles of a voided cross or in three lines across the field. The coins of Plegmund omit his portrait. After his time coins struck by the archbishop's moneyers cannot be distinguished from the regal coins of Canterbury.

36 Archbishop of Canterbury, Jaenberht, Æ penny, naming King Offa

37 Archbishop Ceolnoth, Æ penny, moneyer Wunhere

BISHOP OF LONDON

It seems likely that the thrymsas and sceattas with the mint name of London were issued by an ecclesiastical authority. A unique penny inscribed EADBERHT EP on the obverse and OF⁻R M (Offa king of Mercia) on the reverse can be attributed to an Eadberht, Bishop of London, who died in 789. It is probable that after his death the right of the Bishop of London to mint coins was withdrawn.

KINGS OF MERCIA

During the seventh century Northumbria had been the most powerful of the Anglo-Saxon kingdoms but under a series of energetic rulers, of whom Offa (757–96) was the greatest, Mercia became the dominant power. The Mercians conquered most of their neighbours and drove the Britons further into Wales, Offa's Dyke being constructed to mark the western boundary of their territory. Offa himself was recognized by Charlemagne as being a ruler of considerable power. The sceatta coinage of the earlier period of Offa's reign was entirely anonymous, but in his later years, probably about 780–5, he reorganized the Mercian coinage by switching to the new penny which had been introduced by the Kentish kings. Offa had conquered the kingdom of Kent at the battle of Otford in 774 and the new Mercian coins were minted at Canterbury by the same moneyers who coined for the kings of Kent and the archbishops of Canterbury. Offa also struck coins at a mint in East Anglia.

Offa's pennies completely overshadow those of his contemporaries and successors by their excellence of design and manufacture. The standard of portraiture on some of his coins is extremely high (**38**) and the style of lettering on some of his non-portrait coins is very elegant. The early pennies of Offa tend to weigh a little under 20 grains, about the same as the better quality sceattas, but later coins appear to have been struck to a heavier standard of 21 grains.

38　Mercia, Offa, Æ penny, moneyer Ealmund

Offa, following the practice of the Roman emperors, had pennies struck with the name and portrait of his wife Cynethrith, the only coins known of a Saxon lady. A unique gold penny or solidus is known of Offa and there is also an intriguing copy of a gold Arab dinar of El-Mansur, the Caliph of Baghdad (754–75) which has the name OFFA REX surrounded by an Arabic inscription. The reason for the issue of such a coin remains a mystery. Was it intended for trade with Moorish Spain or perhaps part of a gift of gold sent with some embassy to Baghdad?

Offa was succeeded briefly by Egfrith, of whom no coins are known, and then by Coenwulf (796–822), Ceolwulf I (822–4), Beornwulf (824–6), Ludica (826–8), Wiglaf (828–39), Berhtwulf (839–52), Burgred (852–74) and Ceolwulf II (874–7). Under Coenwulf (**39**) coins were minted at

London and Rochester as well as at a mint in East Anglia. After the reign of Ceolwulf, when the power of Mercia declined as that of Wessex rose, the Mercian kings were not able to use the Kentish mints so the pennies of Beornwulf and Ludica are only known from London and the coins of Wiglaf were only struck in East Anglia. Some of the later Mercian coins have extremely crude portraits.

39 Coenwulf, Æ penny, moneyer Duda

The Mercians were conquered by Ecgberht of Wessex in 829, but later Wiglaf, Berhtwulf and Burgred continued to rule as tributary kings. The reign of Burgred was continually troubled by Viking raids. His pennies have the moneyers' names arranged in three lines between lunettes (**40**). They are the commonest of all Mercian coins and most of them appear to be made of debased silver. Ceolwulf II was merely a puppet of the Danish armies in the western part of Mercia and he was forced to abdicate after Alfred and Guthrum the Dane divided Mercia between them in 878. His coins, which are rare, copy types of Alfred. 'English' Mercia, south-west of Watling Street, was then placed under Ethelred the *ealdorman* who later married Alfred's daughter Aethelflaed known as 'the Lady of the Mercians'. Henceforth Mercia was an earldom subject to the kings of Wessex and England.

40 Burgred, Æ penny, moneyer Guthere

KINGS OF EAST ANGLIA

Silver sceattas of a mid-eighth-century East Anglian king named Beonna have been mentioned above. In style they mark a transition between the Northumbrian sceattas and the early pence of Offa of Mercia, and they are inscribed partly in Runic and partly in Latin characters. Originally known from a single specimen, a recent small hoard from Norfolk has added

substantially to their numbers. The next king of whom coins are known is
Ethelberht, who was killed on Offa's orders in 794. He issued portrait
pennies with his name and the name of the moneyer on the obverse and
with a 'wolf-and-twins' type on the reverse that must have been copied
from a Roman coin of the time of Constantine (**41**). King Offa and his
successor also issued coins minted in East Anglia. For a brief period after
Offa's death in 796 pennies were minted by an East Anglian king named
Eanred who is only known from his coins.

41 East Anglia, Ethelberht, Æ penny, wolf-and-twins type, moneyer Lul

Soon after 830, when the power of Mercia was on the wane, pennies
were issued by two other kings of whom little is known, Aethelstan I
(*c*.825–40) and Aethelweard (*c*.840–65). Some rare pennies of Aethelstan
show his portrait but the majority of Anglian coins just have the king's
name around a cross or large A. Some of the coins with an A (*alpha*) have an
omega as well (**42**); these first and last letters of the Greek alphabet signifying
'the Beginning and the End' (*Revelations*, 1,8 and 21,6) had long been used
as Christian symbols of the omnipotence of the Deity. Though some
pennies bear the title REX ANG, it seems that the *alpha* was adopted as the
symbol of the East Anglian kingdom. Eadmund, the last of the Anglian
kings, was put to death by the Danes in 870 for refusing to renounce the
Christian faith. He was canonized for his martyrdom and after his death
'memorial' pennies were struck by Danish settlers who had adopted
Christianity.

42 Aethelstan I, Æ penny, REX ANG

KINGS OF WESSEX

The first king of Wessex to strike silver pennies was Beorhtric (786–802)
who had married Eadburgh, a daughter of Offa of Mercia. His coins are
rare and they have an *alpha*, sometimes combined with an *omega*, at the

centre of the obverse. Ecgberht (802–38), his rival and successor defeated the Mercians in 825 and conquered their subsidiary kingdom of Kent. Coins were then struck for him at the mint of Canterbury. After a further defeat of the Mercians in 829 Ecgberht minted pennies in London for a brief period and he also struck coins at Winchester in the later years of his reign which bear the title REX SAXONIORVM. Besides Ecgberht's regal coins struck at the mint of Rochester there was also an ecclesiastical issue by Bishop Beornmod which bears the name of the king on one side and on the other the name SCS ANDREAS, St Andrew, the saint to whom the church of Rochester was dedicated, sometimes with APOSTOLVS added.

Aethelwulf (838–58) had coins issued from Winchester with the title REX OCCIDENTALIVM SAXONIORVM, 'King of the West Saxons'. His other coins were minted at Canterbury, as were those of his son Aethelberht (858–66) and these pennies have similar designs to those of Ecgberht or of the archbishops of Canterbury (**43**). The last and commonest type of Aethelwulf, also used by Aethelberht (**44**), has the name of the moneyer set horizontally and vertically within a voided cross, continuing into the angles, e.g. +BVRNV/ALD MO/N–E–T–A. Aethelberht's brother Aethelred I (866–71) used the same type as Burgred of Mercia, his brother-in-law, the name of the moneyer being arranged in three lines divided by two lunettes.

43 Wessex, Aethelwulf, Æ penny, moneyer Brid

44 Ethelberht, Æ penny, moneyer Luceman

The earliest coins of Alfred 'the Great' (871–99), another son of Aethelwulf, continue the lunette type of Aethelred I, Burgred and Archbishop Ceolwulf, and they frequently have the king's name spelt AELBRED. About 874 the type was changed to an issue of better quality silver with a finer portrait and a cross on the reverse having a lozenge centre, the same type being struck for Ceolwulf II of Mercia and Archbishop Aethered. During this reign new mints were opened as a result of the

Map 2 England in the reign of Alfred

expansion of Wessex into Mercian territory. These included London and Gloucester but most of Alfred's coins were struck without bearing the name of a mint. His London pennies have a large diademed bust of the king on the obverse and a monogram of LONDONIA on the reverse (**45**) and they must have been issued following the capture of London from the Danes in 886. Alfred's commonest coins do not have a portrait, instead there is a small central cross with the king's name set around in three or four groups of letters, AEL FRE DRE or +EL FR ED RE, while on the reverse the moneyer's name is arranged in two lines across the field (**46**). In southern England these pennies were struck to a standard of 24 grains, though a 20 grain penny was still issued in the Danelaw.

45 Aelfred, Æ penny, London monogram type

46 Aelfred, Æ penny, Two-line type, moneyer Dudig

Alfred used the old Roman 'Two seated emperors' design for one of his pennies, a type also used by Ceolwulf II of Mercia and Halfdan the Dane. Several different types of halfpennies were issued during Alfred's reign which suggests that coins were beginning to be used in everyday commercial dealings and that small change was needed. Alfred sometimes used the title REX SAXONVM on his coins but on his 'Two Emperors' pennies he assumes the title REX ANGLOR, 'King of the English', the first occasion this is used by an English monarch. There are also rare pennies with the inscription AELFRED REX SAXONVM set across the field in four lines, whilst on the reverse are the mint names EXA and PIN arranged vertically. These have been attributed to Exeter and Winchester respectively, but like large size 'offering pennies' of similar style with the word ELI/MO, *elimosina*, 'alms', in two lines across the reverse, they have no moneyers' names and they may have been intended for the payment of the 'Romescot' contribution to the church of Rome rather than for domestic use.

Edward 'the Elder' (899–924) extended his authority over East Anglia and all central England, fortifying many of the towns and creating many new *burhs*. He issued two main types of pennies, one with his portrait (**47**) and the other with just a small cross in the centre, the reverses of both types having the name of the moneyer across the field in two lines. The type without portrait, known as the Two-line type, was the normal issue during the next five reigns. Besides his normal pennies there are rare types with floral designs and others that may be commemorative issues. One of these has a church tower with arched windows, another depicts a tower copied from a Roman coin and there is a penny with the Hand of Providence descending from a cloud. Most of these rarer types appear to be products of the Chester mint, one of the new *burhs* constructed to contain the Norse settlers in Lancashire and Cheshire. Apart from a rare penny of Bath none of Edward's coins exhibit a mint name.

47 Edward the Elder, Æ penny, portrait type, moneyer Heremod

THE DANELAW

Although Britain had been subject to raids by Viking pirates for many years the first really major Danish invasion took place in 866. Within a few years a considerable Danish army had been built up, ranging and looting over wide areas of England. Settlement on a large scale took place throughout Northumbria, the East Midlands and East Anglia. Halfdan, the son of Ragnar Lothbrok, was one of the outstanding Danish leaders and in 872 he occupied London holding it for three years during his campaign against Alfred. There is a penny copying Alfred's 'Two Emperors' type with the name VLFDENE RX which has been attributed to this Halfdan but it may be a coin of a later Viking leader of the same name. Halfdan moved to York in 876 but was expelled a year or two later and was succeeded by Guthfrith of whom no coins are known.

In the south Halfdan was succeeded by Guthrum who, after an exhausting campaign against Alfred, secured a treaty in 878 which left him in control of East Anglia and Mercian England north and east of Watling Street, an area which became known as the Danelaw. Guthrum and many of his followers were baptised into the Christian faith and he took the baptismal name of 'Aethelstan', his coins being inscribed ED EL TA RE in the manner of some of Alfred's pennies. Guthrum-Aethelstan was succeeded by Eohric and Guthrum II but no coins are known in their names. Instead, 'memorial' pennies were issued bearing the name of St Edmund, SCI EDMUNDI, the martyred King of East Anglia (**48**). Many of the moneyers who produced the St Edmund coins have Frankish names and they sometimes have FECIT ME (made me) after the name instead of the more usual MONETA. Also from the Danelaw come copies of Alfred's pennies, usually of somewhat cruder style and sometimes with quite blundered inscriptions. Pennies with the name of Alfred and a mint name Orsnaforda, arranged in three lines ORSNA/ELFRED/FORDA (**49**) have been tentatively attributed to Oxford or to Horsforth in Yorkshire, but these and rare coins of an unknown Earl Sihtric, SITRIC COMES, from another uncertain mint, Sceldford, arranged GVNDI/SCELDFOR/BERTVS, may come from the southern Danelaw.

48   The Danelaw, St Edmund memorial coinage, Æ penny, moneyer 'Aoleri' (Albert)

49   Penny in name of Alfred, 'Orshaforda' mint, moneyer Bernvald

Also from the closing years of the ninth century is an intriguing group of coins which come principally from the great Viking treasure hoard of coins, ornaments and 'hacksilber' (cut or broken silver ornaments used as bullion) discovered at Cuerdale, Lancashire, in 1840. This hoard contained over 900 coins of Alfred, 51 of Edward the Elder, 65 of Archbishop Plegmund, over 1800 'St Edmund' pennies, over a thousand silver deniers of the Carolingian Franks and some three dozen Islamic silver dirhems, but the most controversial part of the hoard includes some 3000 pennies and some halfpennies in the names of a King Cnut and a King Siefred. These coins are generally attributed to the city of York, *Eboracum*, as many bear the mint name EBRAICE CIV(itas), though others have the strange name CVNNETTI. No Northumbrian 'Cnut' of this period is known from historical sources though there was a king named Harthacnut in Denmark.

The general style of these coins suggests Carolingian rather than Anglo-

Saxon influence and, like Carolingian deniers, they do not exhibit names of moneyers. The Cnut coins have a plain cross or an inverted patriarchal cross and the king's name, if it is a king's name, is set around the cross with the letters C–N–V–T arranged as if making the sign of the cross, with REX in the angles (**51**). Siefred's coins have his name in the Latin form SIEFREDVS REX, the Germanic form SIEVERT R, or as C SIEFRE, the C possibly representing the Scandinavian *cununc*, 'king'. Some coins bear a 'Karolus' monogram copied from the Frankish deniers of Charles the Bald, while others in the group have a religious inscription, DNS DS O REX/MIRABILIA FECIT (**51**), which can probably be expanded to *Dominus deus omnipotens rex mirabilia fecit* (The Lord God, Almighty King, has done wondrous things). The workmanship of the Cnut and Siefred coinage varies considerably and there is extensive 'muling', the mixing of different obverse and reverse

50 'Cnut', Æ penny, CVNNETTI *rev.*

51 Anonymous Æ penny, DNS DS O REX/MIRABILIA FECIT

types. Some coins of Cnut of degenerate style bear the mint name of 'Quentovic', the Carolingian port at Étaples in the southern Boulonnais. Despite the fact that in the main the coins are closer in weight to the Anglo-Saxon standard than to the Carolingian, the writer is not yet convinced by arguments for the attribution to York and until there is further evidence to substantiate that theory he is inclined to think that a continental origin must be considered at least a possibility.

During the early years of the tenth century a number of pennies were issued in the Danish kingdom of York. Some of these cite the name of St Peter, S̄ CI PE/TRI MO, in two lines. Others with the name of RAIENALT (Regnald) have a crude head and a Karolus monogram, or an open hand, a hammer or a bow and arrow. In 919 the Viking kingdom of York was seized by an army from Dublin led by Ragnall, the first of a dynasty of Hiberno-Norse kings of York. He was succeeded by his brother Sihtric

Caoch, 'One Eye', in 921 and by another brother Guthfrith in 926. Coins of 'St Peter' type continued to be issued but from about 920 a sword divides the two lines of inscription bearing the saint's name and sometimes a Thor's hammer appears on the other side (**52**), a reminder perhaps that at this period Christianity was not universally dominant amongst the Scandinavian settlers. The sword appears again on pennies of the Lincoln mint which cite the name of St Martin, patron saint of that city. It has been suggested that this sword represents the celebrated sword of Carlus which was regarded as a symbol of sovereignty by the Scandinavian kings of Dublin.

52 St Peter's of York, Æ penny, Sword type

In 927 Guthfrith was expelled from York by Aethelstan of Wessex who now ruled all England south of the Humber, but Guthfrith's son Anlaf (or Olaf) returned to York in 939 and extended his kingdom to include the confederated Danish Five Boroughs of the Midlands: Derby, Nottingham, Leicester, Lincoln and Stamford. Anlaf issued pennies in the style of those of Aethelstan and also struck pennies bearing the Viking raven device (**53**). On some coins he used the Latin title *rex* but on others the Norse *cununc*, and on pennies of the Derby mint his title is REX TO D, possibly *rex totius*

53 Anlaf Guthfrithsson, Æ penny, Raven type, moneyer Athelferth

danorum (King of all the Danes), in imitation of Aethestan's REX TO BRIT. In 941 Anlaf Guthfrithsson died and was succeeded at York by his cousin Anlaf Sihtricsson who, besides issuing coins of Anglo-Saxon type, struck pennies bearing a triquetra (triple-shield) device and a battle-standard, a type also coined by his cousin Ragnall Guthfrithsson. Sihtric Sihtricsson appears at York about 942 also issuing a triquetra type penny (**54**).

In 942 King Eadmund had captured the Five Boroughs and in 944 he occupied York. However, Eadmund's death in 946 presented an opportunity for Eric Blood-axe, a son of Harald Fairhair of Norway, to establish himself in York where for a short time he issued pennies of Anglo-Saxon type. Anlaf Sihtricsson returned to York to expel Eric and he then issued pennies with his name spelt ONLAF. Eric retook York for a second time in 952 when he issued pennies of the 'sword' type, but he was expelled by King Eadred two years later. From 954 an independent kingdom of York ceased to exist, being replaced by an earldom of Northumbria which was largely autonomous though nominally subject to the English kings.

54 Sihtric Sihtricsson, Æ penny, Standard type, moneyer Ascolv

ANGLO-SAXON KINGS OF ENGLAND FROM 924

Aethelstan (924–39), the eldest son of Edward the Elder, extended his overlordship into Wales, expelled Guthfrith the Norse ruler of York in 927, campaigned in Scotland in 934 and in 937 heavily defeated an alliance of Norse, Scots and Strathclyde Britons at the famous Battle of Brunan-burh. Aethelstan's early coins are of similar type to the Two-line type of his father. Later issues have a circular inscription, frequently with the title REX TO BRIT (*rex totius Britanniae*, King of all Britain) (**55**). A portrait type with a crowned bust was also introduced, but the most important innovation was

55 Kings of all England, Aethelstan, Æ penny of York, moneyer Regnald

the inclusion of the name of the mint on many coins and some thirty mint towns have been recorded.

In a code of laws pertaining to southern England promulgated by Aethelstan at Grateley, Hampshire in 928, one ordinance stipulated that no one was to mint money except in a borough and another laid down the number of moneyers allowed: eight at London, seven at Canterbury (four for the king, two for the archbishop and one for the abbot of St Augustine's), six at Winchester, three in Rochester (two for the king and one for the bishop), two at Lewes, Southampton, Wareham, Shaftesbury and Exeter, and one at other boroughs. Though not all coins bear a mint name some can be attributed to particular mints from the names of moneyers who appear on coins with a mint signature. Other coins can be attributed to certain areas from the style of engraving, the dies having been prepared at regional die-cutting centres: Winchester, London, Chester, York and probably Lincoln. Aethelstan's coins from the North-West region normally have a rosette of pellets on one or both sides, some of his coins from York have a tower with a pointed roof and other coins with a helmeted bust and a cross-crosslet on the reverse have been attributed to Lincoln.

Eadmund (939–46), a half-brother of Aethelstan, also issued coins of both Two-line and Circular Inscription type, as well as Rosette coins from Chester and North-West Mercia, portrait pennies principally from the eastern Danelaw and helmeted bust coins from Lincoln. A few rare halfpennies of Eadmund have survived.

Eadred (946–55) issued coins of similar type to those of his brother Eadmund though few of them have a mint signature. The Norse kings were finally expelled from York during this reign and Eadred was acknowledged as overlord by the king of Scotland. A unique penny of Two-line type exists with the name HOPAEL REX which has been attributed to Howel Dda, King of Wales *c*.942–50.

Eadwig (955–9), the elder son of Eadmund, was king of all England for less than two years, then the Mercians and Northumbrians revolted and for the remainder of his reign he only ruled over southern England. He issued both Two-line and Circular Inscription type coins and a Three-line type was also introduced with a mint name in the centre contracted to two, three or four letters: BE+DA (Bedford), D+E (Derby), +WIN+ (Winchester) (**56**) etc.

56 Eadwig, Æ penny of Winchester, moneyer Otic

Eadgar (959–75) was acclaimed king in Northumbria and Mercia in 957 and was recognized as successor to his brother Eadwig in southern England in 959. His earliest coins continue the Two-line, Three-line and Circular Inscription types, the latter being known from some twenty-five mints, and he also issued an early portrait type, both with and without mint names. Then, in 973, Eadgar instituted a major reform of the currency, calling in and demonetizing the diverse types in circulation and reissuing new money of uniform type throughout the country. These coins had a diademed bust to left with the inscription EADGAR REX ANGLO(*rum*) and, on the reverse, a central cross pattée with the names of the moneyer and mint around (**57**). These are known of some forty mints. The few pre-Reform round halfpennies of this reign were the last known of the denomination until the early twelfth century apart from a reported coin of Edward the Confessor, but another means of providing small change was to cut a penny into two halves. Sometimes this was done by scoring across the flan, the central cross acting as a guide line, and then breaking the coin in half.

57 Eadgar, Æ penny of Stamford, Reform type, moneyer Wulgar

Eadward the Martyr (975–8), the son of Eadgar and his first wife Aethelflaed, continued the Reform type instituted by his father and these pennies are known from some thirty-eight mints. Eadward was murdered at Corfe, probably on the orders of his step-mother.

Aethelred II *Unraed* (the Imprudent, more commonly called 'Unready'), 978–1016, was the son of Eadgar and his third wife Aelfthryth. The last two decades of the tenth century and the early years of the eleventh century saw a resumption of Danish raids on a very large scale with great quantities of plunder secured or the Viking forces bought off by the payment of many thousands of pounds. The Anglo-Saxon Chronicle records, for instance, that in 994 a Danish fleet under Olaf Tryggvason and Swein Forkbeard was bought off with £16,000 in cash (3,840,000 silver pennies), that £30,000 was paid in 1007 and £48,000 in 1012, and that in 1009 the men of East Kent alone paid £3,000. These payments of tribute account in large part for the many hoards of late Anglo-Saxon pennies found in Scandinavia and around the Baltic coasts.

The six-year cycle of Eadgar's Reform type design was completed in 979 and the coinage was then changed to the Hand type. This had a diademed bust to right (though a few coins still retained a left-facing bust) and on the reverse a Hand of Providence emerges from a cloud or sleeve with an *alpha* and *omega* at the sides (**58**). Six years later the design was adapted by the addition of a sceptre on the obverse and by additional curves added at the top of the reverse to make it more obvious that the Hand was coming from

Heaven. Further six-year changes were made with the old types being called in. About 991 another variation of the Hand type was introduced at some mints with the king's sceptre terminating in a cross instead of a trefoil of pellets, while on the reverse the Hand is shown with the two smaller fingers folded giving the Latin benediction. This Benediction Hand type is rare and it was apparently discontinued in favour of a new and distinct design, the Crux type, which has a left-facing bust and the letters c–r–v–x in the angles of the reverse cross. In 997 there was a temporary reversion to the Reform type, which is named the Intermediate Small Cross type, but this issue is only known from eight mints and it was obviously quickly replaced by the Long Cross type of 997–1003. This has a plain bust facing left and a long cross on the reverse with triple-crescent ends; it is the commonest of all Aethelred's coins (**59**). The Helmet type, introduced in 1003, shows the king in a radiate helmet copied from a third-century coin of the Roman Emperor Maximian.

58 Aethelred II, Æ penny of London, First Hand type, moneyer Aethelred

59 Aethelred II, Æ penny of Canterbury, Long Cross type, moneyer Leofric

An interesting but rare type was introduced in 1009, the Agnus Dei type, which has the Paschal Lamb on the obverse and the Dove or Holy Spirit on the reverse. The reason for this choice of type is not known for certain but the issue may have coincided with the promulgation of the penitential code of laws (VII Ethelred) of 1009 which had been drafted by Archbishop Wulfstan before Michaelmas that year, 'when the great army came to the country', and which enjoined strict religious observance to stave off national calamity. It seems that before the dies had been issued on a nationwide basis the type was replaced by the Last Small Cross type which was a repetition of Eadgar's Reform type.

At least eighty mints were active during Aethelred's reign, most being boroughs though some were royal manors, such as Bruton, Milborne Port and Warminster. Some mints were set up in hill forts because of emergency, for instance, at Old Sarum near Salisbury after Wilton had been sacked by the Danes in 1003, at Cadbury, Somerset, at a time when Ilchester was threatened by the Danes, and at Cissbury, Sussex, probably for the same reason. During the greater part of the reign a number of different die-cutting centres supplied dies and these appear to have been based on the regions governed by ealdormen who probably shared in the revenue from die manufacture. During the run of Aethelred's last type the word *moneta* before the mint name, which was usually contracted to M ̄ O, M'O, MON or M O, was usually replaced by the word *on*, 'in', e.g. ALFPOLD ON OXNAF, 'Alfwold in Oxford'.

England, with its prosperous agricultural economy, was an irresistible magnet for the Scandinavians in the late tenth and eleventh centuries and in 1013 King Swein Forkbeard of Denmark landed a very large army to seize the kingdom and he was accepted as king in many parts of the country. Aethelred left London to take refuge in Normandy with his brother-in-law Duke Richard II, but returned after Swein died early in 1014. Meanwhile Swein's son Cnut left for Denmark to secure the throne there but he returned to England with an even greater army in 1015. Aethelred died in April 1016 and then the country was divided between Cnut and Aethelred's son Eadmund 'Ironsides'. Eadmund died in November without having issued coins in his own name as far as is known.

THE ANGLO-DANISH EMPIRE

No English coins are known of Swein Forkbeard though he did strike pennies in Denmark copying Aethelred's CRVX type. His son Cnut (1016–35) married Aethelred's widow Emma, brought all England under his control, then re-secured his paternal territories in Denmark and in the mid-1020s extended his dominion over Norway. His first English coin type, the Quatrefoil issue, was not introduced until 1018 and this has the king's crowned bust set within a quatrefoil, with a voided long cross over a quatrefoil on the reverse. His second type, the Helmet type, has a helmeted bust to left (**60**). The final type of the reign, the Short Cross issue, has a diademed bust and a short voided cross on the reverse. So Cnut maintained the currency system of his predecessor, with recoinages every six years in order to ensure that money in circulation was kept at good weight and quality. Cnut's coins are known from more than seventy-five mints. Copies of English pennies were minted in Scandinavia as well as coins of distinctive Scandinavian type.

Following Cnut's death the succession of Harthacnut, his legitimate son by Emma, was disputed by Harold, his son by Aelfgifu of Northampton.

60   Cnut, Æ penny of London, Helmet type, moneyer Lifinc

Harthacnut was engaged in securing Denmark so his mother acted as regent for a time in southern England whilst Harold held Mercia and Northumbria. A new coinage was introduced in 1036, the Jewel Cross issue, so-called from the design of the reverse cross. Initially a dozen or so mints in the South and South-West issued coins under Emma in the name of 'Cnut', then these and other mints, principally in southern England, issued Jewel Cross coins in the name of Harthacnut, whilst the more northerly mints struck similar coins in the name of Harold. As Harthacnut continued to remain in Denmark Harold was recognized as king throughout England in 1037 and Emma fled for protection to Flanders. After a two-year period the Jewel Cross issue was replaced by the Fleur-de-lis type depicting Harold with sceptre and shield and with a voided long cross on the reverse with a fleur-de-lis or a trefoil of pellets in the angles (**61**). Harold died in 1040 and Harthacnut succeeded him as king of all England. A new coin type was then instituted, the Arm-and-sceptre type which shows the king's arm and a sceptre in his hand, the reverse having a quadrilateral set over a voided cross. Some of these coins have Harthacnut's name fully extended but others have the name contracted to 'Cnut'. It would appear that after Cnut's death the cyclical recoinage (*renovatio*) was instituted at intervals of two years instead of six.

61   Harold I, Æ penny of London, Fleur-de-lis type, moneyer Brungar

THE ANGLO-SAXON RESTORATION

On the death of Harthacnut in 1042 Edward (1042–66), the son of Aethelred II and Emma, was elected king. Edward, later to be known as 'the Confessor' on account of his monastic education and character, had been brought up in Normandy. There were ten main types issued during his reign, the first four types each being issued for a two-year period but the later issues being changed at intervals of three years. On the first five types the king is depicted with a beardless head in profile. These are known as the PACX, Radiate Small Cross, Trefoil-Quadrilateral, Small Flan and Expanding Cross types, the last being struck to first a light (18 grain) and then a heavy (27 grain) weight standard (**62**). On his sixth type Edward is shown bearded and wearing a conical helmet, and on his seventh, the Sovereign/Eagles type, he is enthroned, crowned and holds a long sceptre and orb, while on the reverse an eagle is set in each angle of the voided cross. The obverse type appears to be a very close copy of a gold solidus of the sixth-century Byzantine emperor Justin II and a somewhat similar design occurs on Edward's great seal. The eagles on the reverse of the coin may also be taken from the eagle that appears on some regal seals, and one coin is known that has an eagle on the orb in place of the cross.

62 Edward the Confessor, Æ penny of Canterbury, Expanding Cross type, moneyer Edwerd

Edward's eighth type, the Hammer Cross issue, has a crowned bust of the king to right. His ninth type has a crowned facing bust and a small cross on the reverse, and the final type of the reign, the Pyramids type, has a crowned bust to right and a short voided cross on the reverse with a wedge or pile in each angle. Some rare transitional coins of this issue have a crowned facing bust with an orb and sceptre. About seventy-five mints are known to have been active during this reign.

Harold Godwinsson, the Earl of Wessex and Edward's brother-in-law, was the most powerful figure in England in 1066 and as Edward was childless he was able to secure the throne despite the fact that Edward may have nominated William of Normandy, the son of his cousin, as his heir. Harold's single coin type portrays a determined, martial-looking figure, but the choice of the word PAX across the field of the reverse proved to be optimistic rather than prophetic (**63**). Despite his short reign of nine months his coins, though scarce, are not unduly rare thanks to their deposition in a number of coin hoards hidden at the time of the Norman invasion or shortly afterwards. His coins are known from some four dozen mints.

Harald Hardrada of Norway also had designs on the throne of England, but Harold defeated the Norse king at Stamford Bridge in Yorkshire. He

63 Harold II, Æ penny of Lewes, moneyer Oswold

then force-marched his army south to meet the forces of Duke William who had landed in Sussex to claim the English throne. As everyone knows, Harold and many of his followers fell at Hastings before the superior power and tactics of William's cavalry and bowmen.

The weight of the thin silver penny varied over the Anglo-Saxon period. Commencing at about 20 grains (20 dried barleycorns) in the eighth century, it reached 24 grains in parts of England during the reign of Alfred and up to 25 grains under Edward the Elder and Aethelstan, and it would be from the end of the ninth century that the '24 grain = 1 pennyweight' originated. The weight of the penny dropped around the mid-tenth century but it was back at 24 grains early in the reign of Aethelred II, then it varied at $22\frac{1}{2}$, 25 and $27\frac{1}{2}$ grains and several standards appear to have been used concurrently between about 1010 and 1025. Then the standard seems to have been 18 grains until a heavy issue of 27 grains occurs about 1053, afterwards varying between 18 and 20 grains, and rising to $21\frac{1}{2}$ grains under Harold II. There is no suggestion that moneyers were supposed to strike each coin to within a grain of the standard, that would have been impossible, but they would have been required to mint a specified number of pence from a pound of coinage metal.

There are difficulties in determining the value of the Anglo-Saxon silver penny in modern terms, except through a comparison of the value of commodities. For instance, a cow valued at 24 pence and a sheep at 5 pence in the eleventh century could be worth, say, £400 and £35 respectively today. Though the *scilling* appears in Anglo-Saxon documents, the shilling at this period was only a denomination of account and was not struck as a coin. At one time there were five pence to the Wessex shilling and four pence to the shilling of Mercia.

4

THE NORMANS

❧ ⬥❀⬥ ❧

The conquest of England by the Normans had no immediate effect upon the coinage. The standard of Saxon coinage had been remarkably high compared with that of most of Europe and, as the coins of Normandy minted at Rouen were particularly poor, King William evidently thought it better not to interfere with a monetary system that was working so efficiently. So in the main the Saxon moneyers were left in peace to carry on their work, although most estates and offices of state were divided out amongst the Norman aristocracy and their knights and chief retainers. However, a strong central control was exercised over the mints and die-cutting was concentrated at a single establishment in London with Otto the Goldsmith being appointed to supervise the operation, an office which was passed down through his family as *cuneator* (die engraver).

The general style of the coinage remained the same as before the Conquest, with the issue and design being changed every two or three years. There are eight different types of William I, two of them having his bust in profile and the other six having a full-face bust. They are known as the Profile Left, Bonnet, Canopy, Two Sceptres, Two Stars, Sword, Profile Right and PAXS types. The Bonnet type has an unusually large crown with the four *pendulae* clearly visible, a characteristic derived ultimately from a Byzantine prototype. The Canopy type has the top of the king's throne showing above his head and the last type of the reign has the letters P A X S arranged in the angles of the reverse cross (**64**). The reverses all have a cross of different form, variously decorated, and as with the pre-Conquest issues this facilitated the cutting of the coin into two halves for use as halfpence. The PAXS type used to be the rarest type of William's coins

64 William I, Æ penny of Shrewsbury, PAXS type, moneyer Segrim

until a hoard of over 6000 of these pennies was found at Beauworth near Winchester in 1833. Now it is by far the commonest type.

On the pennies of William I and II a minimum number of punches were used to stamp the lettering into the dies, most letters being constructed from an upright, a wedge and a crescent. Two uprights were frequently used for the letters A, U and V and sometimes for H, M and N as well. As a result the inscriptions are sometimes quite difficult to read. The Saxon *wen* (P) and *thorn* (Þ) were still retained for the sounds *w* and *th*, so William's name appears as PILLELM(VS). Over sixty-five mints were active during the reign though some of the smaller ones did not produce large quantities of coin and consequently pennies of some mints are extremely rare. The first five types of William's pennies were struck to a weight below 21 grains, whatever the theoretical standard may have been, but his later types appear to have been issued at about $21\frac{1}{2}$ grains.

There are a number of references to mints and moneyers in Domesday Book, that extraordinary compilation of land holdings, revenues and local administration in late eleventh-century England. At Hereford, for instance, it is recorded that 'There were seven moneyers there. One of these was the Bishop's moneyer ...'. The entry for Worcester states '... whenever the coinage was changed each moneyer gave 20s. at London for receiving the dies for the coinage'. At Malmesbury in Wiltshire, '... from its Mint the Borough itself pays 100 shillings'; and at Wallingford in Berkshire, '... there are fewer properties (than in 1066). ... a moneyer has one, exempt (from geld) so long as he coins money'. In some boroughs it appears that income from fines and from the moneyers was divided between the king and the earl, usually in the ratio of two to one, the earl's portion being known as the 'third penny'.

WILLIAM II RUFUS 1087–1100

On the death of William I his French and English territories were divided between his two eldest sons, Robert, the eldest, becoming duke of Normandy and William Rufus succeeding his father as king of England. The pennies of William II are of a similar style to those of his father but tend to be of somewhat cruder workmanship. There are five different types, the

Map 3 English and Welsh mint towns

Profile, Cross-in-Quatrefoil, Cross Voided (**65**), Cross Pattée-and-Fleury and the Cross Fleury-and-Piles types. Some of the obverses are close copies of coins of William I; for instance, the Profile type looks very like the Conqueror's Profile Right type except that a sword takes the place of the sceptre and Rufus's fourth obverse is almost identical to William I's Sword type apart from the king's crown being a little flatter. About sixty mints are known to have been active in this reign.

65   William II, Æ penny of Chichester, Cross Voided type, moneyer Brunman

HENRY I 1100–35

William II had no children and, as Robert of Normandy was crusading in the Holy Land at the time of his brother's death, Henry 'Beauclerc', the youngest son of William I, was crowned king. The pennies of Henry I, of which there are fifteen different types, are all scarce or rare except for the last two types of the reign. Owing to a lack of coin hoards deposited during the middle years of the reign the correct order of types may not have been established conclusively, though the evidence of a large hoard from Lincoln, found in 1971–2, appears to confirm the suggestion that what was once thought to be the 'tenth' type was actually issued after the 'eleventh' type.

It seems that there was a lessening of control over the output from the mints during the early part of the reign as contemporary accounts speak of numbers of light weight and base coins in circulation. In 1108 the king threatened severe penalties against any moneyers found to be guilty of fraudulent minting. There certainly seems to have been a temporary improvement in the production of dies about this time as the first four types were of poor workmanship but the fifth and sixth types are of greatly improved engraving on dies of larger diameter and with finer lettering which has serifs at top and bottom of the uprights. Owing to the amount of poor quality coin in circulation and the common practice of bending or nicking the edges of pennies to see if they were made of good silver, complaints were made that these damaged coins were frequently not accepted in trade. The official response was to order the mutilation of all newly minted coin by having a cut made in the edge and this continued to be done for a period of some ten or twelve years, probably until 1125. In that year, according to the *Anglo-Saxon Chronicle*, Henry I ordered a trial of all the moneyers in England and the justiciar, Bishop Roger of Salisbury, had them come to Winchester where, it is said, they were all castrated and deprived of their right hands. The Margam Annals gives the number mutilated as ninety-four and this may not be an exaggeration. There seems to be an improvement in the standard of minting of the later types of Henry I (**66**) but the final type of the reign again tends to be poorly minted. It is only the last three types of Henry's reign that approach the standard weight of $21\frac{1}{2}$ grains.

66 Henry I, Æ penny of Southwark, Pellets in Quatrefoil type, moneyer Lefwine

Some of the types of Henry I show rather more originality than types of the previous two reigns. A three-quarter facing bust is shown on Henry's fifth type and on the Double Inscription issue the reverse inscription is arranged in two concentric circles. A new miniscule letter *h* supersedes the capital H and towards the end of the reign the letters *Th* and *W* begin to be used in place of the Saxon *thorn* and *wen*. Moneyers with Norman personal names, such as Andreu, Eustace, Geffrei, Paien, Ricard and Walter, begin to make their appearance, alongside moneyers with established Anglo-Saxon names. The last type of the reign was only issued at about twenty mints compared with some fifty mints for the preceding types.

A contemporary chronicle records that the halfpenny was ordered to be made round, but it is only a little over thirty years ago that the first Henry I round halfpenny was recognized as such, the only coin of this denomination to be found to date, and probably they were never minted in large quantities.

STEPHEN (1135–54), MATILDA (1139–48) AND HENRY OF ANJOU (1149 & 1153–4)

Stephen of Blois, count of Boulogne and grandson of William I, sailed for England and secured the throne immediately on hearing of the death of Henry, his uncle. His cousin Matilda, the only surviving legitimate child of Henry I and designated by him as his successor, landed in England in 1139 with the support of Robert of Gloucester, her half-brother, her uncle David I of Scotland and a number of other barons, and set up a rival court at

Bristol. This Matilda, not to be confused with Matilda (or Mahaut) the wife of Stephen who was the heiress of Eustace III of Boulogne, was known by the courtesy title of 'Empress' since her first husband had been the German emperor Henry V. After the death of her first husband, Henry I insisted that she took as her second the young Count Geoffrey of Anjou, thus securing the southern border of Normandy. A long civil war ensued between Stephen and the supporters of Matilda which neither side was able to win outright. Stephen was captured at the battle of Lincoln early in 1141 and was imprisoned at Bristol, but he was exchanged six months later for Robert of Gloucester who had been captured in the aftermath of the siege of Winchester.

Stephen made a notable innovation when he extended the period of issue of his first coin type to about fourteen years. This coinage, the Cross Moline type, is sometimes known as the 'Watford' type from the large hoard of pennies found there in 1818. It shows the king in right profile holding a sceptre and on the reverse is a cross moline with a fleur-de-lis in each angle. Early coins of this issue usually have the inscription STIFNE REX, but later this changes to STIEFNE RE, then STIEFNE R (**67**) and finally to just STIEFNE. The type is known from some forty-five mints throughout the country.

67   Stephen, Æ penny of Lincoln, Cross Moline type, moneyer Gladwine

Coins of Cross Moline type were also issued by Matilda at Bristol, Cardiff, Wareham and Oxford, these having the inscription MATILDIS IMP, etc. (**68**), or just IMPERATR:. During the period of Stephen's captivity in 1141 Matilda reached London for a few days before being rejected by the citizens but no coins in her name are known of the London mint. There are, however, coins from half a dozen mints, including London, which have the strange inscription PERERIC. This is possibly a blundered form of *imperatrix*, perhaps used by the die-engravers when there was some uncertainty as to the outcome of the dynastic struggle. Some of Matilda's pennies have a different reverse type, a cross fleury over a cross pattée, and were issued mainly at Cardiff, Robert of Gloucester's principal fortress in Glamorgan. In the mid-1140s Stephen was able to regain much of the territory that had been lost in the West of England and early in 1148 Matilda finally left England for Normandy.

Matilda's son Henry had made an abortive raid on Wessex in 1147 but he

68 Matilda, Æ penny of Oxford, Cross Moline type, moneyer Swetig

undertook a more effective though brief expedition to the West of England in 1149 and it may be on this occasion that coins of Cross Moline type were struck in his name at the mints of Gloucester and Hereford. In the north of England, at a time when Cumbria, Northumberland and Durham were under Scottish control, pennies of Cross Moline type were issued in the name of King David at Carlisle and of Earl Henry, David's son, at Corbridge near Newcastle.

Following a dispute with the Church in 1148 and the exile of Archbishop Henry Murdac from York and Archbishop Theobald from Canterbury, the country was placed under interdict for some weeks and Stephen himself was threatened with excommunication. To this period are now attributed coins which have been defaced, either by having the king's name and title hammered out or by the dies being defaced with crosses or other marks struck over the king's face (**69**) or sceptre or over the initial cross. These coins come from mints in East Anglia and from Stamford, Lincoln, Nottingham and York, and possibly also from Salisbury, Chichester, Hastings, Steyning and 'Delca' (an uncertain mint), all in areas which may have been outside the immediate control of the king at this time.

69 Stephen, Æ penny of Norwich, defaced obverse die

During the later years of the Cross Moline coinage some regional variations began to appear. Some coins from Suffolk mints have large roundels incorporated into the reverse design; from Hampshire come coins with a voided cross moline on the reverse, possibly minted at Southampton at a time when Winchester had suffered severe damage during the siege of 1141; from East Sussex there are pennies with a large star at the end of the obverse inscription and from the upper Thames valley mints are coins with a large rosette of pellets after the king's name (**70**). Pennies with a long cross fleury superimposed on the cross moline are known of the Leicester mint,

70 Æ penny, Cross Moline variant with rosette of pellets by sceptre

other variations come from the West Midlands and from Northumberland there are pennies with a voided cross extending to the outer circle of the reverse. These local issues would seem to indicate that there was a decentralization of minting organization at this period. Many of the local issues were struck to a 16–18 grains weight compared with the $21\frac{1}{2}$ grains standard weight of the substantive regal type.

A new coinage, the Cross-and-Mullets type, was instituted by Stephen, probably in 1149. This has a bust facing half-left and, on the reverse, a voided cross pattée with irregular mullets in each angle and three pellets at each extremity of the cross (**71**). These pellets possibly pertain to the roundels on the arms of Boulogne and to the three stones associated with the martyrdom of St Stephen, the king's name-saint. With the possible exception of two mints this issue appears to have been restricted to mints in south-east and eastern England, the area that Stephen held most firmly. In the Midland counties, which were held by powerful barons loyal to Stephen to a greater or lesser degree, coins of a variety of types were issued which are apparently contemporary with this second coinage. Some have a reverse on which the cross pattée is not voided. Pennies of the Derby mint struck from very crude locally made dies have a bird (an eagle?) in each quarter of a voided cross. There are some Cross-and-Mullets coins of Leicester with the name ROBERTV in place of the king's name, presumably struck by Robert de Beaumont, the Earl of Leicester, at a time when he was in rebellion.

71 Æ cut half penny of Canterbury, Voided Cross and Mullets type, moneyer Rodbert

Stephen's third and rarest coinage, the Cross Fleury type, was probably issued *c.*1151–3 and this has a bust in left profile with a cross fleury on the reverse and a trefoil of pellets in each angle. Again, this was only issued in East Anglia and the south-east of England, but there are also some associated types from mints in the Midlands. A somewhat similar type was issued by David of Scotland and his son Earl Henry of Northumberland, though these have a right-facing bust. Probably contemporary with the Cross Fleury coinage were the pennies minted by Earl William of Gloucester, Robert of Gloucester's son, and by Henry of Anjou, the latter having invaded the West of England again in January 1153. These have a crowned or diademed bust to right and, on the reverse, a cross fleury set over a quadrilateral fleury. This reverse copies exactly the last type of Henry I and may well have been adopted by Henry of Anjou, who was now Duke of both Normandy and Aquitane, having married Eleanor of Aquitaine the divorced wife of Louis VII of France, to symbolize his superior right to the succession to the throne of England over any claim that Eustace Fitz-Stephen may have had. Other pennies with a similar reverse but with a helmeted head on the obverse may have been issued by Patrick Earl of Salisbury.

Stephen's last coinage, the Double Cross Pommée issue, sometimes known as the 'Awbridge' type, was introduced during 1153, probably only in eastern England initially but later at some forty or so mints throughout the country. It has a half-left bust and a double cross pommée on the reverse with a fleur-de-lis in each angle. The type continued to be minted after Stephen's death in 1154 until a new type was instituted under Henry II in 1158. Duke Henry also issued two cross pommée types at western mints during 1153. They both have a facing bust between two stars, a type used by William I and William II. The first reverse has a cross botonée set over a quadrilateral pommée and this type was also issued by William of Gloucester and by another baron, possibly Brian FitzCount Lord of Wallingford, always a loyal supporter of Matilda and her son Henry. The second of Henry's 'pommée' types, also issued by William of Gloucester, has a double cross pommée set over the quadrilateral pommée. At the seige of Wallingford in the summer of 1153 negotiations for a peaceful settlement were begun. Stephen's son Eustace died in August and a treaty was finalized before Christmas under which Stephen recognized Duke Henry as his heir.

There is an interesting group of coins of the reign of Stephen that, in the past, have been attributed to the mint of York. These include pennies in the name of Stephen which show the king holding a banner instead of a sceptre and others with two standing figures (Stephen and Matilda?) holding a tall sceptre between them; pennies in the name of a Eustace depicting a lion or a standing knight holding a sword (**72**) which have been attributed to Eustace FitzJohn, a north country baron, but which are probably coins of Eustace the king's son; pennies of a 'Rodbertus' with a knight on horseback, which have been attributed to Robert de Stuteville, another baron of the north of England, and coins of a Bishop Henry, probably

Henry of Blois Bishop of Winchester, the king's brother. These coins do not have the normal moneyer's name and mint name found on all English coins of this period and most of the types have ornamental devices interspersing or replacing the inscriptions, some of these devices also occurring on coins of western Flanders. Despite the fact that some of the coins of Eustace have the name EBORACI DE FL (etc.) on the reverse, recent research suggests that they may have been minted in Stephen's county of Boulogne or adjacent areas.

72 Eustace, Æ penny of uncertain mint, Knight type, no moneyer's name

5

THE EARLY PLANTAGENETS

❧ ✿❀✿ ☙

HENRY II 1154–89

After the Treaty of Winchester Henry had to wait only nine months before he succeeded to the throne. He was already Duke of Normandy and Count of Anjou, Maine and Touraine, and he held the Duchy of Aquitaine through the right of his wife, the Duchess Eleanor. Stephen's last type was continued until 1158 with the king's name unaltered, but it was then discontinued to be replaced by a new coinage, the Cross-and-Crosslets issue, commonly known as the 'Tealby' coinage from the large hoard of these pennies found at Tealby, Derbyshire, in 1807. These coins have a facing bust with sceptre, the king's name being spelt hENRI, sometimes followed by the title REX ANG (or an abbreviation), and there is a cross pattée on the reverse with a small cross pattée in each angle (**73**). It is unusual for

73 Henry II, Æ penny of London, 'Tealby' type, moneyer Geffrei.

more than half the inscription to be visible on these coins since they tend to be just as poorly struck as coins of the previous reign, whilst in shape they are frequently more square than round. Apart from minor variations in the king's portrait the same design was continued until the type was changed in 1180. The coinage was produced at thirty mints in its earlier years but, as the work of the Exchequer became more sophisticated and the administration of government became more centralized, it became a matter of policy to concentrate the manufacture of coin and by the end of the 'Tealby' coinage the number of mints had been reduced to thirteen. Canterbury was the most prolific of all these mints, but from the exile of Archbishop Becket in 1164 until his return and murder in 1170, and from then until his successor was appointed in 1173 all the revenue from the archiepiscopal mint was in the hands of the king.

In 1180 the coinage was redesigned by Philip Aimery, an Angevin goldsmith, whose name FIL AIMER occurs on some early Short Cross coins, but for some unknown reason he was soon discharged in disgrace. On the obverse of the Short Cross coins there is a crude facing head with the king's crown being merely a row of pellets, his hand and sceptre extending outside the inner circle, whilst on the reverse there is a voided cross with a small cross of pellets in each angle (**74**). In the early years of the Short Cross coinage some 70 moneyers were operating at thirteen mints. By the end of the reign the number of moneyers had been reduced to some two dozen confined to the mints of London, Carlisle, Exeter, Lincoln, Northampton, Norwich, Winchester, Worcester and York. By 1189 the standard of die engraving had deteriorated substantially. What was extraordinary was that the designs were continued with only minor alterations during the reigns of Richard I and John and for the first thirty years of the reign of Henry III, the inscription hENRICVS REX being retained throughout.

74 Æ penny of London, Short Cross type Ib, moneyer Fil. Aimer

From the second half of the twelfth century surnames began to come into use and they are sometimes found on coins of the period, especially if two moneyers of the same name were working at the same mint. For instance at London during the Cross-and-Crosslets coinage the names PIRES MER and PIRES SAL occur, and in the Exchequer Pipe Rolls these two Peters are recorded as Pires Merefin and Pires de Salerna.

In 1170 Henry had his eldest son crowned as joint-king and successor by the Archbishop of York during the time when Thomas Becket was in exile. Henry 'the Young King' rebelled against his father and was aided by his two younger brothers in a major revolt in 1173–4, but neither of these events is reflected in any change in the coinage. The young Henry predeceased his father in 1183 after a further rebellion.

RICHARD I 1189–99

Richard, being the eldest of Henry's surviving sons, became king on his father's death but spent only some five months of his ten-year reign in this country. Most of his time was spent in baronial wars in his Norman and Angevin possessions or crusading in the Holy Land. This may have been one of the reasons why the name hENRICVS was not altered on the coinage.

Richard's early Short Cross pennies have a rather odd-looking portrait with a well-defined beard (**75**). They are scarcer than the Short Cross pennies of Henry II, which is not surprising since a vast amount of money must have been required to finance the Third Crusade. Also, on returning from Palestine, Richard was captured in Austria and held prisoner by the Emperor Henry VI who demanded that Richard should hold the kingdom of England as in imperial fief and pay a huge ransom of 150,000 marks (£100,000). This sum was collected and paid over several years and if much of it was hastily raised in silver coin this may account for the poor workmanship of the dies of the later coins of Richard's reign. Of the forty-five moneyers recorded for this reign probably no more than twenty-eight were working at any one time at the ten mints that were active. The only coins bearing Richard's name were those minted for his French possessions in Aquitaine, Poitou and Berri.

75   Richard I, Æ penny of London, Short Cross type IVa, moneyer Stivene

JOHN 1199–1216

The first issue of John's Short Cross pennies are of even cruder workmanship than those of his brother Richard, the king's head being a grotesque caricature of a face. However, in 1205 there was an enquiry into the work of the mints and as a result a recoinage was ordered, any coins in circulation having lost more than one-eighth of their standard weight being demonetized and reminted. The general design of the new Short Cross pennies remained the same, but there was a great improvement in the standard of die-engraving (**76**). Strangely, the name hENRICVS was still retained, the design having become a *type immobilisée*. Over seventy moneyers were engaged on the work of recoinage.

The Short Cross coinage has been divided chronologically into a variety of classes and sub-classes and these can be distinguished by a study of differences of lettering and style of portraiture, class 1 being attributed to Henry II, classes 2 to 4b to Richard I, classes 4c to 6a to John and classes 6b to 8b[3] to Henry III. The letter E occurs with a round back after class 1a, particularly ornate ES and CS occur on some coins in classes 5a and 6c, and the form of the letter X in REX often provides a quick guide to detailed classification.

The only coins of John to bear his name are his Irish coins (see page 183).

76 John, Æ penny of London, Short Cross type Va, moneyer Henri

HENRY III 1216–72

The first issues of Henry III's Short Cross pennies are similar in style to the last issue of John except that they have rather taller lettering. Coins of rather different style with a portrait having no neck were struck from about 1223 for a period of some twenty years, providing some of the commonest coins in the English series, many of them coming from the hoard of over 10,000 silver pennies found at Colchester in 1902. Only eight mints were active at the beginning of the reign and Henry's last Short Cross coins were produced at just four mints. London and Canterbury now both came under the control of one master moneyer, Nicholas of St Albans, while Durham and Bury St Edmunds continued as the only ecclesiastical mints.

In 1247 a new coinage was ordered and, as security for a huge loan to the king from his brother, Richard, Earl of Cornwall, the coinage was leased to him with a half share in the profits. As a prevention against the practice of clipping, the cross on the reverse was now extended to the edge of the coin, hence the name of Long Cross coinage. On these pennies there occurs for the first time the ordinal TERCI or III' to indicate the third Henry, an innovation that was not repeated until the reign of Henry VII. The earliest Long Cross coins bear no mint name, then there was a brief issue with the mint names LON and CAN(London and Canterbury, still under the control of Nicholas of St Albans) and AED (Bury St Edmunds), but omitting any moneyers' names, the king's title being continued onto the reverse (hENRICVS REX ANG/LIE TERCIE LOND, etc.).

In 1248 sixteen mints were brought into operation to assist in the recoinage and a number of documents have survived which tell us something about the recoinage. There is, for instance, a writ from the king addressed to the bailiffs and men of Wallingford ordering them

> in full town court to choose, by the oath of twenty-four good men four men of the most trusty and prudent of the town for the office of moneyer and four other persons for the keeping of the King's mint, and two fit and prudent goldsmiths to be the assayers of the money to be made there, and one fit and trusty clerk for the keeping of the exchange, and to send them to the Treasurer and Barons of the Exchequer, to do there what by ancient custom and assize was to be done in that case.

From another document we know the full names of the moneyers, custodians of the dies, the assayers and the clerk of every mint: for instance, at Bristol the coins inscribed ELIS ON BRVST were struck by Elias de Aby, and pennies inscribed IVRDAN ON WINCE were minted by Jordan Draper at Winchester.

The early Long Cross pennies are without a sceptre but this symbol of sovereignty was reinstated on later issues (**77**). Most of the provincial mints were closed down after the main recoinage had been completed and for the remainder of the reign the only active mints were London, Canterbury, Durham and Bury St Edmunds, Durham being under the control of the Palatine-bishop and Bury under that of the abbot. If the inscriptions on these coins seem a little difficult to read at first it is because some letters are ligatured, the most usual letters to be joined together being AN, AR, EN, ON, ND and NR. Over 13,000 Long Cross pennies were found in another Colchester hoard in 1969, though even this quantity seems relatively small compared with the enormous hoard found in Brussels in 1908 which contained more than 75,000 of these pennies.

77 Henry III, Æ penny of London, Long Cross type Vb, moneyer Henri

Western Europe had been without a gold coinage since the ninth century though Byzantine *solidi*, known as 'bezants', and Arab gold *dinars* were used in the Mediterranean lands. About 1230 the German emperor Frederick II introduced a gold coinage of *augustali* in southern Italy and in 1252 the republic of Florence began striking gold *fiorinos* or 'florins' which circulated and were copied in many parts of Europe. The following year the city of Genoa began minting gold *genovinos* and in 1257 King Henry ordered the minting of pennies of gold which were valued at twenty silver pence. These coins weighed twice as much as the silver penny, but the ratio of 10:1 between the two metals undervalued the gold content and large numbers of them must have been melted down. The coins were struck only at London under the supervision of William the royal goldsmith who had succeeded Nicholas of St Albans as master moneyer. They have a rather fine image of the king enthroned holding an orb and sceptre on the obverse and a long voided cross with rosettes and pellets in the angles on the reverse (**78**). Fewer than a dozen of the gold pennies are known today. Within eight years of having been issued they were passing at a value of twenty-four pence.

78 *N* penny (of 20d.) of London, mon⟨ ⟩er Willem

EDWARD I 1272–1307

For the first seven years of Edward's reign the Long Cross coinage continued to be struck with the name ʜᴇɴʀɪᴄᴠꜱ. However, though the king's name remained unchanged, the king's portrait was improved by the substitution of realistic bushy hair in place of the crude crescent-shaped curls shown on the pennies of his predecessor (**79**). These last Long Cross pennies were only minted at London and the ecclesiastical mints of Durham and Bury St Edmunds. Their neater style was some indication of the reform to come.

The Venetians had instituted a large silver coin of good quality in 1202, the silver *ducato* or 'grosso' (large coin) as it came to be called. Philip Augustus of France had established a regal coinage based upon the type of denier anciently minted by the abbey of St Martin's at Tours, the *denier tournois*, and in 1266 his grandson, (St) Louis IX, revolutionized the coinage

79 Edward I, *Æ* penny of London, Long Cross type VII, moneyer Phelip

of western Europe by introducing a large fine silver *gros tournois* equivalent to twelve base deniers. Edward I was a great statesman and an able administrator, so it is not surprising that after his return from the crusades in 1274 he should have turned his attention to reforming the coinage. The Long Cross coinage was in a poor state owing to wear and clipping. The latter was alleged to be the fault of the Jews and it became one of the excuses for a persecution which only ended in 1290 with their expulsion from the realm.

In 1279 a new coinage was ordered which was to consist not only of pennies but also of round halfpennies and farthings and a new denomination, the *groat* of four pence. The Long Cross pence were called in to be melted down and the new coins were issued in their place. The design of these new coins was so far in advance of previous designs that not only did they become the model for the English coinage for the next two centuries but they were also copied extensively by a number of the feudal states in the Low Countries, France and Germany. The groat of Edward I is a handsome coin (**80**). It has a crowned facing head framed in a large quatrefoil and

80 Æ groat (four pence) of London

around it the legend EDWARDVS DI GRA REX AnGL, while on the reverse there is a large floriated cross dividing an inscription arranged in an outer and inner circle, the outer having a continuation of the king's titles, DnS hIBnE DVX AQVT (*dominus hiberniae et dux aquitaniae*, Lord of Ireland and Duke of Aquitaine). It seems that these groats were never minted in very large quantities and they are now quite rare, the majority of existing specimens probably having been removed from some chain of office as they show signs of having been soldered on one side and gilded on the other. The handsome unbearded bust of a young king is not a true portrait, merely a conventionalized representation of a monarch and it was to remain as such for the next two hundred years. The obverses of the penny (**81**) and smaller denominations have a facing bust with a crown ornamented with three fleurs-de-lis and sometimes a rose or star is placed on the king's breast, the reverse having a long cross extending to the edge of the coin with three pellets in each angle. Though the design of the coins had been standardized, the coins can be reasonably closely dated as they have been classified into ten main varieties distinguished by variations in the legend, lettering, shape of crown, etc.

The chief official at the mint was now the Master and assisting him were the Comptroller and Warden of the Mint, the Keeper of the Dies, the Engraver, the King's Assay-Master, the Clerk and various other minor officials, with the actual moneyers headed by their Provost whom they elected themselves. There was also the Warden of the Exchange who was concerned with the issue of coins to the merchants who had brought bullion to the mint to be made into coin. There was now no need for the moneyers to be named on coins though the name of the mint continued to be given, such as CIVITAS EBORACI(city of York) and VILL NOV' CASTRI (town of Newcastle). There was one exception: a moneyer's name, ROBERT DE hADELIE, is still found on some of the pennies of the abbey of Bury St Edmunds. Other ecclesiastics who retained their minting rights during this reign were the Archbishop of York, the Bishop of Durham and the Abbot of Reading. The Archbishop of Canterbury shared the profits of the Canterbury mint with the king. The York pennies of the archbishop are

81 Æ penny of London, class Id, annulet on breast

distinguished from those issued by the king's mint in that city by having a small quatrefoil in the centre of the reverse cross and the Durham pennies of Bishop Bek bear his personal mark, a moline cross. Besides the royal mints of London and Canterbury additional mints were brought into operation to cope with the work of recoinage at Bristol, Chester, Lincoln, Newcastle and York. The standard weight of the penny was now reduced by quarter of a grain to $22\frac{1}{4}$ grains to make an additional profit of $2\frac{1}{2}$d. from every pound of silver, the traditional fineness of the sterling silver being maintained at 11 oz. 2 dwt. fine, i.e. in each pound of silver there was 11 oz. 2 dwt. of pure silver and 18 dwt. of alloy. The early farthings had a larger amount of alloy added to them to make them a little larger to handle. These had the inscriptions EDWARDVS REX and LONDONIENSIS. However, in 1280 the farthings too were minted in sterling silver and these are inscribed E R ANGLIE and CIVITAS LONDON (**82**).

The illegal importation of quantities of continental *esterlings* made in imitation of the new English pennies was a continual source of complaint at

82 Æ farthing of London, class IIIg, E R ANGLIE

this time. The penny at this period was frequently referred to in medieval Latin as a *sterlingus*, the halfpenny and farthing being called *obolus* and *ferlingus*. These foreign imitations were often called 'lushebournes', many being made in Luxembourg, and others were known as 'crockards' or *rosarii* and 'pollards', the former having a head wearing a chaplet of roses and the latter the polled head of a priest, having been issued by some foreign ecclesiastical mint. These imitations easily got into circulation in this country as is proved by their presence in many coin hoards, but they were often made of base silver or were underweight. In 1299 these imitations were officially devalued to halfpence and the following year they were called in to be melted down and reminted. This involved a major recoinage and the provincial mints were opened again with the exception of Lincoln but with the addition of Kingston-upon-Hull and Exeter. An English mint was opened at Berwick-on-Tweed about 1296 at the time of Edward's expeditions into Scotland. The town changed hands several times over the next quarter century and some of the coins struck in Edward's name are of quite crude style.

EDWARD II 1307–27

Pennies, halfpennies and farthings were the only denominations issued during this reign. The coins are similar in design to those of Edward I, but they have been classified into five principle varieties which can be distinguished by minor variations of design and lettering. The king's name is given as EDWA or EDWAR and whereas all except the last class of Edward I's coins have triple-petalled fleurs as side ornaments to the king's crown those of Edward II have double-petalled fleurs.

Pennies were struck at the royal mints of London, Canterbury (**83**) and Berwick, and at the ecclesiastical mints of Durham and Bury St Edmunds. Halfpennies and farthings were only struck at London and Berwick. On the pennies of Durham issued during this reign there are found the personal marks of three bishops. The early coins have the cross moline of Bishop Bek (†1311), pence of Bishop Kellawe (1311–16) have one of the arms of the reverse cross bent into the form of a crozier, while from 1317 the coins of Bishop Beaumont have a small lion rampant with one or more fleurs-de-lis taking the place of the normal initial cross. When the bishop's seat was

83 Edward II, Æ penny of Canterbury, class XI

vacant the King's Receiver used a plain initial cross as a distinguishing mark.

Edward II was dethroned in 1326 by Queen Isabella and her favourite Roger Mortimer. Edward was shortly afterwards murdered in Berkeley Castle and was succeeded by his son, Edward III.

EDWARD III 1327–77

Edward was only fifteen years of age on his accession and for three years the country was governed by a council of regency. After an intitial period of some fifteen years, during which time much money was drained out of the country to finance the wars in France and relatively little new coin was issued, a number of monetary experiments led to the establishment of a successful and permanent English gold coinage. The developments in the coinage of the period reflect in some measure the general prosperity of the country based on the wool trade, fine quality English wool being in great demand at the periodic trade fairs of Flanders and Champagne.

For the first eight years of the reign the coinage continued the type and style of that of Edward II, but one distinguishing feature is the use of a Lombardic 'n' in place of the Roman 'N'. Pennies of Durham have a minute crown within a lozenge panel at the centre of the reverse cross, and coins of the mint of Berwick have a small bear's head in one or two quarters of the reverse – a rebus on the name of the town. Between 1327 and 1335 only small quantities of pence were minted at London, Canterbury, York, Durham and Bury. From the years 1335 until 1343 no pence at all were coined. Instead, in order to attract bullion to the mints and to prevent new coin being melted down or exported, a new coinage of halfpennies and farthings only was undertaken which was minted in 10 oz. silver (.833 fineness, i.e. one-sixth alloy) in place of the normal sterling silver. This was the second time since the Conquest that coins had been officially issued below sterling standard and they were declared not to be legal tender for the payment of the king's taxes. The coins of this issue are easily recognized by the star placed immediately to the left of the initial cross on the obverse. Halfpennies of this issue were minted at London (**84**) and Reading, the abbot of Reading having earlier been granted the privilege of a moneyer at

84 Edward III, Second coinage, Æ halfpenny of London

London by Henry I. His new Reading coins are now distinguished by an
escallop shell badge in one quarter of the reverse.

Charles IV of France had died without male issue and when his successor
Philip VI invaded Edward's province of Gascony in 1336 Edward retaliated
by assuming the title of 'King of France' the following year, basing his
claim upon the fact that his mother was the sister of Charles IV. King Philip
had been issuing a handsome gold coinage of a variety of types and in 1344
Edward III followed his example and ordered the production of a new
English gold coinage. Two Florentine goldsmiths were appointed to
supervise this operation and it was decided to issue a large gold piece
together with half and quarter denominations which would outshine the
coins of the French. The largest coin, the 'Florin' or 'Double Leopard', was
valued at six shillings and was twice the weight and value of the continental
florin. It depicted the king enthroned below a canopy and flanked by two
crowned leopards' heads, with a tapestry of fleurs-de-lis behind him, and it
has his new title REX ANGLI Z FRANC DNS HYB (King of England and France,
Lord of Ireland) proudly displayed. It was a design that was probably
influence by King Philip's *Parisis d'or* which showed the French king
enthroned with a lion at his feet. The 'leopard' or half-florin has a
beautifully designed English crowned leopard sejant with a mantle
blazoned with the new royal arms, the French fleurs-de-lis quartered with
the three leopards of England, flying out behind him (**85**). The English

85 Third coinage, *AV* leopard (half florin)

royal beast appears to have been named a 'leopard' by the heralds until the
end of the fifteenth century. The 'helm' or quarter-florin is equally
heraldic, with a helmet having a royal crowned leopard crest set against a
background of fleurs-de-lis. The reverses of the gold coins carry biblical

texts as their reverse inscriptions, possibly intended as a deterrent to clipping. On the double-leopard is the legend IHC AVTEM TRANSIENS PER MEDIVM ILLORVM IBAT (But Jesus, passing through the midst of them, went his way, *Luke 4,30*); the leopard has DOMINE NE IN FVRORE TVO ARGVAS ME (Lord, rebuke me not in Thine anger, *Psalms 6,1*) and the quarter-florin or helm reads EXALTABITVR IN GLORIA (He shall be exalted in Glory, *Psalms 112,9*). Unfortunately these coins had been overvalued in relation to silver with the result that they were discontinued after only a few months and only a relatively small quantity can have been minted. The Florin denominations are all extremely rare, only two examples of the double-leopard being known. This difficulty in adjusting the constantly changing values of coins struck in different precious metals was a problem that plagued the monetary economies of all nations which sought to establish fixed values for their coins based on their intrinsic values. It was a problem not finally solved in this country until Britain officially went on to a gold standard in 1816.

Before the end of 1344 a second attempt was made to provide an acceptable gold coinage. A new large coin named a 'noble' was struck weighing $136\frac{3}{4}$ grains, compared with the 108 grains of the double-leopard, and valued at 6s.8d., i.e. one-third of a pound or half a mark, the mark (of 160 pence) being only a denomination of account. This coin has an impressive design of the king standing in a medieval ship with furled sail and a banner flying from the masthead. The king is mailed and wears a surcoat and he holds a large sword and a shield bearing the royal arms. No half noble of this issue has been found yet but the quarter-noble bears the royal arms of England on a shield in a tressure. Both coins of this issue have a floriate cross on the reverse with a letter L for London at the centre (**86**).

86 Third coinage, *A*/noble, heavy issue

The reverse inscriptions repeat the same biblical texts that appeared on the Florin denominations. This coinage was not quite as unsuccessful as its forerunner but now gold was somewhat undervalued in relation to silver and in 1346 the weight of the noble was reduced by about eight grains to give a gold/silver ratio of 12.4 : 1. On this second noble issue the letter in the centre of the reverse is changed from L to E (for Edward), the reverse inscriptions remaining unchanged.

The silver coins of the third (1344) coinage are known by the name of the 'Florin' issue, named after the gold denomination, and the weight of the penny was adjusted downwards from $22\frac{1}{4}$ grains to $20\frac{1}{2}$ grains and then in 1346 to 20 grains. Pennies were struck at London (**87**), Canterbury, York, Durham and Reading. The coins of Durham normally have a crozier head as part of the reverse cross and those of Reading have the abbot's escallop shell badge in one quarter. Halfpennies were struck at London and Reading and farthings at London only. With few exceptions the Florin silver coins are easily recognizable by the neat bust with wide shoulders, a crown with large fleurs and lettering that is more ornate than on previous issues.

87 Third coinage, Æ penny of London, 'Florin' issue

The Black Death which swept through England in the years 1348 and 1349 is estimated to have wiped out about forty per cent of the population, leading to the abandonment of perhaps as many as a thousand villages. It left much social and economic dislocation in its wake, one factor being the sudden increase in the amount of money in circulation per head of the remaining population. The resulting inflation led to attempts to regulate wages and prices and to control the mobility of scarce labour by measures such as the *Statute of Labourers* enacted in 1351. The same year adjustments were made to the coinage, with the noble being reduced in weight from $128\frac{1}{2}$ to 120 grains and the penny from 20 to 18 grains.

Edward's fourth coinage can be divided into three periods: the pre-Treaty (1351–60), Treaty (1360–9) and post-Treaty (1369–77) issues. The pre-Treaty coins bear the king's French title but Edward's quarrel with John II of France was patched up for a time in 1360 when, under the Treaty of Bretigny, he relinquished his claim to the French throne in exchange for a grant of sovereignty over the Duchy of Aquitaine, the County of Ponthieu and the Calaisis. From then until 1369, when war was resumed against John's successor Charles V, Edward dropped the French title from his coins, the larger coins reading REX ANGL DNS HYB Z AQT, etc. (King of England, Lord of Ireland and Aquitaine). In 1347 Edward had captured the port of Calais, most of its French inhabitants were expelled and it became the headquarters for English trade in Europe, being given the privilege of returning two members to the English parliament. A mint was established at Calais in 1363 and both gold and silver of English type were produced there.

The noble and its fractions of the fourth coinage retain the same essential design of the previous issue though with smaller and less ornate lettering. Some of the gold coins of Calais can be readily distinguished by a banner flying from the stern of the ship (**88**) and most of the nobles and half-nobles have a small c at the centre of the reverse. In addition to the penny, halfpenny and farthing, a new groat of fourpence (**89**) was now issued together with a half-groat. These two large silver coins have the stylised royal bust set within a tressure and on the reverse a plain long cross pattée dividing two circular inscriptions, the outer being POSVI DEVM ADIVTOREM MEVM (I have made the Lord mine Helper, *Psalms* 54,4) and the inner having the mint name, e.g. CIVITAS LONDON. The design of these coins is a close copy of silver coins of the Flemish monetary alliance of *c*.1337–45 issued by John of Luxembourg, William of Namur and Bishop Adolph of Liege.

88 Fourth coinage, A/ noble of Calais, post–Treaty issue, ship with flag

89 Fourth coinage, Æ groat of London, pre–Treaty issue

Groats, half-groats and pennies of the fourth coinage were struck at the royal mints of London, York and Calais, halfpennies and farthings being minted only at London. Pennies of the ecclesiastical mint of York have the usual quatrefoil at the centre of the reverse and most of those of Durham have a crozier. Silver of the post-Treaty period is relatively scarce as a decreasing amount of silver was being taken to the mint during the closing years of the reign. The coins of Edward III are outstanding for the variety of 'privy marks' that can be found on them. In order to keep a close check on the coin being produced a different mark was used periodically, probably at quarterly intervals. Besides changes in the form of the initial mark, usually a cross, there were intentional mis-spellings of words, the use of a broken or mis-formed letter, the insertion of particular stops between words or other marks hidden in the design. A number of coins from each batch of coins produced were placed in a locked box or pyx and periodically these were assayed by independent goldsmiths, a procedure known as the Trial of the Pyx, the quality of the metal being checked against trial plates of known fineness. This custom has survived to the present day, though now it is only an annual occurrence, and the Chancellor of the Exchequer, who today is *ex officio* Master of the Mint, is usually present in person to hear the verdict of the jurors, all freemen of the Goldsmiths' Company.

Both Edward III and Edward the Black Prince, his eldest son, struck coins for their possessions in France. The Black Prince died in 1376, the year before his father, the succession then passing to his son Richard who was only ten years of age.

6

THE LATER PLANTAGENETS

RICHARD II 1377–99

Richard's coinage closely follows that of his grandfather. In fact, some of Edward's dies were used with the first three letters of the name altered from EDW to RIC and the E on the reverse of the gold overstruck with an 'R'. Gold coins of this reign are not common and the silver coins are also rare with the exception of pennies of York and halfpennies of London.

As in the later years of Edward's reign, English silver was undervalued compared with the price on the continent and it was found impossible to prevent the flow of bullion to the other side of the Channel. As a result, hardly any bullion was brought to the mint to be coined into money and, in addition, the expense of maintaining a large army in France was a drain on the country's finances. The French wars had dragged on for a long time and all the English possessions in France had been lost apart from small areas around Calais and Bordeaux. Richard's coins have the same design and portrait, if it can be called a portrait, as coins of the previous reign. The obverse inscriptions range from RICARD DEI GRATIA REX ANGL & FRANC DNS HIB & AQT on the gold nobles to RICARD REX ANGLIE on the farthings. Nobles and half-nobles, which have an R in the centre of the reverse cross, were struck at London and Calais but quarter-nobles (**90**) are only known of

90 Richard II, $A\!V$ quarter noble

London. On these coins distinguishing marks such as a crescent, annulet, lis, escallop and trefoil are inserted into the design to distinguish different periods of issue. During the reign three different styles of lettering were employed. No silver coins were struck at the Calais mint, but small quantities of groats, half-groats, pence and farthings were struck at London and pennies were also produced at the ecclesiastical mints of Durham and York.

It seems that 'lushebournes' were still being imported from Flanders and apparently small base silver Italian coins, known as 'galley halfpence', were being illegally imported for use as halfpennies. To suppress these poor coins and to alleviate the shortage of small change Parliament frequently petitioned the king for three-quarters of all silver coined to be made into halfpence and farthings and the relative commonness of the halfpennies of Richard II (**91**) is no doubt the result of these appeals.

91 Æ halfpenny of London

In 1399 Richard was dethroned by his cousin Henry, the eldest son of John of Gaunt, Duke of Lancaster. Henry had been banished some years previously, but when Richard confiscated the Lancastrian estates on the death of John of Gaunt Henry landed in England and with the support of many of the nobles forced Richard to abdicate. Richard died in prison a few months later.

HENRY IV 1399–1413

The coins of Henry IV are the scarcest of those of any king from the time of the Conqueror to the present day with the exception of coins of Edward V. For the first twelve years of the reign the problem of how to produce enough money became increasingly difficult. The silver famine became more and more acute and records show that the manufacture of gold reached the same low level until the mint ceased operating altogether for considerable periods. Gold nobles, half-nobles and quarter-nobles of what is known as Henry's heavy coinage were minted at London and Calais but they are extremely rare. Silver half-groats (**92**), pennies, halfpennies and farthings were minted at London, the two larger denominations having a star on the king's breast. No groats are known but a specimen may yet come to light. Pennies were struck for the archbishop of York with the

92 Henry IV, Æ half-groat of London, heavy coinage

usual quatrefoil on the reverse. As in the previous reign halfpence are the
least rare of the heavy coins as in 1402 the king ordered that one third of all
silver reaching the mint should be coined into this denomination.

In 1412 a long overdue reform took place when the weights of both gold
and silver coins were changed, the weight of the noble being reduced from
120 to 108 grains and the penny from 18 to 15 grains. This established a
more satisfactory ratio of 11 : 1 between gold and silver instead of 12 : 1,
making it unprofitable for merchants to export coin and bullion to the
continent. Gold and silver now begin to flow into the mint again and
though Henry died the year after the new coinage was introduced his light
coins are less scarce than those of the heavy issue which had been produced
over the previous twelve years. Besides the London coins of all denominations there are light coinage pennies of York and Durham. The London
groats, half-groats and pennies all have an annulet and pellet by the king's
crown to differentiate them from the earlier issue and the gold also has
distinguishing marks on the side of the ship or by the royal arms. No light
coins were issued at the Calais mint which was closed down until the reign
of Henry VI.

During the reign of Charles V of France the French arms were altered by
substituting three fleurs-de-lis for the semée of fleurs-de-lis shield. Henry
IV, like his grandfather, claimed the throne of France and some time during
his reign he, too, made a corresponding change in the English arms. So the
gold coins struck during the latter part of his reign bear only three lis in the
first and fourth quarter of the royal arms.

HENRY V 1413–22

Though he had but a nine-year reign the coins of Henry V are considerably
commoner than those of his father, thanks to the monetary reform of 1412.
All denominations were minted from noble to quarter-noble and groat to
farthing. The mintmark or initial mark which, with a few exceptions in the
reign of Edward III, had normally been a plain cross pattée from the time of
Edward I, was now changed first to a cross with a pellet in the centre and
then to a pierced cross. Most of the silver coins bear privy marks such as a

broken annulet by the crown or a mullet on the king's breast (**93**). The mullet mark is also found on the commonest issue of gold coins, being placed by the king's sword arm on the noble and half-noble and by the side of the shield on the quarter-noble.

93 Henry V, Æ half-groat of London, mullet on breast

York and Durham continued their issue of ecclesiastical pennies as in earlier reigns. No coins are known of Calais though arrangements were being made to reopen the mint there just before the king's death. At one time some Calais coins were attributed to Henry V but it is now established that they were minted in the following reign.

The farthing is one of the scarcest of all denominations, as it is in all reigns from Edward I to Edward IV. There were never enough of them to satisfy public demand because, being the smallest coin, they were the most uneconomical to manufacture, the expense involved in coining them being almost as much as in the minting of larger coins. Being so small they were easily lost and there was less likelihood of them being deposited in savings hoards with coins of higher value.

HENRY VI 1422–61

Henry was only a baby when his father died and he grew up subject to fits of insanity. When still under one year of age he inherited the kingdom of France from his grandfather Charles VI under the terms of the Treaty of Troyes, though the Dauphin was recognized as Charles VII in much of central and southern France and most of the remaining English-held territory fell to the French, aided initially by Joan of Arc, between 1429 and 1450. In England a powerful faction was led by Richard Duke of York who considered the Lancastrian branch of the Plantagenets to be usurpers. The feud between the two parties developed until an armed clash in 1455 led to a civil war which continued intermittently for thirty years – the Wars of the Roses.

Henry's coins follow the same general pattern as those of his father. However, the system of privy-marking was extended as, besides having 'privy' marks hidden in the design, there were prominent marks placed on the coins which were only changed every two or three years. The coins of this reign can, therefore, be divided into eleven different issues based on these markings and are known as Annulet, Rosette-mascle, Pinecone-mascle, Leaf-mascle, Leaf-trefoil, Trefoil, Trefoil-pellet, Leaf-pellet, Unmarked, Cross-pellet and the Lis-pellet coinages. Nobles and half-nobles (**94**) of the Annulet issue, for instance, have an annulet by the king's sword arm and below the inner circle of the reverse and silver coins of the same issue have annulets in two quarters of the reverse and, in the case of Calais coins, on either side of the king's neck. Various types of crosses are used as initial marks on the silver coins but the gold coins all have a fleur-de-lis as a reverse intitial mark.

94 Henry VI, *A*/half-noble of London, Annulet issue

On Henry's accession royal mints were opened at Calais and York in addition to London and all began the manufacture of both gold and silver coins. The York mint was not open for long and gold of this mint is scarce and the silver extremely rare.

Although small quantities of gold were mined in Britain during the Middle Ages, the great bulk of gold bullion used at the mint was obtained from abroad, mainly from Flanders in payment for English wool. Following the defeats of the English in France, the Duke of Burgundy, whose territory included Flanders, formed an alliance with the French in 1435 and forbade the export of gold from Flanders to Calais. As a result, though the early gold coins of Henry VI are common enough, very little gold was struck after 1435. The Calais mint had ceased to strike gold quite early in the reign. The early silver coins of Calais (**95**) are commoner than those of London, but they were later produced in decreasing quantities and the Calais mint was closed for good in 1440.

95 *R* groat of Calais, Rosette-mascle issue

Ecclesiastical coins of the York and Durham mints were struck intermittently. Most of the pennies of York have a quatrefoil at the centre of the reverse, some of the Durham pennies issued for Bishop Neville have two interlinked rings at the centre of the reverse, while those issued by Bishop Laurence Booth have an initial B and a cross by the king's neck (**96**).

At the battle of Wakefield in 1460 Richard of York was killed but a few weeks later his son, Edward Earl of March, defeated the Lancastrian army at Mortimer's Cross and he was acclaimed king on reaching London. Henry VI escaped to Scotland but was later captured hiding in disguise and was put in the Tower of London where he remained for the next nine years.

96 Æ penny of Durham, Cross-pellet issue, Bishop Booth

EDWARD IV, FIRST REIGN 1461–70

The coins of Edward's first reign can be divided into two different coinages, the heavy coinage of 1461 to 1464 and the light coinage of 1464 to 1470. Two interesting features of these coinages are the introduction of new gold coins and the extension of the system of dating coins by changing the mintmarks (initial marks) at regular intervals. To begin with it appears that the marks were changed every year but later, in the sixteenth century, the periodic change seems to have been extended over two or three years at times. Sometimes coins are found with a different mark on one side to that on the other and there are some rare coins of Edward IV with two marks on the same side of the coin. Coins are often found with a mintmark struck over an earlier mark.

The first coins of Edward's heavy coinage are very similar to those of the last (lis-pellet) issue of Henry VI. Until the discovery of the great hoard of 1,337 gold coins found at Fishpool, Nottinghamshire, in 1966, only five nobles of Edward IV were known. This was the largest find of medieval gold yet to come to light in Britain and it added a further sixty-two specimens of Edward's nobles. Many of these coins have the king's name commencing to the left of the king's head instead of to the right. No half-nobles are yet recorded and only one quarter-noble is known.

Various marks appear on the silver coins of the heavy issue, such as a lis, crescent or trefoil below the king's head, annulets or quatrefoils by the king's neck or an eye in the reverse legend. Groats of London and pennies of Durham are the least rare of the silver denominations. It appears to have been the normal practice during the fifteenth and early sixteenth centuries for the London mint to concentrate chiefly on the production of groats, halfpennies and farthings (when issued) and for the ecclesiastical mints to produce the bulk of the pence. Later, Canterbury and York turned out most of the half-groats as well. The farthings of Edward's reign are extremely rare – only two heavy issue pieces are known.

In 1464 it was decided to improve the poor supply of coin by using the same remedy as was applied in 1412 by Henry IV. To begin with, the weight of the penny was reduced from 15 to 12 grains which resulted in a much greater flow of silver to the mint. The next year a new gold coinage was commenced with the noble being revalued and redesigned. The new coin was called a *ryal* or, more commonly, a 'rose noble', and the weight was restored to 120 grains (as it had been prior to 1412) but it was now valued at ten shillings instead of one-third of a pound (**97**). This handsome coin retained the essential design of the noble but it has the (white) rose of

97 Edward IV light coinage, *A*/ ryal or 'rose noble' of London, mm. crown

York placed on the side of the ship and a square banner bearing a large E flies from the stern. In the centre of the reverse is another rose superimposed on a radiant sun, the sun and the rose both being Yorkist badges. The half-ryal, equal to five shillings, is a small version of the ryal. The earliest thirty-penny quarter-ryal has an obverse similar to the quarter-noble, but later coins have the royal arms on the obverse set within a quatrefoil instead of a tressure of eight arcs, and they have an E, rose and sun around the sides of the shield (**98**). All these coins retain the same biblical inscriptions as the noble denominations. The 'rose noble' proved to be a very popular coin in international trade and numerous imitative pieces were produced by states in the Low Countries and Germany, some still being issued late in the sixteenth century.

To cope with the recoinage needed to replace the old issues several provincial mints were temporarily brought into operation, namely Bristol,

98 *A*/ quarter-ryal, mm. crown

Coventry, Norwich and York, and these have the letters B, C, N or E (for *Eboracum*, York), placed in the waves below the ship. Though gold coins of new values were now being produced it was decided not to abolish the old one-third pound coin, so a new gold coin, the *Angel*, valued at 6s. 8d., was produced which was smaller than the noble it superseded, the angel weighing only 80 grains compared to the 108 grains of the noble. The obverse of the angel depicts the Archangel Michael standing with one foot on a prostrate monster (representing Satan) and thrusting a cross–shafted spear down its throat. It has been suggested that this design symbolized the defeat of the Lancastrians by the house of York. The reverse of the angel has a ship similar to that on the old noble but in place of the figure of the king there is a solid cross surmounted by a sun in splendour, at the sides of the cross are a smaller sun and rose and on the side of the ship a shield bearing the royal arms. The reverse legend of the angel is PER CRVCEM TVAM SALVA NOS XPC REDEMPTOR (By Thy Cross save us, O Christ our Redeemer), taken from the liturgy. It seems that relatively few of these early angels were minted as they are extremely rare.

Angels of later reigns are sometimes found with a neat hole punched through them near the edge for use as 'Touch pieces'. These were hung around the necks of the sufferers at the ceremonies of Touching for 'the king's evil'. Presented by the sovereign, who was credited with the divine gift of healing this disease, these amulets were much treasured. St Michael, venerated for his role as captain of the heavenly host in driving Satan out of heaven, was also associated with the casting out of devils and thus was looked upon as a guardian of the sick. The last English monarch to hold a Touching ceremony was Queen Anne but Prince Charles Edward was the last known member of the royal family to exercise the rite in 1745. From the time of Charles II, when the angel denomination was no longer minted for coinage, special gold angel-like medallets were struck for use at the ceremonies.

Though there was a reduction in the weight of the silver coins in 1464 no effort was made to change their design so the old stylised portrait and the cross and pellet reverse remained. The provincial mints that struck the new gold coins also helped in the production of the new lightweight silver denominations and, in addition, a royal mint was opened at Canterbury.

Canterbury did not mint groats, Coventry and Norwich made few half-groats and no pennies or halfpennies, and the royal mint at York produced no pence. The silver coins of Bristol are all rare except for the groats. Groats of London are the commonest of Edward's coins and they usually have a quatrefoil either side of the king's neck. The provincial groats all have the initial letter of the mint (B, C, E or N) on the king's breast as well as the full mint name on the reverse.

In 1463 Archbishop Bourchier of Canterbury was granted the right to strike coins. Since the time of Edward the Elder there had been no separate ecclesiastical mint at Canterbury though the archbishop seems to have had a share in the profits of the royal mint when it was operating there. Archbishop Bourchier struck half-groats and halfpennies as well as pennies and his coins are distinguished by his personal badge, the Bourchier reef knot, placed below the bust of the king as well as by having a distinctive mintmark, an archbishop's pallium.

From now on most of the coins issued for the clerics bear their initials or some other distinguishing marks. For instance, the pennies of Archbishop George Neville of York usually have a G and key at the side of the king's head and some of the coins issued for Bishop Booth of Durham have his initial B with either a D (for *Dunelmensis*) or a cross placed in the obverse field. Coins struck at the ecclesiastical mints during a *sede vacante* (the period between the promotion or death of a prelate and the appointment of a successor) usually omit the distinguishing marks. The same thing happened during the suspension of the temporalities of a prelate who was out of favour and in these cases the profits from the mint went to the king.

THE RESTORATION OF HENRY VI 1470–71

In October 1470 Richard Neville, Earl of Warwick, 'the Kingmaker', landed in England having been exiled by Edward IV for conspiring with the Lancastrians. He quickly raised an army and forced Edward, in his turn, to flee the country. Henry VI was released from the Tower and restored to the throne, but he was no more than a puppet as the reins of government remained firmly in the hands of Warwick.

The coins issued during Henry's restoration are similar to those of Edward IV except for the change of name, which on most of his silver coins is spelt HENRICV. As is to be expected in a reign of only six months, the coins that were issued are now scarce and some are extremely rare. The production of the gold ryal and its fractions was not continued, but the angel was struck with the Yorkist radiant sun omitted at the masthead and with a letter 'h' and a lis by the side of the cross (**99**). A half-angel or Angelet was now added to the coinage, being similar in design to the angel but with the reverse inscription O CRVX AVE SPES VNICA (Hail! O Cross, our only hope), from the hymn *Vexilla Regis* which is part of the Good Friday mass. One peculiarity found on both gold and silver coins of this reign, as well as on the immediately preceding and succeeding coinages, is the form of the letter 'R' which appears at first glance to be the same as the letter 'B'.

99 Henry VI restored, *N* angel of London

All the royal provincial mints had been closed down before Henry's restoration with the exception of Bristol and York. Like London, Bristol continued to mint both gold and silver but only groats and half-groats are known of the York royal mint. The mint of Archbishop Bourchier at Canterbury had been closed before Henry's return and the Bishop of Durham's mint was now closed as well. Archbishop Neville was allowed to retain his mint at York, presumably because he was a brother of the Earl of Warwick. Pennies of Archbishop Neville and groats of the royal York mint are the commonest of the restoration coins.

EDWARD IV, SECOND REIGN 1471-83

After fleeing to the continent Edward was not slow to plan for his return. He found an ally in Charles the Bold of Burgundy who had married Margaret of York, Edward's sister, and the following April he landed in England again at the head of an army. The Earl of Warwick was slain at the battle of Barnet and the Lancastrians were finally defeated at Tewkesbury. Edward sent poor Henry VI to the Tower again where he was probably murdered.

The coins of Edward's second reign differ little from those of his first though they can be distinguished easily by their mintmarks. The angel and angelet (**100**) continued to be the only gold denomination issued, the London coins being relatively common, angels of Bristol less so. The silver coins omit the quatrefoils by the king's neck found on so many of his first reign coins, but some groats have roses by the king's neck or a half-rose on the breast and others have a rose and sun inserted into the reverse legend.

The royal mints of Bristol and York were working early in the reign and a royal mint was opened at Canterbury in the closing years for the production of half-groats, pennies and halfpennies. On the coins of the ecclesiastical mint of York the personal marks of three archbishops are found: the G and key or G and rose of George Neville, the B and key of Laurence Booth and the T and key of Thomas Rotherham. Shortly after Edward's return George Neville was suspended for three years and during this time the York pennies are either found without his personal mark and the quatrefoil on the reverse or they have an E and rose by the king's bust.

100 Edward IV second reign, *A/* half-angel of London, mm. pierced cross

On the episcopal coins of Durham the pennies of Bishop Laurence Booth and his successor William Dudley have the initials of their surnames B or D, with sometimes a D for Durham in the centre of the reverse. Bishop Booth was apparently granted the right to strike halfpennies as well as pennies and these also bear his initial. During the Wars of the Roses many of the coins of York and Durham were made from locally produced dies which are often of much cruder workmanship than the dies produced at London. During these troubled times it was doubtless dangerous to send valuable dies on the long journey from London to the north.

EDWARD V APRIL–JUNE 1483

Before Edward IV died he had appointed his brother Richard, Duke of Gloucester, to be the guardian of Edward, his twelve-year-old son. However, before the queen could have Edward V crowned Richard was proclaimed Protector and the boy-king and his younger brother were detained in the Tower. The crown was then offered to Richard and at some time later it seems that his two nephews were disposed of, though not, it is now argued, until some time in the next reign.

There has been some controversy as to exactly which coins were struck during the eleven weeks of Edward's reign. At one time it was thought that coins with the mark sun-and-rose-united were coins of Edward V, but these are now considered to be the last issue of his father, though they might have continued into the reign of the son. What can certainly be attributed to the young king are gold and silver (**101**) with the name EDWARD and the mintmark boar's head on the obverse, this being the personal badge of Richard, the king's 'protector'. On the reverse these coins have the sun-and-rose mark. All these coins are extremely rare.

101   Edward V, Æ groat of London mm. boar's head (*obv.*) halved sun and rose (*rev.*)

RICHARD III 1483–5

Richard did not enjoy the throne for long. He put down one abortive rebellion led by the Duke of Buckingham, but in 1485 Henry Tudor, Earl of Richmond, returned from exile and Richard was slain at the battle of Bosworth.

Richard's angels (**102**) and angelets are similar to those of previous reigns. His groats of London are the commonest coins of the reign, groats of York being rare. Richard's only known penny of London was stolen in a burglary in 1962 and has not been seen since. York pennies of Thomas Rotherham have a T and key by the king's bust whilst Durham pennies of Bishop Sherwood have an s on the king's breast. The mintmarks boar's head and sun-and-rose both appear on Richard's coins.

102   Richard III, A̸ angel, similar mintmarks

7

THE TUDORS

❧ ✦❀❀✦ ☙

Henry Tudor, Earl of Richmond, was a Welshman descended from the kings of Deheubarth (S. Wales), Gwynedd and Powis (N. Wales) and he could also trace his descent through his mother, Margaret Beaufort, from John of Gaunt and Edward III. Shortly after his coronation he strengthened his position on the throne by marrying Elizabeth, the daughter of Edward IV. This event was later to be commemorated on the coinage by the use of the double 'Tudor' rose made up of the white rose of York and the red rose of Lancaster. Henry was an outstanding statesman who concentrated his energies on repairing the ravages of the civil wars and building England into one of the great commercial powers of Europe. He took an interest in the coinage and introduced two denominations that were to have a long history in the British coinage – the gold sovereign and the silver shilling.

For the first four years of the reign Henry's coins were to differ only in name and mintmark from those of his predecessors. Initially angels and half-angels continued to be the only gold coins issued. The early silver coins of Henry retain the familiar facing head with the open crown. Groats, half-groats, pennies and halfpennies were struck at London and there was a revival of the farthing. These farthings are very rare and quite difficult to distinguish from the halfpennies. As in the previous reign Archbishop Rotherham and Bishop Sherwood placed their initials on their respective pennies of York and Durham. At Canterbury Archbishop Morton regained the privilege previously granted to Bourchier of minting half-groats, pennies and halfpennies which all have a small M in the centre of the reverse.

In 1489 some radical changes were made to the coinage. Most important was the order for the issue of a new large denomination valued at twenty shillings and called a 'Sovereign'. On this magnificent coin the king, who is given a very large head, is shown seated on a low-backed throne set against a backcloth embroidered with fleurs-de-lis. On the reverse, which has the IHC AVTEM legend of the old nobles and ryals, the royal arms are superimposed on the centre of a Tudor rose. This design seems to have been influenced by the equally fine *grand real d'or* struck two years earlier in the Burgundian Netherlands by the emperor Maximilian. Later sovereigns designed by the German engraver Alexander de Brugsal are much better proportioned (**103**), with the king wearing a lace ruff and a far more elaborate throne with the king's personal badges, a dragon and a greyhound, set on the side columns. The latest of Henry's sovereigns have a portcullis, another royal badge, placed below the king's feet. Also issued in 1489 was a revived ryal of ten shillings, only seven examples of which are now known. These have a figure of the king in a ship holding a sword and shield, with a banner bearing an ƕ at the prow and another bearing a dragon at the stern. On the reverse is a large Tudor rose and a shield bearing three fleurs-de-lis, the arms of France, perhaps not surprising as Henry was involved in hostilities with France following the French invasion of Brittany, and may have wished to emphasize the claim of the English crown to the throne of France. The issue of these ryals may have been discontinued after Anne of Brittany married the French king in 1491, an event followed by a peace treaty between Henry and Charles VIII in 1492.

103 Henry VII, N sovereign (20 shillings), mm. dragon

The obverse type of groat (**104**), half-groat and halfpenny was slightly altered in 1489, the king being shown wearing an arched 'imperial' crown surmounted by an orb and cross. The penny, however, was completely redesigned and depicts the king seated on a throne holding an orb and sceptre, the reverse having the royal arms over a cross fourché. From their similarity to the design of the sovereign these coins are usually known as the

'Sovereign' type pennies and they were issued at Durham and York as well as at London. The York pennies of Archbishop Rotherham have the keys of St Peter below the shield and those of Bishop Sherwood of Durham have a crozier in place of the king's sceptre, another in place of the top limb of the reverse cross and the letters D and S at the sides of the shield (**105**). His successor at Durham, Richard Fox, had the letters R D at the sides of the shield on his pennies. After the death of Archbishop Morton the Canterbury coins have no archbishop's mark as the mint was then worked jointly for the king and the archbishop. At York a royal mint was opened for the manufacture of half-groats and these have a lozenge panel in the centre of the reverse cross. At a later date Archbishop Savage struck half-groats at York with keys either side of the king's bust and halfpennies with a key below the king's head.

104 Æ groat, with arched crown, mm. anchor

105 Æ penny of Durham, 'Sovereign' type, Bishop Sherwood

During the second half of the fifteenth century Renaissance art forms were being applied to coinage design in the cities of Italy. The Sforzas of Milan, the Gonzagas of Mantua, the D'Estes of Ferrara and other princely houses were producing impressive gold ducats and double-ducats (*doppias*) and silver *testone* (from *testa*, 'head') with fine large naturalistic portraits. In England the first step moving from medieval to Renaissance style was taken about 1494, perhaps coinciding with the appointment of Alexander de Brugsal, a German goldsmith, as engraver to the mint. On the angel the Archangel Michael was now transformed from a fully-fledged aerial spirit to a winged and mailed warrior in plate armour who looks more the part of the captain of the heavenly hosts as he now stands with both feet trampling on his dragon-like opponent. Then, in 1504, there were produced at the London mint coins with a profile portrait which compete for excellence with the finest portrait pieces issued by the Italians. This new coinage consisted of testoons of twelve pence (the first of this denomination to be issued), groats (**106**) and half-groats, though only the last two coins appear to have been minted in any quantity. These portrait pieces have usually been attributed to Alexander de Brugsal, though as he moved to Antwerp in 1504 it is possible that they were the work of some other engraver. The earliest of the portrait shillings and groats must have been in the nature of experimental pieces and most of them have the portrait neatly framed by a wire-line circle within the normal hatched inner circle but one rare variety of the groat has the king's head set in a tressure. The king's name is variously given as HENRICVS, HENRIC', HENRIC' SEPTIM and HENRIC' VII. Half-groats of the Profile issue were also produced at Canterbury and the ecclesiastical mint of York, the latter being issued for Archbishop Christopher Bainbridge, his early coins having two keys below the royal arms but one rare issue having his initials X B beside the shield.

106 Æ groat, Profile issue, mm. pheon

HENRY VIII 1509–47

It may seem extraordinary, after the interest taken in the coinage by Henry VII, that Henry VIII should have been content to retain his father's portrait on his own coins for the first fifteen years of his reign. Only by the numeral VIII after the name and the mintmarks portcullis and castle can Henry's first coinage be distinguished from the Profile coinage of the previous reign. It may be that it was not yet considered necessary to have a likeness of the reigning monarch on the coinage and relatively few of the population can have seen the king or have known what he looked like.

Henry's first coinage (1509–26) included gold sovereigns, angels and angelets. At London, the only royal mint open for most of the reign, there were issued groats, half-groats, sovereign-type pennies, halfpennies and farthings. No testoons were issued at this period. The halfpenny continued to be struck with the facing head and arched crown introduced by Henry VII but the type of the farthing, which is now a great rarity, was changed to prevent confusion with the larger coin. In place of the king's head there appears a portcullis, a badge used by all the Tudors, whilst on the reverse there is a cross with a rose at its centre. Rare groats, similar to the English coins of this coinage were struck at Tournai in the Low Countries, the city having been ceded to England in 1514 though redeemed by the French four years later at a price of 600,000 crowns. Instead of the normal POSVI DEVM reverse legend these coins read CIVITAS TORNACEN (City of Tournai) and have a crowned T mintmark.

At the ecclesiastical mint of Canterbury Archbishop Warham issued half-groats and pennies with the letters W A by the shield and halfpennies with W A below the king's bust. At York only half-groats were issued, those of Archbishop Bainbridge having the initials X B by the shield, whilst those of Thomas Wolsey have the keys of St Peter and a cardinal's hat below the shield and sometimes the initials T W as well. The Durham pennies of Bishop Thomas Ruthall have the letters T D above or beside the royal arms.

107 Henry VIII, second coinage, A/ George noble, mm. rose

In 1526 a new coinage was introduced when Cardinal Wolsey, Chancellor of the Exchequer, took measures to alter the standard of the English gold coinage to bring it more into line with continental currencies and so prevent the drain of gold coin or bullion overseas. This meant altering the ratio between gold and silver and this was done in three ways: firstly, by altering the values of the existing gold coins; secondly, by introducing new coins made from somewhat debased gold and thirdly, by adjusting the weights of the silver coins. To begin with the sovereign was initially revalued at 22s., later increased to 22s.6d., and the value of the angel was changed from 6s.8d. to 7s.6d. To replace the old 6s.8d. denomination a smaller coin of the same value was introduced called a George noble together with its half. This rare coin has on its obverse a ship similar to that on the angel but in place of the royal arms above the side of the ship there is a Tudor rose and above it are the initials H K for Henry and his queen Katherine of Aragon (**107**). On the reverse St George on a charger is depicted transfixing the dragon and the legend is TALI DICATA SIGNO MENS FLUCTUARI NEQVIT (Consecrated by such a sign the mind cannot waver) from a fourth-century hymn by Prudentius. These coins were issued for only a short time and only a single specimen of the half-George noble is known to have survived.

Another gold coin that was only issued for a few months was the crown-of-the-rose, only two of which are known. This was valued at 4s.6d. and was the equivalent of the French *écu au soleil*. Its obverse shows the royal arms surmounted by a large crown and the reverse, which owes its design to the French coin, has a cross fleury but with a Tudor rose at the centre and the legend HENRICUS RVTILANS ROSA SINE SPINA (Henry, the dazzling rose without a thorn). The significance of this issue was that it was made from 23 carat gold, the same fineness as the écu, and that it was the first time that English gold had been debased below the standard fineness of 23 carat $3\frac{1}{2}$ grains. Although the idea of bringing the English coinage into line with continental currencies might have been laudable in itself, Henry soon saw that further debasement of the coinage would provide a new source of revenue for his expensive tastes. To this end the crown-of-the-rose was superseded by the crown-of-the-double-rose (**108**) and its half-crown, both struck from gold of only 22 carat. These have a large Tudor rose crowned on the obverse with the initials of Henry and one of his consorts, Katherine of Aragon (divorced 1533), Anne Boleyn (executed 1536) or Jane Seymour (died 1537), after which Henry's later queens go unrecognized on the coinage, the cypher H R (for *Henricus rex*) sufficing. The crown-of-the-double-rose and its half-crown were issued concurrently with the sovereign and angel which were still being made of 23 carat $3\frac{1}{2}$ grain gold, the two standards of fineness being known as 'standard gold' and 'crown gold'.

108 *N* crown-of-the-double-rose, Henry and Katherine, mm. arrow

The first actual portrait of Henry VIII is found on the silver groats and half-groats of the second coinage where he is shown as a clean-shaven young man – he was then thirty-five years of age. The 'sovereign' design is retained for the second coinage pennies and on the halfpennies the old conventional facing head is seen for the last time, both the halfpenny and the rare portcullis farthing having the old cross-and-pellets reverse. The silver of the second coinage was not debased but the weights of the coins were reduced, the penny now being minted under $10\frac{1}{2}$ grains, so a considerable profit was made on all the silver coin sent in for reminting. From the time of King John the Kings of England had been Lords of Ireland (DNS HIB, etc. on coins from the Edward I onward) but in 1542 Henry took the title 'King of Ireland' and some rare gold crowns, half-crowns, silver groats and half-groats bear the title HIB REX.

109 Æ groat of York, Thomas Wolsey, cardinal's hat below shield

The ecclesiastical issues of the second coinage are the last of a long and interesting series as, after Henry's quarrel with the Pope which was followed by the closing of the monasteries and the establishment of the Church of England, the clergy were never again allowed the privilege of minting their own money. Cardinal Wolsey, who from 1523 was both Archbishop of York and palatine-bishop of Durham, struck at York the only groat to be issued by an English cleric (**109**). The minting of groats had always been the prerogative of the sovereign and one of the charges formulated against Wolsey, if he had lived to stand impeachment, was that he had usurped the royal prerogative in minting coins of this denomination. Wolsey's York and Durham coins have his cardinal's hat set below the royal arms and most have his initials T W. Wolsey was succeeded at York by Edward Lee and at Durham by Cuthbert Tunstall and their coins have their respective initials E L (or L E) and C D. At Canterbury Archbishop Warham struck half-groats, pennies and halfpennies which bear the first two letters of his name, W A. His successor at Canterbury, Thomas Cranmer, who was burnt at the stake during the reign of Mary, issued half-groats, pennies and halfpennies with his initials. He also used the mintmark Catherine-wheel, a badge that might seem to be associated with Katherine of Aragon, and this seems rather strange in view of the fact that both before and after his elevation to Canterbury he facilitated Henry's divorce from the queen.

It was not until 1544, when the third coinage was begun, that Henry proceeded with a further debasement of the coinage. Then for the last three years of the reign coins were struck in metal of gradually increasing baseness. Gold coins were issued of 23 carat, then 22 carat and finally only 20 carat fineness and silver was issued of 9 oz., 6 oz. and 4 oz. fineness instead of the traditional sterling 11 oz. 2 dwt. standard. The last 'silver' coins of the reign, therefore, had only one-third silver content, the remainder being copper alloy. It is small wonder then that Henry became known as 'Old Coppernose', for after his basest coins had been in circulation for only a short time the copper showed through on those parts of his face that were in the highest relief and received the most wear.

The king is shown on the portrait coins of the third coinage with a much older, bearded facing head reminiscent of the well-known portraits by Holbein. The gold sovereigns and halves still have the king seated on his throne but he now has a Tudor rose at his feet instead of a portcullis and on the reverse the royal arms has two supporters, a leopard on the left and a dragon on the right. The sovereigns of this issue were now brought back to the 20s. value that they had at the beginning of the reign, but at the same time the weight was reduced, first to 200 grains and later to 192 grains. Also issued were gold crowns, half-crowns, angels, now valued at 8s., half-angels and a new denomination, the quarter-angel valued at 2s. Gold was also struck at the Bristol mint which was reopened in 1546, the coins produced there having a W S monogram as their mintmark, the initials of William Sharington the mintmaster.

Silver coins of Henry's last coinage were struck at London at the Tower and at Suffolk Place in Southwark and at the provincial mints at Bristol, York and Canterbury. The testoon or shilling which had not previously been minted for Henry VIII was now produced at the Tower, Southwark and Bristol. On the obverse the testoon has a large bearded facing head of the king and on the reverse a large Tudor rose surmounted by a crown (**110**). The smaller silver coins were struck at all the mints but they retain the royal arms reverse as on the second coinage. Strangely, the groats and half-groats of the Southwark mint have the inscription CIVITAS LONDON while the Tower of London coins retain the POSVI DEVM legend. Towards the end of Henry's reign the older medieval Lombardic lettering begins to be replaced by Roman lettering, though the former reappears on the last coinage of Edward VI and during the reign of Mary.

110 Third coinage, Æ testoon (shilling), mm. pellet in annulet

EDWARD VI 1547–53

Edward was the son of Henry VIII and Jane Seymour and, since he was only nine years of age when his father died, a council of regency was formed led first by the Duke of Somerset and later by Lord Dudley, Duke of Northumberland. In his diary the young king declared his intention of restoring the coinage to its old standards, but owing to the immensity of the task it was to get worse before it got better. The Exchequer could only afford to finance the operation of recoinage in stages and with the mints producing coin of various weights and degrees of fineness there was a period of monetary chaos which provided the unscrupulous with a fine opportunity for profiteering. Coins were minted in London at the Tower and at a new mint set up at Durham House in the Strand, and at Southwark, Bristol, Canterbury and York. In many cases the mintmarks indicate under which mintmaster coins were made: for instance, a bow mark was employed by Sir Martin Bowes at Durham House, a Y was used by Sir John Yorke at Southwark and the Tower mint, a T or 't' by William Tillesworth at Canterbury and a TC monogram by Thomas Chamberlain at Bristol.

To disguise the fact that base coin was still being issued the name and portrait of Henry VIII were retained on the 'silver' testoons and smaller coins and these are only distinguishable from similar coins of the previous reign by their mintmarks or by minor details such as the variety of stops used between words or, in the case of the smaller coins, by the decoration at the end of the cross arms. These 'Henry' coins, of which the groats are by far the commonest (**111**), were issued until 1550 and thus overlap other issues which bear Edward's name and portrait. The first sovereigns issued by Edward have his father's name and closely follow the design of his father's coins but the half-sovereigns, though they have the name HENRIC' 8 depict the enthroned figure with a youthful head (**112**). The rare groats, half-groats and pennies struck at Durham House are distinct in that the inscription on the reverse is REDDE CVIQVE QVOD SVVM EST (Render to each that which is his), appearing in an abbreviated form on the smaller pieces.

The first issue of coins bearing Edward's name read EDWARD' 6,

111 Edward VI, base Æ groat with Henry's name and portrait, mm. lis

112 *A* half-sovereign with Henry's name but youthful head, mm. E

113 Second issue *A* half-sovereign, mm. arrow

EDOARD'6 or ED'6 on the smallest coins. The gold half-sovereigns depict the young king enthroned and the crowns and half-crowns have the crowned Tudor rose, all issued in 20 carat gold. All the silver coins with Edward's profile portrait are rare and difficult to find even in 'fine' condition.

In 1549 an improvement in the gold was effected when the fineness was raised from 20 to 22 carat. Coins of this issue have the Roman numeral VI instead of 6 after the king's name. A sovereign reduced in weight to $169\frac{1}{2}$ grains was now issued with Edward's name, having a neat figure of the young king enthroned, with the crowned arms reverse having leopard and dragon supporters and an E R cypher on a scroll below. The half-sovereign, gold crown and half-crown have either a charming bareheaded bust (**113**) or a crowned bust. The normal reverse legend is SCVTVM FIDEI PROTEGET EVM (The shield of faith shall protect him) but there are rare half-sovereigns which have the TIMOR DOMINE FONS VITE (The fear of the Lord is the fountain of Life *Proverbs* 14,27) inscription which is normally found on the shillings. Some rare Durham House half-sovereigns have the legend LVCERNA PEDIBVS MEIS VERBVM TVVM (Thy Word is a lantern unto my feet *Psalm* 119,105). The half-sovereigns and smaller gold coins omit the supporters by the royal arms.

During 1549 shillings of two different standards were issued. First, there was a coin of improved quality of 8 oz. fine silver but with a weight reduced to 60 grains, not all that much larger than the 40 grain groat, then a larger coin of 80 grains with a reduced fineness of 6 oz. silver. These shillings both have a crowned profile portrait and a date in Roman numerals at the end of the reverse inscription. Those issued at Durham House between January and March 1549 are dated MDXLVIII since the new year did not commence at that time until 25 March. Other shillings are dated MDXLIX (**114**) or MDLX. Some Durham House shillings have the inscription INIMICOS EIVS CONFVSIONE (As for His enemies I shall clothe them with shame, *Psalm* 103,19). No small coins were issued with Edward's name at this time as the exchequer still needed to raise revenue by striking the smaller denominations of 'Henry' type in base 4 oz. silver. In fact, in October 1550 the standard of both the 'Henry' type coins and of shillings with Edward's name and portrait was lowered to 3 oz. silver, one quarter silver and three-quarters alloy, the basest metal to be used for English 'silver' coins until 1947.

114 Base Æ shilling, mm. swan

The following year, 1551, the Exchequer had sufficient funds available to embark upon a new coinage of 11 oz. 1 dwt. fineness, almost restored to the old sterling standard. At the same time the sovereign and the angel and its half were issued again in the old standard 23 carat 3½ grain fineness. The sovereign, which reverts to the original arms on Tudor rose reverse design, was now returned to its original weight of 240 grains but its value had to be increased to thirty shillings and the angel had to be revalued at ten shillings. These 'fine' gold coins are extremely rare and only one specimen of the half-angel is known. A new 'crown' gold issue was also made in 1551 consisting of a one pound sovereign, a half-sovereign of ten shillings and a crown and half-crown. These all have a half-length figure of the young king in armour holding an orb and sceptre, the sovereign having the royal arms with supporters and the smaller gold coins an E R cypher by the arms. Both sovereigns have the IHS AVTEM legend, the smaller coins having the SCVTVM FIDEI inscription with the exception of the angel and its half which have the PER CRVCEM legend.

Two new silver coins now appear, the crown and half-crown which previously had been struck only in gold. These handsome coins depict the king in armour and holding an unsheathed sword seated on a richly caparisoned horse, the date 1551 (**115**), 1552 or 1553 being shown below in arabic numerals for the first time. All the crowns and some of the half-crowns have the king on a galloping horse but some of the half-crowns of 1551 and 1553 show a walking horse. Two more new denominations also appear at this time, the sixpence and the threepence. These, with the shilling, have an almost facing crowned bust of Edward who is depicted wearing an ermine cloak (**116**). To the left of the king's head is a Tudor rose and to the right the value in pence is shown in Roman numerals, XII, VI or

115 'Fine' coinage Æ crown, 1551, mm. Y

116 Æ shilling, mm. tun

III, this being the first time that a mark of value appears on English coins. Sixpences and threepences of this type were also struck at York, all the other provincial mints now having been closed. Base pennies, half-pennies and farthings continued to be minted, the penny and its half having a Tudor rose on the obverse and the farthing being of the portcullis type. A 'fine' silver penny of sovereign type was also issued but is extremely rare.

MARY TUDOR 1553–8 AND PHILIP OF SPAIN 1554–8

The Duke of Northumberland, who had been Protector and head of the council of regency during Edward's lifetime, had hoped to remain the power behind the throne after the young king's premature death from consumption at the age of fourteen. He had arranged for Lady Jane Grey, his daughter-in-law and a granddaughter of Henry VII to be proclaimed queen, but Mary, the daughter of Henry VIII and Katherine of Aragon, was looked upon by many as the rightful heir to the throne and received much popular support. Within nine days Jane was forced to abdicate and was later executed on Tower Hill; Northumberland suffered the same fate. No coins were struck in her name. The coins struck for Mary can be conveniently divided into two issues: those minted in the first two years of her reign and those issued after her marriage to Philip of Spain.

Mary's coins issued prior to her marriage have the name MARIA M'D'G' ROSA SINE SPINA, 'the rose without a thorn', on the pennies and they are unusual in that they have no mintmark at the beginning of the inscriptions, though most of them have a pomegranate inserted after the first or second words. The pomegranate (O.Fr. *pome + grenate*, 'apple with many seeds') was adopted as a personal badge by Mary's mother Katherine, being taken from the arms of Castille and Aragon, the pomegranate fruit having been added to the blazon to commemorate the capture of Granada in 1492, the last Moorish kingdom in Spain to be reconquered.

Mary's gold sovereigns show the queen enthroned and most have the date MDLIII (**117**) or MDLIV inserted at the end of the obverse inscription. A new reverse inscription was introduced for the gold coins of this reign – A DOMINO FACTVM EST ISTVD ET EST MIRABILE IN OCVLIS NOSTRIS (This is the work of the Lord and it is marvellous in our eyes, *Psalm 127,23*), the legend being abbreviated on some coins. A gold ryal was reintroduced valued now at 15 shillings and this has Mary standing in a ship, somewhat after the style of the old rose-noble. It is an eagerly sought after rarity. Mary's angel and angelet are rare, the latter omitting the last phrase of the inscription. No coins of 'crown gold' were issued during this reign.

117 Mary, 'fine' sovereign of 30 shillings, MDLIII (1553)

The silver coins of the early part of Mary's reign consist of groats (**118**), half-groats and pennies, the last two being rare. They have the queen's portrait facing left, but it is in rather low relief, the features being quickly worn flat on coins that remained in circulation for any length of time. The legend on the reverse of these coins is VERITAS TEMPORIS FILIA (Truth is the daughter of Time), perhaps chosen as a rebuttal of the proclamation of her illegitimacy passed by the parliament of 1533 and reaffirmed by Northumberland's council on Edward's death. Simultaneously with the output of good silver coins of 11 oz. fineness the issue of billon pennies was continued, these containing only one-quarter silver. Like the similar coins of the previous reign they have a large Tudor rose on one side and the royal arms on the other.

118 Æ groat, mm. pomegranate after first word

In 1554 Mary, who was an ardent Catholic, made a most unpopular marriage when she wedded Philip (later Philip II of Spain) the son of the Emperor Charles V, heir to a great Catholic empire on the continent. The event was made the occasion for a new coinage on which Philip's name was placed before that of his wife. The marriage was by proxy and though Philip later joined his wife for a few months he soon departed and returned to Spain, ascending the throne of that country on his father's abdication in 1556. It is said that Philip was disappointed in Mary and angered by her courtiers' ill-disguised contempt for foreigners.

The only gold coins issued after Mary's marriage were angels (**119**) and angelets, both of traditional design. Silver shillings and sixpences (**120**) were now issued again and these have two fine portraits of Philip and Mary facing each other with a single crown above. Early coins of these denominations have their combined titles, PHILIP Z MARIA R ANG FR NEAP PR HISP (King *and* Queen of England, France and Naples, Prince *and Princess* of Spain), but after Philip's return to Spain these titles were changed to REX ET REGINA ANGL. Mary was never crowned Queen of Spain. The reverses of the shillings and sixpences have a crowned shield with the arms of Hapsburg Spain impaled with those of England and most of them have the value x – II or v – I divided by the crown. The reverse legend on these coins is the plural form of the usual text used on Tudor silver, namely POSVIMVS DEVM

ADIVTOREM NOSTRVM (*We* have made the Lord *our* Helper). The same legend appears on some of Philip's coins struck for Naples and Sicily. The groats, rare half-groats and 'fine' pennies bearing the names or initials of the two monarchs were probably not struck until the latter part of the reign as only the bust of Mary is shown on the obverse and only the arms of England appear on the reverse. Mary's portrait on these coins is rather more angular and less flattering than that on the coins issued prior to her marriage. No halfpennies were issued during this reign.

119 Philip and Mary, *N* angel, mm. lis

120 *R* sixpence, 1557, mm. lis

ELIZABETH I 1557–1602/3

This reign is especially interesting to the numismatist as more different denominations were struck for this monarch than at any time before or since. They include the gold 'fine' sovereign of 30s., the ryal of 15s., the angel of 10s. and its half and quarter, the 'pound' sovereign of 20s., half-pound, gold crown and half-crown, the silver crown and half-crown, shilling, sixpence, groat, threepence, half-groat, three-halfpence, penny, three-farthings and halfpenny – twenty coins in all.

The 'fine' sovereign, ryal and angel denominations are all of 'standard gold' and are of similar type to those of Mary, except that on the ryal an Elizabethan caravel with high stern and low pointed prow supersedes the medieval cog with its raised decks fore and aft. The 'fine' sovereign was only issued in the years 1558–61 and 1582–96 and the ryal in the years 1582–92. All the 'crown gold' coins have a profile portrait of the queen on

the obverse (**121**), often in a richly embroidered costume which is especially
finely engraved on the pound (**122**) and its fractions issued from 1592 to the
end of the reign. These coins have on their reverses the royal arms
surmounted by a crown and the letters E R by the shield, though the silver
coins have only the royal arms on a cross fourché without the crown or the
initials. The ryal has the IHS AVTEM TRANSIENS reverse legend and the 'fine'
sovereign and the angel and its half have A DNO FACTVM EST, etc., but on the
quarter-angel the usual titles of the queen are extended to ET HIBERNIE
REGINA FIDEI (and Queen of Ireland, ... of the Faith) to fill the inscription
space on both sides of the coin, the first occasion that the title '(Defender) of

121   Elizabeth, *N* half-pound, mm. castle

122   *N* pound, mm. 1 (1601)

the Faith' appears on an English coin. The 'crown gold' coins all have the
inscription SCVTVM FIDEI PROTEGET EAM; the larger silver denominations
have the POSVI DEVM legend and the half-groat and smaller values have E' D'
G' ROSA SINE SPINA on the obverse and the mint name CIVITAS LONDON on the
reverse. The halfpenny was only issued from 1582 and has no inscriptions,
just a portcullis and mintmark on one side and a cross and pellets on the
other. The groat was only issued in 1558–61; the threepence, three-
halfpence and three-farthings were introduced in 1561 but were discontinued in 1582.

   In 1559 the recoinage of base 'Henry' silver coin was put in hand, but while the groats and smaller denominations were being reminted the base shillings were retained for a time in circulation with their values substantially reduced. Those of 6 oz. silver were countermarked with a portcullis to pass at $4\frac{1}{2}$d and the baser sorts of silver were stamped with a greyhound's head and 'cried down' to $2\frac{1}{4}$d.

The coins of Elizabeth, unlike some of the coins of Edward VI and Mary, had no mark of value and as the smaller silver might have been difficult to distinguish one from another, the sixpence, threepence, three-halfpence and three-farthings (**123**) all have a Tudor rose behind the queen's head and a date above the royal arms. The shilling, groat, half-groat and penny have neither, but from 1582 the half-groat has two pellets placed behind the queen's head to indicate two-pence. The silver crown (**124**) and half-crown

123 Æ three-farthings, 1561, mm. pheon

124 Æ crown, mm. 1 (1601)

were not issued until 1601 and these have a rather more mature portrait of Elizabeth who is depicted with an orb and sceptre in her hands. Nearly thirty different mintmarks were used during this reign and as one mark was sometimes used during three different calendar years there are a great number of different date/mintmark combinations. The last three mintmarks are the numerals 0, 1 and 2, used to indicate the years 1600, 1601 and 1602.

An important development in the manufacture of coins took place in the early years of Elizabeth's reign. Machinery was introduced into the mint by a Frenchman, Eloye Mestrelle. The coins produced by him are of much finer workmanship than those made by the old method of hammering the dies by hand. The new coins became known as 'milled money' as the various machines used were operated by a mill driven by horse or water power. The dies used in the screw-press minting machine were very finely engraved and due to the even pressure exerted over the whole die the coins produced did not suffer from the weak striking in some areas that was a common fault with hammered coins.

Between 1561 and 1571 Mestrelle produced milled gold half-pounds, crowns and half-crowns and silver shillings, sixpences (**125**), groats, threepences, half-groats and three-farthings. There was, however, a great deal of opposition amongst the mint workers to the introduction of machinery as they feared it might affect their employment and in 1572 Mestrelle was removed from his post at the mint on the grounds that his machines were too slow. Hammered coins had continued to be made concurrently with the milled money and after Mestrelle's dismissal hand-hammering remained the only method of production until the reign of Charles I. In 1578 Mestrelle was hanged at Norwich for forgery.

125 Æ milled sixpence, 1562, mm. star

Throughout the later Middle Ages and during the sixteenth and seventeenth centuries it had been a continual cause for complaint that insufficient small change was being minted. It was found to be more profitable for the mint to strike groats, half-groats and pennies than the smaller halfpennies and farthings. Though the two smaller coins were inconveniently small when struck in silver the monarchy considered it to be beneath the royal dignity to issue coins made of base metal. Lead token coins are known to have been issued illegally by local tradesmen in Elizabeth's reign and though proclamations were made prohibiting their manufacture and use these do not seem to have had much effect. The first official step to alleviate the problem was taken in 1577 when the city of Bristol was granted a licence to make its own copper farthings. These were square or diamond-shaped and have c b (for *Civitas Bristollie*) on one side and a ship issuing from a castle gateway, the arms of the city, on the other. In the closing years of Elizabeth's reign various patterns were produced for a base metal coinage but none of these were put into production for general circulation.

Perhaps mention should be made here of the first English coins to be struck specifically for overseas trade. In the year 1600 a charter was granted to the 'Governor and Company of Merchants of London trading to the East Indies' (later the East India Company) and to assist the new enterprise special silver coins were minted which became known as 'Portcullis Money' from the use of a crowned portcullis as the reverse type. These coins were intended as a competitor to the Spanish 8 *reals* (or 'dollar') and its fractions which were so extensively used by traders in the Indies and in the New World. The Portcullis coins consisted of the one, two, four and eight testerns (**126**), the testern being the equivalent of the Spanish real.

126 R̵ eight testerns (dollar) of the East Indies Company, mm. o (1600)

8

JACOBEAN TO
COMMONWEALTH ENGLAND

❧ ⚜❦

JAMES I 1603–25

James I (James VI of Scotland) was the son of Mary Queen of Scots and
Henry Lord Darnley. He ascended the Scottish throne in 1567, when only
one year old, and he was adopted heir to Elizabeth I of England as he was
the great-grandson of Margaret, the daughter of Henry VII, who had
married the Scottish king James IV. James took a great interest in his
coinage, both English and Scottish, and within two days of the death of
Elizabeth he issued his first orders relating to English currency. The union
of the two countries under one monarch is marked on the coinage by
changes in the king's titles and in the royal arms and by the introduction of
new reverse legends. The lions of England and the fleurs–de–lis of France are
now placed in the first and fourth quarters of the royal arms, the rampant
lion of Scotland within its tressure fleury counter-fleury is set in the second
quarter and the harp of Ireland in the third quarter. James's titles are set out
on his earliest English coins as IACOBVS D' G' ANG' SCO' FRAN' ET HIB' REX
(James, by the Grace of God, King of England, Scotland, France and
Ireland).

The coins of James's first issue, 1603–4, were made to the same weights as
the last coins of Elizabeth's reign and he also continued the minting of gold
coins of two different standards. All denominations higher than one shilling
are rare. The 20s. sovereign has a half-length portrait of the king holding an
orb and sceptre and around the royal arms on the reverse is the new
inscription EXVRGAT DEVS DISSIPENTVR INIMICI (Let God arise and let His
enemies be scattered, *Psalms* 68,1) and the half-sovereign has the same
legend but with a profile bust without the orb and sceptre. The gold crown
and half-crown have the inscription TVEATVR VNITA DEVS (May God protect

the united *realms*). A quarter-angel is known but as it has the same reverse as the gold half-crown it may be only a pattern piece.

The silver crown (**127**) and half-crown both show the king on horseback and these, together with the shilling and sixpence of the first issue which have a head and shoulder portrait of the king, all have the EXVRGAT legend. The half-groat and penny have a similar portrait and read I' D' G' ROSA SINE SPINA and have no reverse legend around the royal arms. The halfpenny of this issue continues the portcullis type. No groats or threepences of James were issued. There are six main varieties of bust on the gold and silver coins of this reign. The sixpence is the only denomination to have a date.

127 James I, first coinage, Æ crown, mm. thistle

Although there was a ratio of one to twelve between the English and Scottish currencies at this time, James changed the designs of the Scottish coinage to conform more closely to the English issues. The Scottish 60 and 30 shilling pieces, equivalent to the English crown and half-crown, can be distinguished by the thistle on the trappings of the horse, the English coins having a rose. The smaller coins of the two realms can be distinguished by the type of crown (see p. 216).

Due to a shift in the ratio between gold and silver James found it necessary to make an alteration in the weights of the gold coins in 1604. At that time vast quantities of silver were being transported to Europe from the mines in Spain's American colonies. On his second coinage, 1604–19, James uses for the first time the title 'King of Great Britain', MAG BRIT (*Magnae Britanniae*) appearing instead of ANG SCO. He struck a complete set of 'standard gold' coins as well as the commoner 'crown gold' denominations. The 30s. sovereign was now reduced in weight to 213 grains and is termed the 'rose-ryal' from the use of the Tudor rose on the reverse, and its half is the 15s. 'spur-ryal', so-called from the radiant sun at the centre of the reverse being likened to the rowel of a spur. The angel and its half are of

normal type and these, with the two larger coins, all have the A DNO FACTVM
EST legend.

In the 'crown gold' series the 20s. sovereign or pound (**128**), now
reduced in weight from 172 to 155 grains, is renamed a 'unite' and it
commemorates the union of the two realms under one monarch with the
reverse inscription FACIAM EOS IN GENTEM VNAM (I will make them one
nation, *Ezekiel* 37,*22*). The half and quarter unite of the second coinage are
known as the 'double crown' and 'Britain crown' respectively. They have
the same design as the unite, a crowned profile bust of the king and the
royal arms surmounted by a crown, but they have the inscription HENRICVS
ROSAS REGNA IACOBVS (Henry *united* the roses, James *united* the realms). A
new gold coin of four shillings value was also introduced called the 'thistle
crown' (**129**). It has a crowned rose on one side and a crowned thistle on the
other and the TVEATVR legend on the reverse. A similar coin was minted in
Scotland which can be recognized by the thistle mintmark. The gold half-
crown also has the TVEATVR inscription.

128 Second coinage, A/ unite (of 20 shillings), mm. lis

129 A/ thistle crown (of 4 shillings), mm. cross

Though James had decreased the weights of the second coinage gold it
was soon found that the adjustment was inadequate to prevent gold leaving
the country. In 1612 it was decided that, instead of lowering the weights
again, the values should be 'called up' by 10 per cent instead. So the rose-
ryal was revalued at 33s., the unite at 22s., the angel at 11s. and the thistle
crown at (of all ridiculous amounts) 4s.4¾d.!

The silver crowns, half-crowns, shillings and sixpences (**130**) of the second coinage are somewhat similar in design to those of the first coinage but they have a new inscription which also refers to the two realms under one crown: QVAE DEVS CONIVNXIT NEMO SEPARET (Those whom God hath joined together let no man put asunder, *Matthew* 19,6). The designs of the half-groat and penny were now changed, the king's portrait and the royal arms being replaced on the half-groat with a crowned rose on one side and a crowned thistle on the other, both coins having the TVEATVR legend. The penny and the halfpenny have an uncrowned rose and thistle, the smaller coin having no inscriptions.

130 Æ sixpence, 1606, mm. rose

In 1613 the king put an effective stop to the issue of illegal lead and pewter tokens by private traders. Though he did not go as far as to authorize a regal base metal coinage he did grant a licence to Lord Harington allowing the striking of farthing tokens on condition that the profits were shared with the crown. These 'Harington' farthings, as they were called, have the royal name and titles IACO D G MAG BRIT with a crown superimposed on two crossed sceptres on the obverse, perhaps symbolizing two realms under one monarch, and FRA ET HIB REX and the Irish harp on the reverse. They were given mintmarks rather like the coins issued by the Tower mint, though as the marks are far more numerous it is likely that they were changed at more frequent intervals. The first of this series of farthing tokens were of so small and insignificant an intrinsic value that they were tinned so as to make them look more like silver coins. These were soon superseded by larger untinned farthings of similar design (**131**). Like the smaller coins, they were only grudgingly accepted as their intrinsic value was so much lower than their face value and though twenty-one shillings-worth were issued for a pound, twenty-one shillings-worth had to be accumulated to get a pound's worth of silver in exchange. They were extensively forged. On the death of Lord Harington his licence was purchased by the Duke of Lennox and some of the 'Lennox' farthings were struck on oval flans. In 1616 an exchange was set up in London for the sale and purchase of these tokens and there is still a Tokenhouse Yard in existence in the City.

In 1619 it was decided to adjust the coinage again. The awkward gold
denominations were discontinued, the rose-ryal being restored to its
original 30s. value, the unite to 20s. and the angel to 10s. and, to
compensate, the weights of the gold coins were reduced by just under 10
per cent. All the gold coins of this third coinage, 1619–25, were given new
designs and they also have their value in shillings expressed in Roman
numerals. The reverse of the rose-ryal now has the royal arms set within a
circle of lis, leopards and roses, instead of being on a Tudor rose. The spur-
ryal has a facing crowned lion holding a shield and sceptre instead of the
king standing in a ship, and on the angel a three-masted carrack replaces the
medieval cog found on earlier issues. The unite, now reduced in weight
from 155 to 142½ grains, is known as a 'laurel' from the uncrowned bust of
the king which is depicted with a wreath of laurel in the manner of a
Roman emperor. The 'half-laurel' (**132**) and 'quarter-laurel' are similar.
This design owes much to the king's interest in classical art and history and
it was to set a pattern for the English coinage which persisted in one form or
another for some two hundred years.

131 'Harington' Æ farthing

132 Third coinage, *N* half-laurel (10 shillings), mm. mullet

The silver coins of this coinage have more or less the same designs as
those of the previous issue but they can be distinguished by their
mintmarks. On the larger silver coins the words of the obverse legend are
separated by colons whereas earlier coins have a stop and apostrophe. One
new feature appears on some of the larger silver coins minted during the last
three years of the reign when coins made of silver sent to the mint from
mines within the principality of Wales were distinguished by the Prince of
Wales's plumes set as a crest over the royal arms.

CHARLES I 1625–49

The coins of Charles I are amongst the most fascinating of all the English coinages as not only do they consist of a great many varieties from a number of different mints, but they also record the varying fortunes of a civil war, the outcome of which had a profound effect on the subsequent history of the country. Charles, a man of principle passionately convinced that he ruled by divine right at a time when new philosophical ideas were beginning to permeate Europe, found himself embroiled in an intensifying struggle against a parliament determined not to allow any interference with its ancient privileges, a battle that was finally decided by force of arms. The coins of the Civil War period will be dealt with in the next section. From the numismatist's viewpoint the most important event during the earlier part of the reign was the re-introduction of minting machinery.

The coins of Charles struck at the Tower were of the same weights and values as those of James I, the one exception being a brief issue of light-weight shillings in 1626. The general design of the early coins is similar to that of the previous reign except for the change in name, portrait and inscriptions. No 'fine' sovereigns or ryals were issued, the only 'standard gold' being angels and of these no halves or quarters were minted. The King's bust varies considerably: first he appears in a large ruff, later in armour and he is finally depicted in a falling lace collar in a style reminiscent of Van Dyke's famous portraits. The majority of coins struck during this reign except the crowns, half-crowns, half-groats, pennies and halfpennies, bear a mark of value.

The reverse inscriptions chosen for some of Charles's coins may seem to have been a little optimistic in view of his eventual end, but they are interesting as they stress his devoutness, his view of justice and divine protection and the assumed loyalty of his subjects. AMOR POPULI PRAESIDIVM REGIS (The love of the people is the king's protection) appears on the angel, FLORENT CONCORDIA REGNA (May the kingdom flourish) on the unite and CVLTORES SVI DEVS PROTEGIT (God protects His worshippers) on the gold double-crown and the Britain-crown (**133**). On the silver coins CHRISTO AVSPICE REGNO (I reign under the auspices of Christ) is used for the larger denominations and IVSTITIA THRONVM FIRMAT (Justice strengthens the throne) for the half-groat and penny. The halfpenny, however, has no inscription; it is too small.

The gold unites and its fractions are not uncommon due, in part, to the number of hoards concealed during the Civil War. These have the king's crowned bust on the obverse and crowned arms, with or without the initials C R, on the reverse. As in the previous reign the silver crowns (**134**) and half-crowns show the king on horseback, this time facing left, while the shilling and sixpence have his bust to left. As on the gold coins, the shape of the shield on the reverse varies, early coins having a flat-topped shield, then a shield with rounded 'corners', an oval shield and finally, on the shillings and sixpences, a square-topped shield again. Some coins have the initials C R above or at the side of the arms. Sixpences continued to be dated until 1630 but from then on the Tower mint sixpences can only be dated from their mintmarks. There are two distinct types of half-groat and penny. The earliest follow the style of those of James I but have a large rose on both sides. Later coins have a portrait and a shield reverse as on the sixpence. Both denominations have the king's name (normally CAROLVS) reduced to the initial 'C', and the halfpenny has a rose on both sides without any inscription.

133   Charles I, Tower mint, *AV* crown, mm. anchor

134   *AR* crown, with Welsh plumes on reverse, mm. plumes milled

In the first year of Charles's reign Nicholas Briot, a brilliant French engraver, settled in England and he began work at the Tower mint both as a medallist and a designer for the king's portrait on coinage. He introduced the latest types of machinery and not only struck coins and medals of outstanding design and workmanship but also produced many beautiful patterns that were never minted for general circulation. Briot's screw-press could not produce nearly enough coin to satisfy demand and so hand-hammering was still used to produce the bulk of the coinage. In fact, his milled money amounted to only a very small proportion of the total coin struck, but, even so, the use of machinery was viewed with much hostility by the English mint workers.

Milled coins struck from Briot's dies are well-rounded and evenly struck, and they usually display his initial B by the mintmark or below the king's bust. His first group of coins, issued 1631–2, have a flower as mintmark and he also struck a later series of coins, 1638–9, with mintmark anchor. Some of his gold coins are great rarities though his silver coins are not unduly rare (**135**), all denominations being known except for the halfpenny. As well as making dies for his milled series Briot appears to have made some of the punches for dies of some hammered coins. However, the dies for most of the hammered coins were prepared by far less skilled hands and the actual striking of many of Charles's coins could hardly have been done more carelessly. Little attempt was made to round the blanks carefully for coins struck late in the reign, many being so irregular in shape that at first glance they appear to have been fraudulently clipped.

135 Briot's milled coinage, Æ half-crown, mm. anchor

Until 1637 coins made from Welsh silver were minted at the Tower mint and have the Prince of Wales's plumes set over the royal arms as a provenance mark. These include all denominations from the silver crown down to the half-groat. In 1637 a provincial mint was opened at Aberystwyth, close to the mines, and this obviated the transportation of unwieldy consignments of bullion from Wales to London. All the coins struck at Aberystwyth, which was under the management of Thomas Bushell who held the lease of the Welsh mines, have the distinctive plumes emblem but they also have as mintmark an open book (**136**). On the half-groat, penny and halfpenny the plumes form the main reverse design. On the outbreak of civil war in 1642 Bushell moved his mint to Shrewsbury.

In 1624 the Duke of Lennox died and his licence for striking copper farthing tokens passed to his widow, the Duchess of Richmond. These 'Richmond' farthings have the king's name CARO instead of IACO but otherwise they are very similar in design to the 'Lennox' farthings of the previous reign. In 1634 the licence was transferred by purchase to Lord Maltravers and his coins, known as 'Maltravers' farthings, have the king's name extended to CAROLVS. A later type, known as the 'rose' farthing, has a crowned rose on the reverse in place of the Irish harp (**137**). These are somewhat smaller and dumpier than the earlier issues and most of them have a brass plug through the flans in order to make forgery more difficult.

136 Aberystwyth mint, Æ threepence, mm. book   137 Æ 'Rose' farthing

CIVIL WAR COINAGES 1642–9

One of Parliament's main quarrels with the king lay in the fact that he usurped its privileges by levying taxes without its consent and when members remonstrated with him he dissolved Parliament and did not call another one for eleven years. The situation was further complicated by religious differences, for Charles was very much of High Church inclination and supported Archbishop Laud in his suppression of the Puritans. The final break came when the king went in person with an armed party to arrest five Members of Parliament who were opposing him. They took refuge in the City of London, which was not on friendly terms with the king and, expecting an armed rising, Charles left the capital to raise an army.

If it seems strange that, after Charles was forced to flee from London in 1642, Parliament should have allowed the king's name and portrait to be displayed on coins issued under its authority until his execution in 1649, it should be remembered that Parliament still recognized Charles as the legal, though erring ruler until after his conviction for high treason. The coins struck at the Tower mint during the Civil War have essentially the same designs as those issued earlier, but they can be easily distinguished by their mintmarks – (P), (R), eye, sun and sceptre. Exactly what these marks symbolised is not certain, but perhaps (P) indicated Parliament, (R) stood for *reipublica*, the eye was for the Eye of Providence, the sun (it also appears on Commonwealth coinage) (**138**) for the dawning of a new era and the sceptre for the sovereignty of Parliament and people.

On leaving London Charles stayed at York for several months and established a mint there. Half-crowns, shillings, sixpences and threepences of good design were struck there, some of which were minted from dies engraved by Nicholas Briot who went to York secretly whilst working for Parliament at the Tower mint. All the York coins have a mintmark lion and most of them have the mint name EBOR (Eboracum) on one side or the other. One group of half-crowns was struck in base silver. This mint remained open until the surrender of the city in July 1644 following the battle of Marston Moor. Some of the York half-crowns have slightly oval flans that are not quite flat and these appear to have been pressed between dies engraved on cylindrical rollers or in a rocker press instead of being struck by the usual method. Some of the crowns and half-crowns struck by Briot in London and Edinburgh have the same characteristics.

138 Parliament, Æ shilling, mm. sun

In August 1642 Charles raised his standard at Nottingham and in September he made a declaration of war against the Parliamentary rebels at Wellington in which he promised to defend 'the Protestant religion, the liberties of Parliament and the laws of England'. These promises were given the widest publicity by being advertised on coins of the Shrewsbury mint which was established in October. Thomas Bushell, the mintmaster at Aberystwyth, had been ordered to transfer his entire mint to Shrewsbury and from gifts of plate and other bullion contributed by the king's supporters he struck silver crowns, half-crowns and shillings and, as there was a dearth of gold, two new silver denominations – pound and half-pound pieces (**139**). These large heavy pieces have designs similar to the crowns and half-crowns. The obverse depicts an equestrian figure of the king on horseback riding over a battlefield strewn with arms and on the reverse is what is known as the 'Declaration' inscription RELIG PROT LEG ANG LIVER PARL across the field in two lines around which is the EXVRGAT legend last used on the coins of James I. Above the Declaration on the Shrewsbury coins is the mark of value xx, x or v and sometimes 2.6, and there are also three plumes which seem to have been adopted by Bushell as his personal mark rather than indicating the use of Welsh silver. Also struck at

139 Charles I, Shrewsbury mint, Æ half-pound, 1642, mm. plumes

Shrewsbury was a small amount of large gold triple unites, now exceedingly rare. Some of the early Shrewsbury silver coins were struck from Aberystwyth obverse dies.

After the battle of Edgehill the king moved to Oxford which became his headquarters for the next three years, and Bushell transferred the mint there before the end of 1642. Many of the early Oxford coins were struck from Shrewsbury obverse or reverse dies and these can be recognized by the form of Bushell's plumes. The Shrewsbury plumes are encircled by a coronet only, whereas the Oxford plumes have a motto scroll below in addition. The Oxford mint produced large amounts of coin, much of the bullion being donated by the colleges of the university. The coins struck consisted of gold triple-unites, unites and half-unites, silver pounds (**140**), half-pounds, crowns, half-crowns, shillings, sixpences, groats, half-groats and pennies. Some of the Oxford coins have the mint name OXON or OX below the date and they either have the Declaration reverse and the EXVRGAT legend or, in the case of the half-groats and pennies, they have a large plume on the reverse as on the Aberystwyth coins.

The gold triple-unites and the unites depict the king holding in one hand a sword and in the other an olive branch. On some of the silver pounds the Declaration on the reverse is contained within a lion-headed cartouche. Most of Bushell's coins struck at Oxford and other mints have a small plumes device before the king's face or, in the case of the larger coins, behind the king's back. Thomas Rawlins, well-known as a medallist, was one of the die-engravers working at Oxford and it was he who produced the famous Oxford silver crown which has a view of the city below the king's horse. It is now one of the great rarities of the English series. The Oxford mint was closed down when the city was taken by the Parliamentarians in 1646.

In July 1643 the city of Bristol was captured by Prince Rupert of the

140 Oxford mint, Æ pound, 1643, mm. plumes, made from donated silver plate

141 Bristol mint, Æ shilling 1644, BR below date

Rhine, the king's nephew, and shortly afterwards Thomas Bushell set up a mint there. Bristol at this period was the most important city in the country after London. The coins struck there are similar to those of Oxford in that, apart from the penny, they have a Declaration reverse, EXVRGAT legend and Bushell's plumes, but most of them are distinguished by a BR monogram used as a mintmark or placed below the date (**141**). Gold unites and half-unites are known to have been minted at Bristol but they are exceedingly rare. The silver must have been struck in some quantity until the mint was closed down shortly before the city was surrendered to General Fairfax in September 1645.

There are coins of Bristol style, some actually from altered Bristol dies, which are dated 1645 and 1646 and must have been minted at other places. At one time those with distinguishing letters A and B or plumelet were tentatively attributed to Appledore, Barnstaple and Lundy Island, but recent research suggests that Devonshire locations are unlikely and that these mints need to be sought elsewhere. Ashby-de-la-Zouche, in

Leicestershire, and Bridgnorth-on-Severn have been put forward as possible mints.

In November 1642 Charles commissioned Sir Richard Vyvyan to open a mint at Truro to ensure a supply of coin to the Royalist forces in the south-west who were cut off from the main mint at Oxford. The coins of Truro broadly follow the pattern of the Tower coinage. The gold is extremely rare; only unites are known and these have either the FLORENT or CVLTORES legends. The silver coins have the CHRISTO AVSPICE REGNO legend, and some rare half-crowns have the king charging across a battlefield littered with various arms. Another interesting coin from this mint is the very rare silver ten shillings which was struck from crown dies on blanks of double thickness. Some half-crowns depict the king with a marshal's baton instead of a sword and on some crowns and half-crowns the king's head is shown half-facing instead of being in profile.

In 1643 the mint was transferred from Truro to Exeter, the latter having been taken by Prince Rupert's brother Maurice. The Exeter mint coins are very similar in style to those of Truro and they have either the mintmark rose in common with the Truro coins, a castle or the mint signature 'Ex'. The crowns of Exeter are perhaps the commonest of all the crowns of Charles I but their flans are often very irregular in shape. Smaller denominations were also minted at Exeter and on the half-groat and penny, which display Vyvyan's rose as the reverse type, the first two words of the IVSTITIA legend are transposed – THRO IVSTI FIRMAT.

A third commission for coinage of the king's monies was given to Sir Thomas Cary, covering the counties of Chester, Shropshire, Herefordshire and Worcester. There are a number of coins which have not yet been positively attributed to specific mints, but some coins can be given to their mints of origin from the mint letters displayed, devices taken from armorial bearings or on grounds of style. At Chester various types of half-crowns were issued, some with the letters CHST below the king's horse and some having three gerbs (wheatsheaves, taken from the city's arms) as the mintmark, whilst on the reverses there is either the Declaration or a variety of shields bearing the royal arms. There is a round shield with scroll garniture copied from late Tower mint coins, a shield with lionskin garniture similar to that on coins of the York mint and also a crowned square-topped shield with crowned C and R at the sides. One half-crown with the letters H C in the lower part of the garnishing of the arms has been attributed to a mint set up at Hartlebury Castle near Kidderminster, the pears that were used as a mintmark doubtless deriving from the arms of Worcester which lies a few miles to the south. There are half-crowns with the letters W or SA below the king's horse and shillings and some smaller denominations of rather crude workmanship which in the past have been attributed to the mints of Weymouth and Salisbury, but which have recently been tentatively re-attributed to Worcester and a mint which re-opened at Shrewsbury in 1644. These have a variety of mintmarks, such as a pear, castle, helmet, bird, lis and lion. From this same West Midland area may come another half-crown dated 1645 which has on the reverse the royal arms set within the Garter and supported by a lion on the left and a unicorn on the right.

The latest conventional coins to be struck with the name and portrait of Charles I are a series of silver pieces, from the half-crown down to the penny, that follow the style of the earlier coins of Aberystwyth but for the mintmark which is a crown instead of a book. At one time attributed to Coombe Martin in Devonshire, recently they have been shown to have been minted at the silver smelting mills at Dovey-Furnace, near Aberystwyth, at a time when the castle at Aberystwyth had been badly damaged.

Perhaps the most interesting of all Charles's coins are the siege pieces. These were emergency issues struck by the besieged towns of Carlisle, Scarborough, Newark, Pontefract and possibly Colchester, in order to pay the troops and provide for the transactions of the townspeople. As there was no proper minting equipment available these curious pieces are of somewhat crude work and were made from pieces of metal cut from hammered silver plate. Some of these coins are occasionally found with parts of the original design of the plate still visible and some rare pieces actually show the plate hallmark.

At Carlisle, which was besieged for nine months in 1644/5, silver three-shilling and one-shilling pieces were issued, all now very rare. These have a crowned C R with a value below on the obverse and OBS CARL 1645 in three lines on the reverse, i.e. *Obsessum Carleolium* (Carlisle besieged). The least rare of the obsidional coins are those of Newark struck in 1645 and 1646. They consist of silver half-crowns, shillings, ninepences (**142**) and six-pences, all on lozenge-shaped flans, and like the Carlisle coins they have a crown, with C R and the value below on one side and OBS NEWARK (or

142 Siege of Newark, Æ ninepence, 1646

NEWARKE) and the date in three lines on the other. The town was besieged several times but was finally surrendered in May 1646. Newark shillings and smaller denominations are sometimes found holed or plugged as they became popular with Royalist supporters for wearing as keepsakes.

In the autumn of 1648 the town of Pontefract was besieged by Cromwell and Lambert and obsidional shillings and two-shilling pieces were minted struck on circular or, more commonly, octagonal or diamond-shaped flans. There are two main issues. The first was struck while Charles was a prisoner at Hurst Castle and later on trial for his life at London and the second, struck after the king's execution, names the king's son as CAROL II or CAROLVS SECVNDVS. Some have a large crown over C R and the inscription DVM SPIRO SPERO (Whilst I breathe I hope) on one side and on the other a view of the castle and a hand holding a sword protruding from the tower on the left, with OBS P C and the date around (**143**). One variety has the value XII in place of the sword. On the latest issue the legend HANC DEVS DEDIT (This God hath given) is inserted below the crown on the obverse and the reverse inscription is POST MORTEM PATRIS PRO FILIO (For the son after the death of the father). All the Pontefract coins, which include octagonal gold unites, have the date 1648 as Charles I was executed in January 1648/49 (1649 then not commencing until 25 March).

143 Siege of Pontefract, Æ shilling 1648

Scarborough was besieged from July 1644 until July 1645 and irregular-shaped uniface pieces of silver plate were stamped with a crudely punched view of the castle and with the value in shillings and pence stamped incuse alongside or below the castle. Some twenty-two different values have been recorded, ranging from 5s.8d. to 4d. One group of coins has an extended view of a rather battered castle with a gateway to the left (**144**) and the other has a gateway flanked by two towers. They are all extremely rare. There are also commoner pieces on rectangular flans with clipped corners depicting a castle of different style and with an inscription in script characters reading *Caroli Fortuna resurgam*: most are probably eighteenth-century concoctions.

In the summer of 1648 Colchester became the centre of a Royalist rising in the eastern counties and it is possible that rare gold half-unites, if genuine, could have been struck there. These are uniface pieces with a view of the castle and OBS COL and the date and value below.

144 Siege of Scarborough, Æ 2s. 6d.

THE COMMONWEALTH 1649–60

After the execution of Charles I a republican coinage was instituted. The new coins were possibly the plainest to have been issued over the previous five hundred years and they were sometimes contemptuously referred to as 'Breeches Money'. Lord Lucas remarked to Charles II some years later that this 'was a fit name for coins of the Rump' – the parliament of 1648 from which ninety-six members had been excluded. All the Commonwealth coins from the unite (**145**) to the penny have a St George's cross (the republican arms of England) surrounded by a wreath of palm and laurel on the obverse and on the reverse the arms of England and Ireland side-by-side with the mark of value above. For the first time in the history of the coinage the inscriptions appear in English as the Puritans considered that Latin smacked too much of Popery. The new inscriptions, THE COMMONWEALTH OF ENGLAND and GOD WITH VS, are used on all coins down to the sixpence. The smaller coins have neither legends nor mintmarks but all denominations have the mark of value in shillings or pence over the shields on the reverse, except for the halfpenny. This coin had the English arms on one side and the Irish on the other and it was to be the last issue of this denomination minted in silver (**146**). The sun mintmark was in continuous use from 1649 until the death of Cromwell in 1658 but during the protectorship of Oliver's son Richard the mintmark was changed to an anchor.

In 1649 Pierre Blondeau, another Frenchman, was invited over from Paris to work at the Tower mint. He had perfected a machine for making

145 The Commonwealth, N unite (20 s.) 1649, mm. sun   146 R halfpenny

coins with inscribed edges and it was realized that here at last was an answer to the problem of clipping. Blondeau produced a series of pattern coins in 1651 with his new invention. His half-crowns of that year have two different edge inscriptions – IN THE THIRD YEAR OF FREEDOME BY GODS BLESSING RESTORED 1651 and TRVTH AND PEACE 1651 PETRVS BLONDAEVS INVENTOR FECIT. Blondeau also made pattern shillings and sixpences but these have a grained edge. In the same year David Ramage produced another set of patterns the edges of which were inscribed TRVTH AND PEACE 1651. These were made by the new machinery but Ramage's work was not quite of the high standard set by Blondeau. Blondeau, like earlier engravers from the continent, met a good deal of opposition at the mint and in 1656 he was retired with a pension.

After some dissension amongst the Parliamentarians their most out-standing general, Oliver Cromwell, was appointed Protector of England. No change was made in the coinage but some beautiful patterns were struck in 1656 and again in 1658 bearing his name and portrait. These were made by means of Blondeau's machinery but were designed and produced from dies engraved by Thomas Simon, a talented medal and seal engraver. Pattern gold pounds and fifty-shilling pieces and silver half-crowns were struck in 1656, all very rare. It was possibly on Cromwell's death in 1658 that another group of crowns, half-crowns (**147**) and shillings was produced, perhaps for sale as memorial pieces. A few sixpences were also made but these are extremely rare. Cromwell may not have accepted the crown, as some wished him to do, but he had acquired the powers of a dictator and it may be significant that Simon portrays him draped and laureate like a Roman emperor. The obverse inscription on these coins is OLIVAR D G RP ANG SCO ET HIB &c PRO (Oliver, by the Grace of God, Protector of the Republic of England, Scotland and Ireland, &c). On the reverse is a quartered coat of arms with the crosses of St George and St Andrew and the Irish harp, and in the centre on an inescutcheon of pretence is a rampant lion, the personal arms of the Cromwell family. The reverse legend is PAX QVAERITVR BELLO (Peace is sought by War). Two different inscriptions were used on the edges of these coins. On the fifty-shilling pieces it is PROTECTOR LITERIS LITERAE NVMMIS CORONA ET SALVS (A protection for the letters: the letters are a garland and safeguard to the coinage), but on the crown and half-crown the edge reads HAS NISI PERITVRVS MIHI ADIMAT NEMO (Let no one remove these *letters* from me under penalty of death). The smaller coins have grained edges. There are in existence Cromwell crowns that were made at a later date in the Netherlands from false dies which are known as the 'Dutch' crowns and there are also other Cromwell coins which were struck from dies made by John Tanner in the eighteenth century. From the prices these forgeries fetch they seem to be more highly prized by collectors than the original coins! After Cromwell's death the mint continued striking coins by the hand-hammering method and Blondeau's machinery was left unused until after the Restoration.

147 Oliver Cromwell, pattern Æ half-crown by Simon, 1658

In 1644 Parliament had stopped the issue of the Maltravers 'rose' farthings in response to the public outcry against them but though several patterns were produced for an official copper coinage none was put into production for general circulation. The shortage of small change was now acute and to supply the deficiency tradespeople began to issue their own private token coins as they had done at an earlier period. Then they had usually been made of lead or pewter, but in the seventeenth century tokens were normally made of copper or brass. Though in some parts of the country penny tokens were issued, the great majority of tokens were farthings, with halfpennies appearing from 1666 (**148**). They were usually struck on round flans but some, mostly halfpennies, were octagonal or heart-shaped (**149**) and there are a few other shapes. It was not only shopkeepers who issued tokens. A number of towns had their own tokens, some being issued by the mayor, bailiff or constable, and others by the Overseers of the Poor. It is not surprising that the town tokens were usually larger or thicker than tokens issued by private persons who expected to make a profit.

148 Token Æ halfpenny of William Aukland, of Askrigg, Yorks. 1666

149 Token Æ halfpenny of William Overend, of Bentham, Yorks. 1668

Tokens were of convenience to local people but they were a nuisance to travellers as they were likely to be unacceptable beyond the area in which the issuer was known. Complaints were made that some people issued tokens at a profit and then decamped before being required to redeem them for coins of the realm. Designs vary considerably but it was usual to have the issuer's name and perhaps his occupation on the obverse with the arms of his guild at the centre or some other device representing his trade. The reverse would normally have the name of the place in which he worked with sometimes the date and at the centre the initials of the issuer and, if he was married, the initial letter of his wife's name. There are some tokens that were issued by women. Halfpenny tokens usually have the words HIS (or HER) HALFE PENNY in the centre of the reverse. Tokens issued in London and a few from Bristol have the name of the street instead of the name of the town, and most of London's streets and lanes are represented amongst the four thousand or so tokens that were issued there. As might be expected, the majority of tokens were issued by grocers and tavern-keepers but a great variety of other trades are represented, such as apothecaries, bakers, coffee-houses, cordwainers, dyers, pastry-cooks, gardeners, postmasters, pewterers, rat-catchers and tallow-chandlers. Tavern tokens often have their inn signs as the main device. Some tokens depict the family arms of the issuer and others have a punning allusion to the issuer's name, such as the halfpenny of Ellinor Gandor of Shadwell whose type is a goose. Tokens issued by local authorities frequently have inscriptions such as FOR NECESSARY CHANGE or THE POORES FARTHING, while other private issues sometimes have legends such as ALTHOVG BVT BRAS YET LET ME PASS and after the Restoration the legend GOD SAVE THE KING is sometimes found. These tokens are a series full of interest for collectors and local historians alike.

9

FROM RESTORATION
TO GREAT RECOINAGE

~⊰ ❦ ⊱~

Two major developments in the history of English coinage took place during this reign, the final abandonment of the hand-hammering method of minting and the commencement of a regal copper coinage. In 1660 growing disillusion with the Commonwealth government resulted in a successful counter-revolution led by General Monk and Charles II being invited to take his rightful place on the throne. On Charles's return to England plans were formed to bring out a machine-made coinage bearing his name and portrait with the least possible delay in order to replace the hated republican issues. However, as neither the necessary minting machinery nor the trained workmen to use it were immediately available the first Restoration coins were, of necessity, hand-hammered.

This first hammered coinage was designed by Thomas Simon. The gold unites, double-crowns and crowns were made to the same weight and value as the Commonwealth coins but in 1661 a rise in the market price of gold made it necessary for the unite to be revalued at 21s.4d. These coins have a very fine uncrowned, bewigged and laureate bust of the king and on the reverse a crowned oval shield with the FLORENT CONCORDIA REGNA legend (**150**). The hammered unites became known as 'broads' after the thicker and smaller milled coins were introduced. No angels were minted but the king had gold medallets made as touch pieces for the Touching ceremonies and these retained the St Michael and ship types.

The hammered silver coins follow the general pattern of the last Tower mint shillings and sixpences of Charles I. They have the king's crowned head facing left and on the reverse the flat-topped shield and the CHRISTO AVSPICE REGNO inscription. The earliest of the gold and silver hammered coins have no mark of value, but later coins had a mark of value added behind the king's head. The first hammered silver coins consisted of the half-crown, shilling, sixpence, half-groat and penny, but later groats and threepences were also issued. No hammered silver crowns were struck although they were authorized. The abandonment of hand-hammering more or less put an end to the clipping of new coin, though as the old hammered money was still allowed to circulate alongside the new milled coins it did not entirely end this nuisance.

150   Charles II, hammered *A*/ 'broad' (pound), mm. crown

The new milled coinage began in 1662 with an issue of silver crowns, the other denominations appearing in 1663 or later years, but the sixpence not being struck until 1674. Pierre Blondeau had been recalled from France after the Restoration and the new coinage was made with his machinery. A family of coin and medal engraver from Antwerp, the Roettiers, who had been of some service to Charles II during his exile, settled in England at this period and John Roettier was given a post at the mint as joint-engraver with Thomas Simon. Following a trial of skill arranged to decide which of the two should design the new coinage the commission was given to Roettier, though Simon was still employed for some time on the production of dies for the groats, threepences, half-groats and pennies. These small coins are particularly well-struck and are considered to be amongst the gems of English milled coinage.

In 1663, smarting over his deposition as chief engraver, Simon produced his *tour de force*, the famous 'Petition' crown (**151**). There are some fifteen specimens known of this beautifully engraved pattern coin and in the sale room a choice specimen would be likely to realize at least £40,000. These coins were made to the same specifications as Roettier's crown but Simon's treatment of the design is quite different, the large bust of the king and the reverse design being most finely engraved in high relief. Simon's 'petition' is arranged around the edge in two lines of minute lettering and reads THOMAS SIMON MOST HVMBLY PRAYS YOUR MAJESTY TO COMPARE THIS, HIS TRYALL PIECE, WITH THE DVTCH, AND IF MORE TRVLY DRAWN &

EMBOSS'D, MORE GRACEFULLY ORDER'D AND MORE ACCVRATELY ENGRAVEN, TO RELEIVE HIM. Other rare pattern crowns produced by Simon, known as the 'Reddite' crowns, have a similar design but another edge inscription reading REDDITE QVAE CAESARIS CAESARI & CT.POST (Render unto Caesar those *things* which are Caesar's, etc.). Simon's petition did not succeed and two years later he was transferred to the Edinburgh mint.

151 Milled pattern 'Petition' crown, by Simon, 1663

The new coins designed by Roettier were struck on smaller but thicker flans than the old hammered money so as to allow for a grained or lettered edge. They have a laureate bust of the king which now faces right (**152**) building up the practice of reversing the direction of the head of a new monarch. On the reverse the royal arms are now divided into four separate shields which are arranged crosswise. The three lions of England appear in the top shield, the fleur-de-lis of France is at the bottom, on the right is the rampant lion of Scotland, on the left is the harp of Ireland, and placed at the centre is the Star of the Order of the Garter. The gold and silver are more or less similar in design but the former have the king's bust undraped. On the reverses of the gold coins are four sceptres dividing the four shields, each one headed by a different device: a cross, a thistle, a lis and a harp. The silver coins do not have sceptres, instead they have the king's cipher – two interlinked Cs – in the angles of the shields. This difference was to prevent silver coins from being gilded and passed off as gold. Even so, gilt shillings are sometimes seen which have had the Cs scraped off and sceptres scratched in their place. Religious texts are now omitted from the coinage and in their place DEI GRATIA appears in full after the king's name and his titles continue onto the reverse of the coins, MAG BR FRA ET HIB REX.

Two new denominations were now added to the coinage, a five pound piece and a two pound piece (**153**) to supplement the pound and half-pound, but a gold crown was no longer minted. Much of the gold for the new coinage was supplied by the Africa Company which was engaged in trade along the Gold or 'Guinea' Coast as it was known. As a special mark of recognition to the company the coins made from African gold were marked with the company's badge. This was either an elephant or an elephant with a castellated howdah on its back, hence the well-known elephant and castle tavern sign. The pound pieces soon became known as 'guineas' and this name was applied to coins with and without the Africa Company badge. It should be noted that when first issued the guineas were coins of 20s. value but they were soon rated at a higher value in silver coin. The milled guinea was first struck at slightly over $131\frac{1}{2}$ grains, some $8\frac{1}{2}$ grains lighter than the hammered unite or 'broad' valued at 21s.4d. With fluctuating metal prices it became necessary to reduce the weight of the guinea in 1670 by a couple of grains to $129\frac{1}{2}$ grains. However the price of gold continued to rise and, though the weight was not altered again, guineas were changing hands at between 21s. and 22s. in the closing years of the reign.

152   Milled Æ half-crown, 1663

153   Milled Æ two guineas, 1664, elephant below bust

The Africa Company's elephant badge, and more rarely the elephant and castle, are also found on some of the silver coins, principally those of 1666. The Welsh plumes reappear on a few rare half-crowns and shillings made from silver from the Welsh mines. This mark is usually placed below the king's bust and in the centre of the reverse in place of the Garter Star, but on a few rare pieces it is found on one side of the coin only. Another provenance mark used during this reign was the rose which was placed below the king's bust on most of the silver crowns of 1662, denoting that the silver had come from the mines in the West of England. The same mark had been used on many of the coins of Charles I from the western mints. These crowns differ from coins of the following years by having the lions of England and the fleurs-de-lis of France quartered together on the top and bottom shields. Silver crowns are by far the commonest of the denominations, probably because there was still a great quantity of hammered coins in circulation which were mostly of the smaller values and silver crowns were also needed to take the place of the gold crowns no longer being minted.

The edges of the five and two guinea pieces and the crowns and halfcrowns have the inscription DECVS ET TVTAMEN (a decoration and safeguard), the letters protecting the coin from clipping. This is followed by the date and, after 1662, by the regnal year, e.g. ANNO REGNI VICESIMO TERTIO (the twenty-third year of the reign), though between 1663 and 1666 the regnal year is given in Roman numerals and not words. Charles dated his accession from 1649, the year of his father's death, as the Commonwealth was considered an illegal usurpation. The graining on the edges of the two and one guineas and the shilling and sixpence was perpendicular at first but from 1669 edges were grained diagonally so as to make imitation by counterfeiters more difficult. John Roettier made several minor adjustments to the king's portrait during the reign and portraits on the coins of the later years do show a marked ageing. The rarity of coins dated 1665 was due to the Great Plague, which had taken firm hold in London in April of that year and rapidly spread through Britain, Thomas Simon being one of the victims.

The smaller silver coins designed by Simon are all undated. These were re-designed by Roettier after Simon's death (**154**), a twopence being produced in 1668 followed by fourpences, threepences and pennies in 1670. The fourpence has four interlinked Cs in the centre of the reverse together with rose, thistle, lis and harp emblems. The threepence has three Cs without the emblems, the twopence two Cs and the penny a single C. It used to be thought that all these smaller coins were Maundy Money but it is now generally accepted that, except perhaps for the penny, they must have been issued for general circulation as they are so frequently found in worn condition.

It had been the custom from time immemorial for the sovereign to perform a public act of humility on Maundy Thursday, the Thursday before Easter, by washing the feet of the poor and giving alms, following the example of Jesus washing the feet of his disciples. Though Charles I had discontinued feet washing, Charles II had renewed the practice. The alms used to consist of gifts of food, clothing and money. The washing of feet was last performed by James II in 1685. As the recipients sometimes scandalized those present at the ceremony by impatiently discarding their old garments and changing into the new before the service had been completed, it was decided in 1724 to substitute woollen cloth for clothes. In 1837 a money allowance was granted in place of provisions and in 1882 a similar allowance was made in lieu of cloth. The monarch at one time had given his own cloak to the poor person considered to be the most needy, but Queen Elizabeth ordered instead that 'redemption' money of 20s. be paid to each poor person present.

154   Small Æ ('Maundy') 4d., 3d., 2d., and penny, 1673-82

For some two hundred years or so the Lord High Almoner used to deputize for the sovereign at the Maundy service but in 1932 George V presented the royal Maundy himself and since then Edward VIII, George VI and our present Queen have each made presentations in person. The amount of Maundy Money proper given to each person varies each year and consists of as many pence as the monarch's age. The recipients are elderly men and women, many of whom have been in royal or public service or have been recommended by the parish where the Maundy service is held, the numbers of each sex being equal to the age of the sovereign. Maundy Money probably consisted only of pennies, sometimes possibly supplemented by half-groats, until the middle of the reign of George III, since when it has been given in sets of pennies, twopence, threepence and fourpence. Thus, in 1984, when Queen Elizabeth was aged fifty-eight, fifty-eight elderly men and the same number of women each received the sum of 4s.10d. (58 pence) in Maundy Money and this was made up of five sets of 4, 3, 2 and 1 pence with two or three other pieces to make up the odd eight pence. In addition to this they received ordinary money in lieu of food and clothing. Maundy Money issued since 1816 is still legal tender for the same number of decimal pence though they are, of course, of far more value as collectors' items.

With each die being individually made it was hardly surprising that errors should occur from time to time. It is possible to find coins of Charles II and later reigns with words mis-spelt, such as GARTIA for GRATIA, DECNS for DECVS, PRICESIMO for TRICESIMO and MRG for MAG, but more unusual mistakes can also be found such as the transposition of the shields of Scotland and Ireland on some shillings of 1663 and the use of an undraped bust from a guinea puncheon used on some shillings of 1666. After 1662 coins of every denomination were dated and mintmarks were no longer used. Just as mintmarks were sometimes altered on hammered coins to extend the life of the dies so on the milled coins dates were sometimes altered so that the dies could continue to be used in the following year.

The establishment of an official base metal coinage in 1672 at last supplied the public with the small change that was needed and, unlike the farthings that had been made under licence and the private issues that followed them, it was of sufficient intrinsic value to be accepted by everyone with confidence. A number of patterns for a copper coinage were produced in the 1660s but the first issue of copper halfpennies and farthings made for general circulation was not until 1672. These have a laureate and cuirassed bust of Charles II with the inscription CAROLVS A CAROLO (Charles from *son of* Charles) and on the reverse there is a figure of Britannia seated and resting on a shield bearing a Union Jack, with a spear in one hand and an olive branch in the other indicating that she was prepared for war or peace. It has been suggested that the reverse design was adapted from the Roman sestertius of Antoninus Pius which has a seated Britannia with spear and standard. Samuel Pepys suggests that Roettier modelled his Britannia on Frances, Duchess of Richmond. Some of the 1665 patterns for this coinage have the inscription QVATTVOR MARIA VINDICO (I claim the four seas), possibly a reference to the successful sea action fought against the Dutch off Lowestoft in that year. That legend was replaced by the simpler inscription BRITANNIA on the coins of 1672 and though it is said that the earlier legend was dropped in deference to Louis XIV it is more likely that the claim to rule the 'four seas' was seen to be patently ridiculous after the destruction of the English fleet by the Dutch in the Medway in 1667.

Copper halfpennies were issued in 1672 and 1673 and farthings (**155**) in most years between 1672 and 1679. The copper for the coinage had come in the form of blanks from Sweden. However, it was suggested that if halfpence and farthings were to be made from English tin this would stimulate the Cornish tin industry. This was agreed and accordingly an issue of tin farthings was made in 1684. These are of similar design to the copper coins but they are slightly thicker and to make them more difficult to counterfeit in lead the edges were inscribed with the date and the legend NVMMORVM FAMVLVS (the servant of the coinage) and the tin blanks were made with a plug of copper through the centre of the flan. Perfect specimens of these coins are rarely found as the metal is very liable to corrosion.

155 Charles II, Æ farthing, 1675

JAMES II 1685-8

When Charles died he left no legitimate male children so the succession passed to his brother James, Duke of York. James was a Catholic and he soon caused considerable consternation by his attempts to restore catholicism in England. An abortive revolt led by the Duke of Monmouth was put down with the greatest severity. The theory of divine right was preached with renewed vigour and James proceeded to act in defiance of Parliament by filling all the offices of state and army with Catholics.

Apart from the change of name and portrait the coins of this short reign are similar in design to those of Charles II except for the fact that there is no C cipher at the centre of the gold coins or in the angles of the shields on the larger silver (**156**). On the small silver coins the value in Roman numerals replaces the former interlinked CS. The Africa Company's elephant and castle badge is known for all the gold coins with the exception of the two-guinea piece. The Welsh plumes is the only provenance mark that appears on any coin of this reign and that is only found on extremely rare shillings of 1685. There are two minor variations in the king's bust and on the reverses most coins have shields with an indented top though some have shields with a top that points upwards.

Tin continued to be used for the base metal coinage and a tin halfpenny was minted. These coins have IACOBVS SECVNDVS around the king's bust which is draped on the halfpence and on the farthings of 1687 but cuirassed on the earlier farthings (**157**). The king's head on these coins faces to the right unlike that on the gold and silver coins where it faces left. As on the copper coinage of Charles II Britannia is depicted on the halfpenny with drapery down to her ankles but on the farthing she is shown with one leg bare to the knee.

When the birth of a son and male heir in 1688 meant the possibility of continued Catholic rule a number of leading Protestants sent an invitation to William of Orange, the Protestant *stadtholder* of the Dutch republics, to come to England and secure the succession for his wife, James's daughter Mary. William landed at Torbay in November 1688 and James fled to France.

156 James II, Æ crown, 1688

157 Tin farthing, 1685, with cuirassed bust

WILLIAM AND MARY 1688–94

Mary, the eldest daughter of James II, had been brought up in the Protestant faith on the instructions of Charles II. In 1672 she had married her cousin Prince William of Orange-Nassau, the son of Mary, daughter of Charles I. When she was invited to England it had been taken for granted that Mary would assume the crown, but William had no plans merely to remain as consort and it was eventually agreed that they would rule as joint sovereigns. It is for this reason that the heads of both William and Mary are shown on the coins, but unlike the earlier coins of Mary I and Philip of Spain, their heads are conjoined with William's to the fore.

On the gold coins and the early silver half-crowns a large single shield replaces the four crosswise shields of the previous two reigns. The shields on the five and two guinea pieces are highly ornamented, those on the guinea and half-guinea are less ornate and that on the half-crown is quite plain. The royal arms on the first half-crowns to be struck in 1649 has the arms of the four kingdoms quartered on a crowned shield and an inescutcheon bearing the arms of Nassau (a rampant lion on a billety field (**158**)). Coins struck later in the year have England and France quarterly in the first and fourth grand quarters. The Africa Company's elephant and castle badge is used on some of the gold coins, appearing as an elephant only on some guineas and half-guineas. No provenance marks appear on the silver coins of the joint reign.

Crowns were not struck until 1691, shillings not until 1692 and sixpences not until 1693 (**159**). In 1691 the design of the reverses of the larger silver coins reverted to the 'crosswise shields' type with the lion of Nassau in a central frame and the royal cipher, w m interlinked, set in each angle of the cross, the date being arranged around the central panel. On the latest type of half-crowns the heads are made larger in size. The portraiture on the smaller silver coins is somewhat crudely engraved, with undraped busts, and on the reverses of these coins the mark of value is given simply as 4, 3, 2 and 1 with a crown above; this was to remain the basic pattern to the present day.

158　William and Mary, Æ half-crown, 1689, first busts, first shield

159　Æ sixpence, 1693

Halfpennies and farthings continued to be struck in tin until 1692 and are similar in design to those of the previous reign. Though these had a copper plug through them it did not prevent them being extensively counterfeited in lead, so in 1694 the tin coinage was abandoned in favour of English copper. The blanks for these coins were cast in moulds and this ensured that the metal was more malleable for striking and extended the life of the dies. On these copper coins and those of William alone the edges often show signs of shearing where the 'gits' joining the moulds were taken off.

WILLIAM III 1694–1702

After Mary's death in 1694 the coinage had to be re-designed and in the following year the coins display the portrait of William alone. On the gold the single shield type was abandoned and the type reverted to the cruciform shield with sceptres in the angles. Much of the gold minted came from the Africa Company and bears the company's badge. The five and two guinea pieces of 1701 and some of the guineas of that year are particularly well engraved with a mass of hair from the king's wig falling down below the truncation of the neck. Coins of this type are referred to as the 'fine work' issue (**160**).

160 William III, *A/* five guineas, 1701, 'fine work' type

The silver coins of William alone drop the W M monogram in the angles of the shields but in their place on some of the later coins of the reign are marks (roses or plumes) indicating the provenance of metal supplied by the chartered mining companies. The Africa Company must have supplied a small quantity of silver in 1701 as there are some very rare half-crowns with an elephant and castle below the king's bust. There are also very rare shillings and sixpences of 1700 that have the Welsh plumes below the royal bust.

In 1695 it was at last decided to demonetize all the old hammered silver coin which was now well-worn and much clipped and replace it with newly minted milled money. This reform was long overdue as some of the coin in circulation dated back to the reign of Edward VI. So as not to cause a great deal of hardship to holders of hammered coin it was decided that the old money would be exchanged for new at face value and not by weight. The loss and expenses of recoinage, which were to amount to over two million pounds, were to be borne by the Exchequer rather than the individual. The loss was made good by instituting the Window Tax on property, and it is still possible to find houses of the period which had windows bricked in for tax avoidance purposes.

As the recoinage was going to take some time to complete and to prevent unscrupulous persons taking advantage of the terms of the exchange by clipping yet more silver off the hammered coins in circulation, it was ordered that all good unclipped hammered coins were to be pierced through the centre in such a way that no metal should be lost. These pierced coins were to pass as legal tender until they could be exchanged for new coin, but any coins which appeared to have been clipped after they were holed were only to be exchanged by weight. Hammered coins can still be found with a hole punched through their centre (**161**).

The operations of the recoinage were supervised by Isaac Newton, the physicist-astronomer, who had been made Warden of the Mint in March 1696 and who was appointed to the Mastership in 1699 when that position became vacant. To assist in the recoinage, which took place between 1696 and 1698, branch mints were opened at Bristol, Chester, Norwich and York. Half-crowns, shillings (**162**) and sixpences were the only denominations to be produced by these mints and their issues can be distinguished by the letters B, C, E, N and Y (or y) placed below the king's bust. Crowns were only struck at the Tower mint as they needed heavier and more powerful presses than the other coins. The small silver fourpence, threepence, twopence and Maundy penny were also only made at London. There is a fourpence dated 1702 which must have been issued posthumously as William died on 8 March, seventeen days before the new year (old style).

161 Hammered half-crown of Charles I officially defaced by piercing prior to recoinage, 1696

162 Æ shilling, Bristol mint, 1696

There are some variations in the engraving of the king's bust on both gold and silver coins. What is known as the 'second bust' on the silver coins was used briefly in 1696, and in 1697 on sixpences, and this shows the king with two long ringlets of his wig falling down across his breast. Crowns, half-crowns and shillings of this type are exceedingly rare, the sixpences less so. The fourth or 'flaming hair' bust occurs only on shillings and this has the hair on the top of the king's head seemingly being windblown up to the edge of the coin.

Though William's copper coins follow roughly the same pattern as coins of previous reigns, with a seated figure of Britannia on the reverse, there are some variations. The first issue shows Britannia holding an olive branch before her and has the date in the exergue; the second has the date following the legend BRITANNIA; the third type depicts Britannia resting her right arm on her knee and the date is returned to its normal place in the exergue. There are no farthings of the third type as they revert to the first type in 1699 and 1700.

10

THE EIGHTEENTH CENTURY

⇥ ❀❀ ⇤

Anne was the younger daughter of James II by his first wife Anne Hyde, and as William and Mary had no children she succeeded to the throne on William's death. She was married to Prince George of Denmark, a consort who took no significant part in public life, and though she had seventeen children, all but one died in infancy, the exception being William Duke of Gloucester who did not live long enough to survive his mother.

In 1707 the two kingdoms of England and Scotland which had been under one monarch since 1603 were formally united by the Act of Union, and the coinage can be divided into pre-Union and post-Union issues differentiated by the blazon of the royal arms. Pre-Union issues have the English lions and Scottish lion on separate shields but after the Union they are impaled together on the top and bottom shields (**163**). The queen's bust was designed by John Croker.

In 1702, following the outbreak of the War of the Spanish Succession, an Anglo-Dutch naval expedition under the command of the Duke of Ormond sacked the towns of Cadiz and Vigo and captured a number of treasure ships in Vigo Bay that had just arrived in Spain from South America and Mexico. Over 11 million 'pieces of eight' (8 *reals*) were seized and much of this was brought back to England where it was made into new coin. In commemoration of the exploit the name VIGO was placed below the queen's bust on some of the shillings of 1702, and on all the crowns, shillings (**164**), sixpences and most of the half-crowns minted in 1703.

Queen Anne was a woman of many virtues and considerable modesty who thought it improper to be represented undraped on her coinage, so she is shown with drapery round her shoulders on her gold coins as well as her silver. A rose takes the place of the Garter Star at the centre of the reverse of the pre-Union gold. A small quantity of gold was brought back by the Vigo expedition to be made into coin but the VIGO gold pieces are extremely rare and the Africa Company guineas of 1707–9 are also rare. No two-guinea pieces were struck before 1709. In the years immediately following the Peace of Utrecht in 1711 large quantities of gold coins were minted as a result of increased trade with the continent, guineas of 1714 being particularly common.

163 Anne, *N* guinea, 1712, post-Union issue

164 *R* shilling, 1703, with VIGO below bust

165 Æ farthing, 1714

There was the normal use of provenance marks on the silver coins during this reign indicating silver brought to the mint by the chartered mining companies as in earlier reigns. For three years before the Edinburgh mint was closed for good, coins of English denomination and type were struck there and these are distinguished by a letter E placed below the queen's bust.

No copper coins of Anne were issued for general circulation but various patterns for halfpennies and farthings were designed in 1713 and farthings of 1714 were actually put into production, Britannia being given the likeness of Anne herself (**165**) with both legs clothed with propriety to the ankles. However, the queen died before they could be put into circulation and as they frequently turn up in a remarkably fine state of preservation it seems likely that they were distributed and hoarded as mementos. At one time it was rumoured that these farthings were of great rarity and worth a large sum of money, and this is probably why numerous forgeries of this coin are found, most being casts.

GEORGE I 1714–27

Anne's nearest relative was Prince James Edward, the Jacobite pretender, but being a Catholic he was not acceptable to the Protestant establishment. The 1701 Act of Settlement stipulated that failing a male heir the succession should pass to Anne's nearest Protestant relative, at that time Sophia of the Palatinate, the granddaughter of James I, but she having also died in 1714 the throne went to her son Georg Ludwig, the Elector of Hanover.

The gold and larger silver coins of George I have his English titles on the obverse and his German titles on the reverse. The obverse inscription reads GEORGIVS·D·G·M·BR·FR·ET·HIB·REX·F·D (George, by the Grace of God, King of Great Britain, France and Ireland, Defender of the Faith) and the reverse reads BRVN·ET·L·DVX·S·R·I·A·TH·ET·EL (*Brunsvicensis et Luneburgensis Dux, Sacri Romani Imperii Archi-Thesaurarius et Elector*, Duke of Brunswick and Luneburg, Arch-Treasurer and Elector of the Holy Roman Empire). On the 'Prince-Elector' guinea of 1714 (**166**), the only denomination of the first year of the reign, the inscription reads BRVN·ET·LVN and ET·PR·EL but on all later issues the PR (*Princeps*) is omitted.

166 George I, A͞ guinea, 1714, 'Prince Elector' issue

On George's accession the royal arms were changed so that the Hanoverian arms could be blazoned in the fourth quarter, the Irish harp now being transferred to the third quarter. The electoral arms of Hanover are blazoned in a far less complex manner than in the German version since they omit the quarterings of the minor estates of the family. Instead they are tierced per pale and per chevron with the two lions passant guardant of Brunswick, the lion rampant with semée of hearts of Luneburg and the leaping horse of Hanover, while on an inescutcheon is the crown of Charlemagne to denote the elector's office of Arch-Treasurer of the Empire.

In 1717, following a report on the coinage by Sir Isaac Newton, the value of the guinea, which during the last decade of the seventeenth century had ranged from about 24s. to 30s. just prior to the recoinage, and subsequently was rated at 21s.6d., was finally fixed at 21s. It remained at this rate for the next hundred years until it was replaced by the sovereign. An undraped bust of the monarch is again used on the gold coins to distinguish them from gilded silver coins. West African gold supplied by the Africa Company is used for the last time during this reign or, at least, it is the last time that the company's elephant and castle badge appears on a few rare guineas and half-guineas. A new denomination, a quarter-guinea, was issued in 1718 to supplement the diminishing amounts of silver that were being brought to the mint for coining. It did not prove to be a popular coin, being inconvenient to handle and easily lost on account of its small size. It was not issued again during this reign.

Silver crowns, half-crowns, shillings and sixpences were minted with the cruciform shields reverse, but the smaller fourpence, threepence, twopence and penny have a large crowned numeral on the reverse and omit the king's German titles. In 1723 a large quantity of silver was brought to the mint by the South Sea Company and the coins produced from this metal have the initials SSC placed in the angles of the shields on the reverses (**167**). This chartered trading company had been reconstituted after the infamous

167 Æ sixpence, 1723, SSC in angles of shields

'South Sea Bubble' scandal of 1720 in which ministers of the crown were implicated. In its later form its activities were confined to trading principally along the west coast of South America and it was from this area that the 1723 silver was obtained. Other companies that supplied silver bullion for coining were the Welsh Copper Company and the Company for Smelting down Lead with Pitcoale and Seacoale. Shillings made from silver supplied by the former company have the initials W.C.C. placed below the king's bust and plumes and interlinked CCs in alternate angles of the reverse. These are rare and were only struck in the years 1723–6. Coins made from 'Pitcoale and Seacoale' silver have roses and plumes in the angles as in the previous reign.

There are two issues of copper coins. The first consists of 'dump' halfpennies of 1717 and 1718 and farthings of 1717 (**168**) which were struck on small thick flans. Later copper coins were struck on larger, thinner flans and these have a rather more attractive portrait than is usual for this somewhat unprepossessing monarch.

168 Æ farthing, 1717, 'dump' issue

GEORGE II 1727–60

The coinage of this reign is readily divisible into two different issues. The earlier coins have a youthful portrait of the king designed by John Croker who had also designed the coins of Anne and George I; a head with older features engraved by John Tanner was introduced between 1739 and 1743. The Maundy coins are an exception as they retained the young head throughout the reign. The arrangement of the king's titles differs from that used on coins of George I as the king's British titles are removed from the obverse to leave the inscription GEORGIVS II DEI GRATIA, while on the reverse the royal style appears as M·B·F·ET·H·REX·F·D·B·ET·L·D·S·R·I·A·T·ET·E (for a translation see p. 134).

The gold coins of George II were given new reverses with the four separate shields and Garter Star being abandoned in favour of a single crowned shield of rather ornate style. In the first quarter are the arms of England and Scotland impaled; the second quarter has the arms of France; the third quarter the arms of Ireland and the fourth the arms of Hanover. On many of the gold coins issued in the early years of the reign the initials E.I.C. set below the king's bust indicate that the gold was supplied by the East India Company (**169**). In 1733 the old hammered gold coins were finally demonetized, called-in and recoined.

In 1745 a great treasure of silver coin had been seized in the North Atlantic by two British privateers, the *Duke* and the *Prince Frederick*, from two French treasure ships that had come from Peru. This booty was transported in forty-five wagon loads from the port of Bristol to the mint in London. As the booty principally consisted of 'pieces of eight' bearing the Lima mintmark it was requested that coins taken from these prizes might bear the name 'Lima' to celebrate the exploit. This was agreed and much of the silver struck in the years 1745–6 has the word LIMA placed below the king's bust (**170**). Some of the gold five, one and half guineas of 1745 also bear the LIMA mark. Apart from the Lima issues the majority of earlier George II silver bears the roses or plumes provenance marks, indicating West of England or Welsh silver, and the combined roses and plumes mark of the 'Pitcoale and Seacoale' company. After 1745 it appears that the supply of silver from domestic sources failed due to the exhaustion of silver-bearing ores. There was a small issue of West of England silver in 1747 but that was the end and though there were further mintages of silver

169 George II, *A/* five guineas, 1729, E. I. C. below bust

170 *R* half-crown, 1745, LIMA below bust

coin in 1750–1 and 1757–8 (only shillings and sixpences in the last two years) these were made from silver obtained from various overseas sources. Owing to the increasing difficulty in obtaining silver at a price the mint could pay, the 1758 coins were the last silver coins to be issued in any quantity for general circulation for nearly thirty years. The bimetallic system of coinage had been in crisis for some decades and, to all intents and purposes, Britain was now on a gold standard.

The copper coins follow the style of previous issues. Up to 1739 they have the cuirassed bust of the king designed by Croker (**171**) and after that date they change to Tanner's 'old head' portrait. No copper coins were struck after 1754 or if they were they were not given a new date. Owing to the great scarcity of small change many light-weight counterfeits of halfpennies and farthings were manufactured about this time.

171 Æ halfpenny, 1733, young head

GEORGE III 1760 – 1820

From a numismatic point of view the reign of George III is as notable for the scarcity of coin as for the coins themselves. There was already a silver famine at the beginning of the reign which was to become even more acute. In addition, the price of copper rose to the point where little copper coin was minted and even gold became so scarce during the Napoleonic Wars that a paper currency virtually took the place of gold. This period also saw the advent of steam power, a form of energy soon applied to the manufacture of coin, new issues of unauthorized private tokens and, early in the next century, the transference of the mint to a new site on Tower Hill leading to the major recoinage of 1816–17.

No five-guinea or two-guinea pieces were issued for George III although patterns for both denominations were produced. Quarter-guineas were tried out again in 1762 but, as in the reign of George I, they were not readily accepted and they were not minted in later years. They were probably kept as curiosities as they frequently turn up in good condition. On the other hand guineas and half-guineas were struck nearly every year between 1761 and 1799. Early coins with a youthful bust of the king were designed by Richard Yeo but on later coins designed by Thomas and Lewis Pingo the king is given a more mature portrait. The reverse design of the gold also varies. A garnished shield is used at first, the coins sometimes strangely being described as 'rose' guineas, but in 1787 a plain flat-topped shield was adopted which, from its resemblance to the old style long-handled spade, earned for the coins the name of 'spade' guineas (**172**). These were to attain considerable popularity as watch-chain pendants in the next century after the coins had been called-in and demonetized. The minting of guineas was interrupted in 1799 owing to the hazards of importing gold from overseas during the war with France and it seems that guineas dated 1798 and 1799 were held in the Bank of England's gold reserves and not released until 1813 as they are seldom seen in worn state. Bank notes were declared legal tender in 1797 for any amounts over one pound. However, to supplement the issues of half-guineas, a new denomination of seven-shilling pieces, one-third guineas, was introduced in 1797, these small coins simply having a large crown as the reverse type (**173**).

172 George III, *A*/ guinea, 1799, 'spade' type

173 *A*/ one-third guinea, 1799, first type

174 *A*R shilling, 1763, 'Northumberland' issue

Owing to the high price of silver, no silver coins were issued during the first half of the reign apart from a substantial quantity of threepences in 1762–3, small amounts of Maundy coins and a very limited issue of shillings dated 1763 (**174**). These last coins are commonly known as 'Northumberland' shillings as numbers of them were thrown to the crowds when the Earl of Northumberland rode in procession through Dublin to be sworn in as Lord Lieutenant of Ireland. Though quite scarce it is likely that considerably more were struck than the 2,000 used on that occasion.

Apart from Maundy money no other silver coins were struck until the year 1787 when the Bank of England commissioned the Mint to coin a quantity of shillings and sixpences, which were produced at a loss to the

Bank. They are amongst the commonest English silver coins issued prior to 1816. A new feature on these coins are the straight-sided shields with crowns in the angles and as on gold coins of the period the lettering is positioned very close to the edge of the coins as an additional deterrent to clipping and re-edging. An interesting error occurs on the earlier strikings of both shillings and sixpences – the minute semée of hearts around the lion of Luneburg was omitted. In 1798 there was a temporary fall in the price of silver and the banking firm of Dorrien and Magens as well as some other banks sent silver to the mint to be coined into shillings and they were struck to the same design as the 1787 coins. However, an Order in Council forbade their issue and ordered them to be melted down so consequently the 'Dorrien and Magens' shillings are great rarities.

By 1797 the dearth of silver coin had become acute as much of the 1787 issue appears to have been hoarded. To remedy the situation the Bank of England began purchasing Spanish silver 8 *reals* or 'dollars' as they were usually called at this time. After being countermarked with a small oval punch bearing the head of George III on the neck of the Spanish king, Carlos III or IV, they were reissued to the public in March 1797 as 'dollars' valued at 4s.9d. (**175**). The punch used for the head of George III was that used at Goldsmiths' Hall for hallmarking silver plate. Some of these coins and some 4 *real* pieces were from Spanish mints, but most originated in the Spanish-American mints of Lima, Potosi and, most commonly, the mint of Mexico City, easily recognized by the mintmark M with a little ° above. The dollars were some 40 grains lighter than English crowns and they were made of silver of inferior fineness, so initially their intrinsic value was a little under their current value. The dollars were extensively counterfeited and given false countermarks; sometimes genuine dollars were given false marks and occasionally counterfeit dollars are found bearing an official counterstamp. In September 1797, as a check to this counterfeiting, the Bank of England began to call in countermarked dollars at 4s.9d. per dollar

175 Spanish Æ 8 reals ('dollar') countermarked with head of George III, current for 4s. 6d.

in lots of not less than 20 pieces and they were declared no longer legal tender from the end of October. The newly coined one-third guineas helped to provide coin for the exchange where payment was not made in bank notes.

No copper coins of George III were issued during the first ten years of his reign and it was about this period that numerous forgeries of George II halfpennies and some farthings appeared, many of very light weight and often with peculiar inscriptions, such as GEORGE RULES, CLAUDIUS ROMANUS and CORNWALLIS IND, etc. A variety of reverse inscriptions occur, such as BRITAIN.ˢ ISLES, BONNY GIRL and DELECTAT RUS, etc. around a figure of Britannia, or NORTH WALES, etc. around a crowned harp. By these devices the counterfeiter avoided the technical offence of forgery as he could claim he was not copying a coin which was legal tender. In any case, though the counterfeiting of gold and silver coin was punishable by death or transportation, the counterfeiting of copper coin was merely a misdemeanour warranting a fine or short term of imprisonment. Many of these curious forgeries were shipped across to the American colonies where they became known as 'bungtowns'.

During the period 1770–5 copper halfpennies and farthings were issued to the same weight and style as the coppers of George II. They have a laureate and cuirassed bust of the king facing right and on the reverse a seated figure of Britannia holding a spear and olive branch. Some of the imitation coppers are also of the same general design. After 1775 there was a gap of twenty-two years during which time no regal copper coins were minted.

In 1787 such was the shortage of small change, particularly in those areas where new industries were growing up, that a flood of new token coins was produced to fill the gap. The first of these was an issue of token pennies by the Parys Mining Company of Anglesey made from copper obtained from their own mines and these were followed by an issue of halfpennies the following year (**176**). These Anglesey tokens have a druid's head on one side and the name and cipher of the company on the other, whilst on the edge in incuse characters are inscriptions such as PAYABLE IN ANGLESEY,

176 Token halfpenny of Parys Mining Company of Anglesey, 1791

LONDON OR LIVERPOOL. These tokens are extremely well struck and contain nearly their full value of copper. Also issued in 1787 and later years were the tokens of John Wilkinson the ironmaster, one of the few tokens to bear a portrait of the issuer. Many other companies began ordering tokens for the payment of their labour force, but many tokens were of very light weight and earned a good profit both for the manufacturers and the issuers. Most tokens bear the name of the issuer as a guarantee of good faith but quite a few are anonymous and were foisted on the public by those who had no intention of redeeming them at a later date. Quite a number of tokens, notably those issued by Thomas Spence and other radicals, were produced for political propaganda. Others were not intended for real circulation at all but were produced for sale to collectors who soon began to take an interest in the series.

As early as 1772 Matthew Boulton, the well-known manufacturer, had campaigned for an improved coinage. In 1786 he had coining presses of the latest design set up at his Soho foundry at Handsworth, near Birmingham, and with these he produced some excellent copper coins for the East India Company. In 1788, in collaboration with James Watt the engineer, he had the first steam driven coining presses erected and by 1790 he was using a steam engine that worked eight presses, each of which could produce 50 large or 150 small coins a minute. Boulton had tried to interest the government in his new method of coining in 1788 and he produced a variety of patterns for both pennies and halfpennies in an attempt to obtain a contract for their manufacture. Due to the obstruction of officials at the Mint he was not immediately successful and it was not until 1797 that he was eventually given a contract for the manufacture of copper pennies and twopenny pieces (**177**). These coins, the first English regal coins to be minted by steam power, are remarkable both for their size and their excellent workmanship. So precisely were they struck by the new machinery that effective forgery was made almost impossible and their

177 George III, Æ twopence, 1797, from Mathew Boulton's mint at Soho, Birmingham

issue in quantity soon put a stop to the manufacture of tokens. The copper twopences weighed exactly two ounces avoirdupois and, being so large, they soon acquired the name 'cartwheels'. The inscriptions which were stamped incuse into the broad raised rim around each side of the coin are an unusual feature of their design. On the reverse the figure of Britannia becomes a symbol of Britain's increasing maritime power with the substitution of a trident for the earlier spear, the addition of waves at her feet and a man-o'-war in the background. The name of Boulton's foundry, SOHO, appears in minute letters on a rock in the foreground. The 'cartwheel' penny of 1797 was still being minted two years later with the date unchanged. In 1799 Bolton started minting halfpennies and farthings of similar design but without the heavy raised rims and with the inscriptions in relief. When the price of copper rose quantities of these heavy coins were taken out of circulation and melted down and Boulton's next issue was to be of a lighter weight.

The coins of George III issued after 1800 are dealt with in the next chapter.

11

THE NINETEENTH CENTURY

⇒❧❦⇐

GEORGE III 1760–1820 (continued)

The formal union of the kingdoms of Great Britain and Ireland took effect by Act of Parliament on January 1801. In the negotiations with France the same year, which led to the Treaty of Amiens, it was agreed to drop the monarch's title to the throne of France. This resulted in changes in the royal arms which appear on the half-guineas of 1801. These are now *Quarterly, 1st and 4th England; 2nd Scotland; 3rd Ireland; overall, ensigned by the Electoral cap, an inescutcheon of Hanover with the Electoral inescutcheon.* At the same time the royal style on the reverse is altered to BRITANNIARUM REX FIDEI DEFENSOR (King of all the Britains, defender of the Faith). In 1804 a new portrait of the king by Nathaniel Marchant appears on the half and one-third guineas and the same head with short hair is used on the guineas of 1813 (**178**). These coins are commonly known as 'Military guineas' as many were used for the payment and provisioning of the army during the Peninsular campaign. They were the last guineas to be minted before the change to a sovereign coin.

In 1787 the government had set up a Committee to look into deficiencies in the coinage and the administration of the Mint. It found that the

178 George III, *AV* 'Military' guinea, 1813

majority of coin in circulation was seriously underweight but, though its recommendation that copper coin should contain its full intrinsic value of metal was eventually implemented with Boulton's 1797 'cartwheel' issue, it proposed little other effective action. Early in 1798 a new enquiry into the coinage was set up in the form of a Committee of the Privy Council. This committee included the Earl of Liverpool, known for his *Treatise on the Coins of the Realm in a letter to the King*, published in 1805, and Sir Joseph Banks who formed a notable collection of coins. John Rennie the engineer was commissioned to investigate the running of the Mint and found it to be grossly inefficient, recommending that up-to-date machinery should be installed in a new building. This recommendation was accepted and in 1804 a new mint building was commenced on Tower Hill.

The Earl of Liverpool had recommended that, to avoid the continual re-evaluation of gold in relation to silver coin, gold should be the standard coin and be of full weight but that silver and copper coin should be token coinages with intrinsic values below their current value and that they should be redeemable in gold on demand. Lord Hawksbury, the Earl's son, was Master of the Mint in the years 1799–1801, an office that had been very much a sinecure throughout most of the eighteenth century, and it was he who, as second Earl of Liverpool (from 1808) and Prime Minister (1812–17), steered through Parliament the 1816 Coinage Act which contained most of his father's recommendations.

The countermarking of Spanish dollars was resumed at the Tower mint early in 1804, but a new form of counterstamp was devised having the king's bust in an octagonal instead of an oval frame, the punch of the Maundy penny bust being used. This type of counterstamp was quickly copied by counterfeiters so later the same year the Bank of England commissioned Matthew Boulton to completely overstrike Spanish dollars with a new design. This was done so effectively at the Soho foundry that the original design of the coins was almost entirely obliterated. These pieces have a new bust of the king designed by Boulton's chief engraver Conrad Küchler and on the reverse a figure of Britannia as a patron of trade and industry with a beehive to her left and a cornucopia in the foreground (**179**). The main inscription on the reverse is BANK OF ENGLAND and the main design is set within a frame inscribed FIVE SHILLINGS DOLLAR and surmounted by a mural crown representing the City of London. The minting of these coins was continued for a number of years, though they all have the date 1804, and occasionally pieces can be found with the date of the original Spanish coin just visible and of a year later than 1804. In 1812 an increase in the price of silver led to the dollars being officially revalued at 5s.6d.

Spanish dollars were privately countermarked by a number of firms in

179 Bank of England Æ dollar, 1804

Scotland (see p. 219) and by a few firms in England, notably by Richard Arkwright for his mill at Cromford in Derbyshire and possibly by John Cartwright for his Revolution Mill at East Retford, Notts., for the Cotton Works at Cark-in-Cartmel, Lancs., and for the Percy Main Colliery near South Shields, Northumberland. The values expressed on the coins are 4s.6d., 4s.9d. and 5s. A large number of unauthorized private silver tokens for lower denominations also appeared in the years 1811–12, followed by copper penny and halfpenny tokens (**180**). The Bank of England intervened to discourage these issues, in advance of pending legislation and a new regal coinage, by having more than £4 million of official silver Bank Tokens minted by the new Mint on Tower Hill. These bank tokens were made from melted down Spanish silver dollars which were coined into three-shilling (**181**) and 1s.6d. pieces and minted in the years 1811–16, but being issued only as a temporary expedient they were withdrawn from circulation in 1817 and demonetized in 1820.

The Committee on Coinage had been so impressed by the superiority of Boulton's steam-powered coining presses installed at the Soho works that Boulton and Watt were given a contract to equip the new mint with steam-powered machinery under the supervision of Rennie. The Mint was constructed on the site of the ancient Abbey of St Mary de Graciis which was destroyed on the dissolution of the monasteries, a naval bakehouse and victualling depôt being built in its place which in turn eventually became a tobacco warehouse. The new mint building was designed by James Johnson and completed by Robert Smirke. The Committee on Coinage produced their final report in May 1816 and the following month a Coinage Act was passed establishing gold coin as the sole standard measure of value and legal tender for any amount. This Act also stipulated that silver coin should be legal tender for amounts up to two pounds only and that in future it should be coined at the rate of sixty-six shillings to the pound Troy instead of the previous sixty-two shillings. The 1816 Coinage Act did not

180 Token Æ penny of Birmingham Workhouse, 1812

181 George III, Bank of England, Æ three-shilling token, 1814

lay down a definite denomination for the new gold coinage but the
opportunity was now taken to drop the somewhat tiresome twenty-one
shilling piece and replace it with a new coin of twenty shillings value
weighing $123\frac{1}{4}$ grains – the 'sovereign'.

Thomas Wyon and his son, Thomas Jnr., came as engravers to the Mint
from Boulton's establishment and they were joined by Benedetto Pistrucci,
an Italian gem engraver. Pistrucci not only produced some finely cut
obverse puncheons for the king's portrait but also the renowned St George
and dragon reverse. There are two versions of this reverse type: on the
sovereign (**182**) St George is depicted grasping the broken shaft of a lance,
the head of which is embedded in the dragon's body, whilst on the silver
crown (**183**) the saint holds a sword with which he presumably hopes to
deliver the *coup de grâce*. This latter type was continued in later reigns on
both crowns and some sovereigns and it is still in use on gold coins
currently being minted. Sovereigns were minted each year between 1817
and 1820, coins of 1819 being exceedingly rare and no half-sovereigns of
this year being recorded. The reverse of the half-sovereign has a crowned
shield with a new version of the royal arms. Napoleon had abolished the
Holy Roman Empire and in 1814 the Congress of Vienna had promoted
the electoral principality of Hanover to the status of a kingdom; the change

is indicated on the new arms by the substitution of an arched regal crown above the Hanoverian inescutcheon in place of the earlier electoral cap.

The first silver coins of the new coinage, half-crowns, shillings and sixpences, were dated 1816 but they were not issued for general circulation until February 1817. The Prince Regent did not like Pistrucci's portrait of his father as shown on the half-crown on which the king is viewed from behind his right shoulder and this type (**184**), now known as the 'bull-head' half-crown, was replaced during 1817 by a smaller less aggressive-looking bust. All three denominations have the royal arms within the Garter though the half-crown has, in addition, the Collar of the Order from which is suspended the Lesser George. The crown was not issued until 1818, the lettered edge with the DECUS ET TUTAMEN inscription and regnal year being

182 Æ sovereign, 1817

183 Æ crown, 1818

184 Æ half-crown, 1816, 'bull-head' issue

formed at the moment of impact of striking by means of an inscribed collar of three segments which sprung open as the coin was being ejected from the dies. Originally it had not been intended to issue the crowns in large numbers for general circulation but merely as examples of the engraver's art. However the coins proved to be so popular with the general public that large numbers were minted in the years 1818–20.

There were four types of Maundy Money struck during the reign. The first had a young head of the king; the second, struck only in 1792, had a middle-aged bust and is known as the 'wire-money' issue on account of the thin wiry numerals on the reverse; the third type is similar but has thicker numerals and the last type, of 1818–20, has the new head by Pistrucci.

Boulton's 1799 coinage of halfpennies and farthings had been minted at the rate of 36 halfpence to the avoirdupois pound. In 1805 a further order was given to Boulton for a new issue of copper coins to include pennies as well as the two smaller coins, but as the price of copper had risen substantially the coins were minted at the rate of 24 pence per pound, i.e. only three-quarters the weight of the previous issue. These coins are dated 1806 and 1807. Though it was the intention to make a further issue of copper after 1815, with all the pre-1797 worn copper being called in as a preliminary step, the Mint was too occupied with the silver recoinage to give further attention to the smaller denominations until early in the next reign.

GEORGE IV 1820–30

The first coinage of George IV has a fine left-facing laureate portrait by Pistrucci which can be seen to best advantage on the silver crowns of 1821–2. Gold sovereigns and half-sovereigns of this type were issued in 1821–5, the former having the St George reverse without the surrounding Garter of the previous sovereigns, and the half-sovereigns having an ornate crowned shield on those issued in 1821 and a plain crowned shield on the coins struck in 1823–5. These reverses and the reverses of the silver coins below crown-size were designed by Johann Baptiste Merlen, a Frenchman of Flemish origin, who also engraved the bare-headed portrait of the king depicted on a two-pound piece which was issued in 1823. The minute initials W.W.P. concealed in the ground of the St George type and at the centre of the triple shamrocks on the other silver coins are the initials of William Wellesley Pole, Chancellor of the Exchequer and Master of the Mint, an elder brother of the Duke of Wellington and later third Earl of Mornington. On the reverse of the half-crown Merlen concealed his own minute initials in the beading around the rim (**185**). As on the half-sovereign, the design of the half-crown, shilling and sixpence was changed in 1823, the silver coins now having a plain crowned shield within the Garter and the half-crown having in addition the Garter Collar. The only inscription on the reverses of these coins is the word ANNO followed by the date.

185 George IV Æ half-crown, 1820, first issue

In 1824 the king requested a new portrait for the coinage. Pistrucci was asked to copy the much admired marble bust sculptured by Sir Francis Chantrey but he refused to do this as he considered that an artist of his calibre should not be expected to copy the work of another. As a result the commission was given to William Wyon and it is his obverse that appears on the third issue coins of 1825–30. Pistrucci's St George design was temporarily abandoned and all the new reverses were designed by Merlen. Both the sovereign and half-sovereign have a flat-topped shield with a crown above; the half-crown has a shield surmounted by royal helm and lambrequins added to garnish the royal arms and below there appears for the first time on the coinage the royal motto DIEU ET MON DROIT (God and my Right). The shilling (**186**) and sixpence both have a large crown surmounted by a royal lion below which is a floral sprig of shamrock, rose and thistle combined, and these coins, known as 'lion' shillings and sixpences, seem to have been highly regarded and treasured once they were superseded by later issues. The third coinage gold and silver all have the date on the obverse below the monarch's head. A set of proofs of the third coinage was issued in 1826 in a leather case, the sale of such coins being a perquisite of the engravers. The set included proofs of a five-pound and two-pound piece and a silver crown, though none of these denominations were issued for general circulation.

The Maundy coins retain Pistrucci's portrait throughout the reign and have the usual mark of value within a wreath on the reverse. One unusual feature is the small head found on the threepence of 1822, the head being formed from the puncheon used on the twopence.

For the first five years of the reign the farthing was the only denomination of copper to be issued as this was the coin most needed for

small change. On these coins Britannia is depicted wearing a plumed
helmet for the first time. In 1825 the first pennies (**187**) and halfpennies of
George IV were minted and these have a head by William Wyon, but
unlike the silver and gold of this issue the king is depicted wearing a wreath
of laurel while on the reverse Britannia loses her sprig of laurel. The little
half and one-third farthings, though similar in design to the larger copper
coins, were only intended for use in some of the colonies which had a lower
standard of living than Britain and they were not current in this country.

186 Æ shilling, 1826, third issue

187 Æ penny, 1826

WILLIAM IV 1830–7

During this fairly short reign there was one set of designs for the coinage.
The king's portrait was engraved by William Wyon from a model by
Chantrey and the larger coins have the initials W.W. on the truncation of
the king's neck. The reverses of the gold and silver were designed again by
Merlen. The obverse inscriptions all read GULIELMUS IIII D G BRITANNIAR REX
F D, the only inscription on the reverse being ANNO followed by the date.

The only gold coins issued for general circulation were the sovereign and
the half-sovereign, though some rare proofs exist of a two-pound piece and
a few extremely rare proofs of a five-pound piece. The royal arms on the
sovereign and its half resemble those on the last issue of George IV but the
garnishing of the shield is slightly different. The first half sovereign issued in
1834 was struck on a smaller but thicker flan than previously to prevent

confusion with the sixpence, but the public did not like the reduced size and in 1835 the denomination was restored to its former diameter.

A silver crown was not issued for general circulation but beautifully engraved proofs of this denomination were made for the proof sets of 1831 and as no ordinary coins are available for collectors these proofs are eagerly sought after and in perfect condition have sold for around £5,000 (**188**). The half-crown, like the crown, has the royal arms draped in a mantle of ermine. On the crown the arms are surrounded by the Collar of the Order of the Garter; on the half-crown the Collar and pendant George are visible below the arms. The shilling and sixpence have the value in words for the first time on a British regal coin, ONE SHILLING or SIX PENCE in two lines within a wreath of oak and laurel. In 1836 a groat (fourpence) was re-introduced into the coinage in addition to those that were part of the Maundy money. They are now usually known as 'Britannia' groats from the seated figure of Britannia on the reverse similar to that on the copper coinage (**189**). This denomination was minted at the instance of Joseph Hume the philanthropist, hence their nickname 'fourpenny Joey'.

188 William IV Æ pattern crown, 1831

189 Æ fourpence or groat, 1836

The Maundy coins retain the same reverse designs as in the previous reign, as do the copper pennies, halfpennies and farthings. Half and one-third farthings were only struck for use in colonial territories, as was the little silver three-halfpence piece which, owing to its resemblance to Maundy money with its '$1\frac{1}{2}$' within a wreath, is sometimes mistaken for an English coin.

VICTORIA 1837–1901

On Victoria's accession the kingdom of Hanover passed to her uncle Ernst August, Duke of Cumberland, as under Salic law women were excluded from the dynastic succession, and so the Hanoverian shield was now omitted from the royal arms which thus attained their present form. The coins of this reign, the longest reign of any British monarch, can conveniently be divided into three main groups: the Young Head coins of 1838–87 (1838–94/5 in the case of the copper and bronze), the Jubilee issue of 1887–93 and the Old Head coinage of 1893–1901. Two new denominations were introduced during the reign, the florin of two shillings and the double-florin.

The Young Head coinage began in 1838 with an issue of gold sovereigns and half-sovereigns, silver shillings, sixpences, groats and Maundy money, and copper halfpennies and farthings. Victoria's portrait on these coins was engraved by William Wyon, whose initials appear on the truncation of the neck of some of the coins. The young queen's hair is bound by two fillets in Grecian fashion and gathered in a loose bunch high at the back of the head.

190   Victoria, *N* sovereign, 1847, young head, shield reverse

From 1838 to 1874 the reverse of the first type sovereign had a crowned shield surrounded by a wreath of laurel leaves (**190**). In 1871, however, Pistrucci's St George reverse was reintroduced and for four years coins of both types were issued concurrently, the shield type then being discontinued. The half-sovereign retains a shield-type reverse throughout the period – a type very similar to that used in the last reign but with the addition of the inscription BRITANNIARUM REGINA FID DEF (Queen of the Britains, Defender of the Faith). No Young Head two-pound piece was struck but a pattern or proof five-pound was issued with the cased proof set of 1839. This famous coin designed by William Wyon is usually known as the 'Una and the Lion' five-pound piece as the queen is depicted standing beside the British lion, guiding him with her sceptre (**191**). These pieces are particularly highly regarded by collectors and have been sold for between £10,000 and £20,000 depending on condition and variety. With the discovery of gold in Australia the Royal Mint set up branches in Sydney and later in Melbourne, and between 1855 and 1870 sovereigns and half-sovereigns of local type were made at Sydney for domestic use in Australia. However, after 1870, sovereigns of United Kingdom type were issued at both mints and much of the coin struck was brought back for use in this country and passed into circulation alongside London-made coins. The Sydney and Melbourne coins have an s or m mintmark below the wreath on the reverse and below the head on the obverse of the St George type, both types being issued concurrently until 1887, the shield type coins being principally used for supplying the gold market in India where they seem to have been preferred.

191 Pattern *Æ* five pounds, 1839, 'Una and the lion' type

The Young Head crown was only struck for circulation in the years 1844, 1845 and 1847; the half-crown was first issued in 1839 but none were issued between 1850 and 1874. Both these coins have the same reverse as the early sovereigns – a plain crowned shield within a wreath of laurel. The shilling and sixpence of this issue follow the same pattern as that of William IV, having the value ONE SHILLING or SIX PENCE within a wreath of laurel and oak. Early Young Head coins have the queen's head modelled in higher relief than coins of later date, the lower relief being adopted when it was found that the dies could be given a longer life with less pressure being needed to strike the coins. Between the years 1868 and 1879 minute die numbers can be found on the reverses of many of the gold and silver coins, these being inserted to check the working life of the dies.

The Britannia groat, which had been introduced in 1836, continued to be struck until 1855 when its issue in the United Kingdom was discontinued in favour of the threepenny piece. During the reign of William IV and in the opening years of Victoria's reign the threepenny piece had been struck only for use in the colonies: it was first issued for general circulation in this country in 1845. This coin has the same design as the Maundy threepence but when in uncirculated condition it can be distinguished by its surface which is not as highly polished as the Maundy coins.

In 1846 William Wyon prepared the pattern for a new crown piece which depicts the queen wearing an arched crown and an ornate gown (**192**). The queen was delighted with the design and in 1847 8,000 pieces were circulated through the banks. It is possible that they were originally conceived as a commemorative issue on the tenth anniversary of Victoria's accession. It is doubtful if they were ever intended for circulation as they would have been expensive to produce in quantity. They were most carefully struck from well-buffed dies and that they were treasured by those who obtained them is apparent from the numbers that are still found in uncirculated conditon. The whole style of the coin reflects the mid-nineteenth-century Gothic revival with all its tressures, lattice work and medieval lettering and it is always known as the 'Gothic' crown. The reverse has four shields with the national emblems, rose, thistle and shamrock in the angles; the *tueatur unita deus* inscription, first used by James I, and the date are arranged between the four crowns. A similar crown dated 1853 was included in the rare proof set issued in that year.

192 Æ crown, 1847, 'Gothic' type

In the late 1840s there was some agitation, both inside and outside Parliament, for a decimal system of coinage and numerous Mint and unofficial patterns were produced for coins with names such as centums, centimes, francs, decades, dimes, and ducats. A decimal coinage had been adopted in France after the Revolution and by the United States in 1792, by the Netherlands in 1817, Belgium in 1832 and Switzerland in 1839, and in Russia Peter the Great had established a monetary system of 100 kopeks to the rouble in the early years of the eighteenth century. After much discussion it was finally decided to take the first step towards decimalization in this country by striking a two-shilling piece, this being a tenth of a pound. The name 'florin' given to this coin did not have any connection with the gold florin of Edward III but was adopted because it was roughly equivalent in size and value to the florin or *gulden* of the Netherlands. It also had an historical basis in that the first medieval *fiorino d'oro* of Florence was rated at one *lira* (pound) and was initially equal to ten silver *fiorinos* (florins). The florin was intended to replace the half-crown, so the larger coin was not issued between 1850 and 1874 but was eventually re-introduced at the request of the banks and was then issued concurrently with the florin until decimalization in the twentieth century.

The first silver florin was somewhat similar in design to the Gothic crown except for the inscriptions which were in Roman lettering and read VICTORIA REGINA 1849 on the obverse and ONE FLORIN ONE TENTH OF A POUND on the reverse. As the usual *dei gratia* was omitted this coin became known as the 'Godless' florin (**193**). The queen is said to have been most displeased at this omission and requested the type be discontinued. In 1851 an amended design appeared which is known as the 'Gothic' florin, the lettering copying the medieval type of the Gothic crown. The date *mdcccli* (*et seq.*) comes at the end of the obverse inscription which now gives the queen's normal style, *d: g: brit: reg: f: d:*. After 1867 the abbreviation *brit:* is changed to *britt:*, the doubling of the last letter of a contraction being the classical method of indicating a plural form (i.e. of the Britains). To the uninitiated these florins sometimes appear to be dateless as the Roman numerals set in Gothic script are not immediately obvious.

193 Æ florin (2 shillings), 1849, 'Godless' type

A major Coinage Act in 1870 made various changes in the constitution of the Royal Mint. The Chancellor of the Exchequer from now on held the *ex officio* post of Master of the Mint and the positions of Deputy-Master and Comptroller were combined in one post to control the administration, with a Chief Clerk to assist. The privileges and contracts of the moneyers had been terminated earlier in 1851. The 1870 Act also tightened up the 'remedy' or error allowed in the variation of weight and fineness from the prescribed standard. This was now reduced in the case of gold to 2 parts per 1,000 in fineness and 1.6 parts per 1,000 in weight for each coin and for silver 4 parts per 1,000 in fineness and 4.17 parts per 1,000 in weight. These alterations had been made possible by technical improvements in machinery and scientific instruments.

Although in the 1870s it had been proposed to move the Mint to a new site, both Somerset House and Whitefriars having been proposed, in 1881 it was decided to reconstruct part of the Tower Hill premises. As stocks of both gold and silver were high at the end of that year coinage operations were suspended entirely from February to December 1882 whilst rebuilding took place. Twelve new furnaces were installed for melting gold and Heaton & Sons of Birmingham supplied fourteen new presses of the German Uhlhorn type.

In 1887 it was decided to alter the designs of the coinage. Despite the fact that the queen was now nearly seventy the portrait on her coins was still basically the one designed when she was a young woman, though the obverse dies had been touched up once or twice to make her appearance more mature. The advent of the Golden Jubilee provided an excellent occasion for a new issue. Sir Joseph Boehm modelled the portrait for the new coins and his initials J.E.B. appear below the queen's bust. Prince Albert had died in 1861 and the queen had remained in mourning so she is portrayed with a widow's veil over the back of her head and she has a miniature crown perched precariously on the top. The 'Jubilee Head' design seems to have been widely criticized and it was replaced in 1893.

Gold five-pound and two-pound pieces were issued in the Jubilee year but they did not circulate to any great extent, being mainly kept as souvenirs. These two coins, together with the sovereign and the silver crown, have Pistrucci's St George reverse. The half-sovereign, half-crown, shilling and sixpence have a shield type reverse; the half-sovereign has the same style of shield as the Young Head issue, the half-crown has a plain shield surrounded by the Garter and the Collar of the Order, and the shilling and sixpence have a plain shield with the Garter but no collar. This sixpence is known as the 'withdrawn' type as it was replaced later the same year by the old SIX PENCE reverse, the 'withdrawn' type being liable to confusion with the half-sovereign if it was gilded. The crown piece was minted for the first time with a grained instead of a lettered edge, possibly on grounds of speed and economy.

A double-florin (four shillings) was introduced with the Jubilee coinage but it did not prove popular, there being no demand for two large silver coins, and it was not issued again after 1890. The double-florin was an enlarged version of the florin (**194**) and they both have a reverse design copied from the early milled gold coinage, four shields with sceptres in the angles. Gertrude Rawlings, writing in 1898, says of the double-florin '... it has been spoken of as "radiating kitchen pokers and tea-trays"'.

194 Victoria Æ Florin, 1892, Jubilee type

A new and improved portrait of the queen was designed by Thomas Brock in 1893 and his initials T B appear below the queen's bust on the new coinage. The portrait is larger and a partly veiled coronet replaces the small crown of the previous issue. The addition of IND IMP to the queen's titles draws attention to the fact that Victoria was now Empress of India. She had been proclaimed Empress in 1876 but the title had not hitherto appeared on the United Kingdom coinage though it had been given on the coins of British India since 1877. On this 'Old Head' coinage Pistrucci's St George reverse was used on all the gold coins and on the silver crown. The reverse of the half-crown has a spade-shaped shield within the Collar of the Order of the Garter, whilst the florin and the shilling (**195**), both designed by Sir Edward Poynter, have the arms of England, Scotland and Ireland on three separate shields over crossed sceptres and with a surrounding Garter. The DECUS ET TUTAMEN legend in raised letters is revived again for the edge of the silver crown, but not for the larger gold coins, and two regnal years appear for each date of issue. The branch mints of Sydney and Melbourne continued to issue gold of United Kingdom type. Similar coins with a mintmark P were produced at Perth from 1899 when a branch was opened there to coin gold produced by the mines in Western Australia.

195 Æ shilling, 1900, Old Head type

There are three main divisions of Victoria's 'copper' coinage, though they do not correspond to the gold and silver issues as there is no special Jubilee design. The first type is the heavy copper issue which has Wyon's Young Head portrait of the queen and the Britannia reverse by the same engraver (**196**). The 1860 coins of this issue are very rare, the type being discontinued in that year. Half, one-third and quarter-farthings of this type were issued for use in the Colonies. Half-farthings were declared legal tender in the United Kingdom in 1842 but though very common it is doubtful if they circulated to any great extent as they are usually found in good condition and they are known to have been sold by street hawkers as curiosities at three-farthings each.

196 Æ penny, 1853, copper issue

197 Æ penny, 1870, bronze 'bun penny' type

In 1860 a bronze coinage was introduced to replace copper. This was made of a copper alloy having a small percentage of tin and zinc to make the metal far harder and therefore more durable, and this meant that coins could remain in circulation for a much longer period before becoming so worn that they had to be replaced. They were made smaller and thinner and were therefore much more convenient for the public. The new coins were designed by Leonard Wyon and have a charming portrait with the queen's bust draped, her head laureate and her hair swept back into a chignon, hence the popular name 'bun' penny (**197**). The queen's titles only appear on the obverse and on the reverse the value in words is inscribed around a helmeted seated figure of Britannia, with a sailing ship and a lighthouse, modelled on the former Eddystone lighthouse, completing the seascape in the background.

During the late 1870s and early 1880s, as the Mint was often working to full capacity and unable to fulfil all its orders, Messrs. Ralph Heaton and

Son of Birmingham minted much of the copper coinage and some of the colonial issues under contract. Bronze coins made by Heaton's are distinguished by a small н below the date. The 'bun' head issue was replaced in 1895 by Brock's Old Head obverse and on the reverse the figure of Britannia was slightly altered, being seated rather more erect and alert, and the sailing ship and lighthouse were now omitted.

In 1887 and 1893 proof sets in leather cases were made by the Mint for sale to collectors and members of the public. These coins were made from specially prepared highly polished dies and were sold in handsome red leather cases with the royal arms on the lid. Before 1887 such proof sets had been sold privately by the Mint Engravers. Maundy money was issued of the Young, Jubilee and Old Head types, the 1887 set being of Young Head design as the Maundy Service came before the Jubilee celebrations. The Old Head Maundy coins are much commoner than present day issues as, until 1909, Maundy sets in cases could be purchased through the banks. Today only sufficient sets are minted to supply the recipients at the Maundy service and those who officiate at the service or are associated with the Maundy ceremony.

12

THE TWENTIETH CENTURY

࿇ ❀❀ ࿇

Edward VII was fifty-nine years of age on his accession and his coins retained the same designs throughout his relatively short reign. The king's head and the reverses of the half-crown, florin and shilling were designed by G. W. de Saulles. The gold five-pounds, two-pounds (**198**), sovereign and half-sovereign and the silver crown all have the Pistrucci St George reverse, and the half-crown has a shield-in-Garter reverse. On the florin there is a windswept figure of Britannia standing on some mythical ancient ship which could hardly be sea-worthy under her weight, but it is, nevertheless, a pleasing composition (**199**). Miss Susan Hicks-Beach, daughter of Sir Michael Hicks-Beach, Chancellor of the Exchequer and Master of the Mint, was the model for Britannia. The shilling has a lion-on-crown reverse somewhat similar to that on the third coinage shilling of George IV. The reverses of the sixpence, threepence, 'coppers' and Maundy money all follow the pattern of the last Victorian issues.

Proof sets were issued in 1902 but these proof coins were given a dull, matt surface instead of being highly polished, the matt finish being achieved by sand-blasting the dies. Some sets contain all the gold and silver coins, but less expensive sets were also issued which omit the five- and two-pound pieces; none of the sets contain proofs of the bronze coins, nor did the sets issued in 1887 and 1893. In addition to the London sovereigns and half-sovereigns and those issued by the branch mints in Sydney, Melbourne and Perth, there were also sovereigns with a mintmark C that were struck at a branch mint opened at Ottawa, Canada (1908–10). The Ottawa mint was opened in 1908 to convert into coin gold that was being mined or panned in British Columbia and the Yukon.

The crown piece was only issued in 1902 and it was the last crown to go into general circulation, crowns of later reigns being issued either for collectors or as commemorative pieces. Farthings continued to be issued with a dark bronze finish to prevent confusion with half-sovereigns. A minor variety of the bronze penny of 1902 shows the level of the horizon set lower against the leg of Britainnia and this is usually known as the 'low-tide' variety.

198   Edward VII, *N* two pounds, 1902

199   *R* florin, 1905

De Saulles the engraver died in 1903 and the post of Engraver to the Mint was then discontinued. In 1901 and 1902 the Mint had purchased Janvier reducing machines and it was then no longer necessary to engrave steel coinage dies by hand. A metal electrotype copy of an enlarged plaster model of a coin could now be reproduced mechanically by means of a tracer on one end of a pivoted arm being moved over the area of the model. A rapidly rotating cutter on the shorter end of the arm was able to cut the design into a steel reduction punch of any size needed and from this puncheon a master die could then be made.

GEORGE V 1910–36

The portrait on the coins of George V was the work of Sir Bertram MacKennal and the initials B M are found on the truncation of the king's neck. No crown pieces were issued at the beginning of the reign and no five-pound or two-pound pieces were issued for circulation, though they were included in the proof sets of 1911.

Sovereigns were struck between 1911 and 1917 and half-sovereigns until 1915. It is doubtful, however, if any gold sovereigns were released for general circulation after 1914. Gold was urgently needed during the First World War for paying for war materials and other essential imports, and for this reason the gold coins in circulation were withdrawn and in their place one-pound and ten-shilling Treasury notes were issued. These first Treasury notes, printed in black and red respectively, were known as 'Bradburys' as they bore the signature of John Bradbury, the Chief Clerk to the Treasury. Sovereigns were struck again at the London mint in 1925 but these were only minted to recoin sovereigns in the Bank of England's gold reserves which were found to be under the legal weight and they were not intended for internal currency. Sovereigns continued to be struck by the branch mints overseas but they were intended for the national gold reserves and were not issued to the general public. From time to time they would have been used for making payments to overseas central reserve banks. Ottawa minted sovereigns until 1919, Sydney until 1926, Melbourne and Perth until 1931, the Pretoria branch of the Royal Mint struck sovereigns between 1923 and 1932 with the mintmark s a (South Africa) and for a short time a branch mint was opened at Bombay in 1918 for minting sovereigns with the mintmark i (for India). In 1928 the issue of one-pound and ten-shilling Treasury notes ceased and their place was taken by Bank of England notes which had previously been of five pounds value or more. With the passing of the sovereign our British coinage became wholly a token currency.

200 George V, Æ half-crown, 1925, second issue (.500 silver)

The first and second issue half-crowns (**200**) and shillings of George V vary from the Edward VII issue only by the omission of the beaded inner circles on the reverses. The florin reverse is a modification of the Victoria Jubilee design with the four shields and sceptres in the angles and the sixpence was now altered to the 'lion' type and thus became a miniature version of the shilling. During and after the First World War the price of silver increased substantially until, at one time in 1920, it rose for a few weeks to the point where the value of silver in a coin was worth more than the face value of the coin. In order to prevent large quantities of silver being taken out of circulation for hoarding or melting as soon as it was issued the minting of .925 sterling silver was suspended and to take its place a new coinage of debased 50% silver was commenced (.500 silver; i.e. 500 parts in 1,000). At first there was some difficulty finding a really satisfactory alloy for the coinage. An alloy of 50% silver, 40% copper and 10% nickel was used at first but it was found that coins from this metal quickly discoloured and in 1922 a more suitable alloy was used consisting of 50% silver and 50% copper.

In 1927 a new coinage was commenced with new designs and of a different alloy consisting of 50% silver, 40% copper, 5% nickel and 5% zinc. The king's portrait by MacKennal was retained for the obverse type but the

201 Æ crown, 1931

reverses of all the silver coins were redesigned by Kruger Gray. Proofs of the new coinage were issued in 1927 but, with the exception of the shilling, the new coins were not issued for general circulation until 1928. A crown piece (**201**) was issued for the first time since 1902 through the prompting of Sir Charles Oman, MP for Oxford and a noted numismatist who was then President of the Royal Numismatic Society. There was only a limited issue of these coins as they were intended for collectors and as presentation pieces and they were seldom seen in circulation. Apart from the proofs of 1927 the issue for any one year never exceeded 10,000 and in 1934 was as low as 932. The coin has a large crown on the reverse within a wreath of roses, shamrocks and thistles, a punning allusion to its denomination, and it has a grained instead of an inscribed edge. The shield bearing the royal arms on the reverse of the half-crown is unusual in that it is a jousting shield with a spear rest indentation on the dexter side, it has a double G cipher either side of the arms and there are rose, shamrock and thistle emblems dividing the inscription. The florin (**202**) has a G at the centre in place of the Garter Star and the crowns which were previously over the shields are now placed over the sceptres instead. The lion and crown design of the shilling becomes more stylized and the date is transferred to the legend; the sixpence and threepence were completely redesigned and have groups of six or three interlinked oak leaves and acorns.

202 Æ florin, 1932, third issue

The bronze coins retained the same design throughout the reign but in 1928 the head of the king was reduced in size slightly on the penny and the halfpenny and this helped to eradicate the 'ghost' image found on the reverse of some of the earlier coppers. Farthings were given a dark finish until 1917 but as the issue of half-sovereigns had by then been discontinued they were given the same bright finish as the pennies and halfpennies. Pennies with a small H mark by the date were struck by Heaton's of Birmingham in 1912, 1918 and 1919, and others with a KN mark were minted by the King's Norton Metal Company in 1918 and 1919. Very few pennies were minted in 1933 as there were large stocks of coins of earlier date in the Royal Mint vaults at the time. Only eight coins of this date are recorded and six of these were placed in museum collections or set under the foundation stones of public buildings. There are two popular fallacies regarding pennies of George V. From time to time the rumour appears in print that 1920 pennies are worth £8 each – untrue; one thousand nine hundred and twenty pennies are equal to £8. Yet another tale is told about a pot of gold being mixed with the metal for pennies of a certain date. This idea may have arisen as a result of some pennies of George V being found with yellow streaks in the flan, but this was only due to poor mixing of the bronze alloy.

In 1935 a special crown piece was issued to commemorate King George's Silver Jubilee and it was the first true commemorative issue in the history of the British coinage. The reverse was designed by Percy Metcalf and depicts a bareheaded St George on a large horse which is trampling a very angular wounded dragon (**203**). The modernistic treatment of the design came as rather a shock to the public and provoked considerable adverse comment at the time, but as a symbol of good overcoming evil it certainly presents a powerful image. The general issue of these crowns, which amounted to nearly three-quarters of a million pieces, had the DECVS ET TVTAMEN ANNO REGNI XXV legend stamped incuse into the edge. There was an additional issue of 2,500 proofs with a raised edge inscription made for the benefit of collectors and a special issue of 25 pieces struck in gold for which a ballot was held. The edges of the current crowns were impressed in a separate process from the actual die-stamping of the faces, so when viewed from the obverse some coins appear to have an inverted edge inscription.

203 Æ crown, 1935, proof Silver Jubilee commemorative

Proof sets were issued in 1911 and 1927. The former have all four or the two smaller gold coins together with the silver from the half-crown to the Maundy penny; the latter have only the six silver coins from the crown to the threepence. The Maundy coins are of the now customary reverse design with the mark of value within a wreath. In 1932 King George distributed the Maundy in person, the first monarch to do so for more than two centuries.

EDWARD VIII 1936 (LATER DUKE OF WINDSOR)

King Edward came to the throne in January 1936 and abdicated in December of the same year due to the opposition to his proposed marriage to Wallis Warfield (Mrs Simpson), an American divorcée. No coins were issued for circulation in this country bearing the king's name and portrait as he had abdicated before his new coins were ready for issue. However, a few pattern twelve-sided nickel-brass threepenny pieces were produced in order to assess the problems involved in the introduction of a twelve-sided coin into general circulation (**204**). These and other patterns have the king's head facing left by his special request as he preferred his profile viewed from his left. Thus they break the accepted tradition that a new sovereign's head shall face in the opposite direction to that of his or her predecessor. The reverse of the nickel-brass threepence is a clump of thrift designed by Madge Kitchener which is rather more naturalistic than the somewhat stylized design chosen for the George VI coin. A small number of sets of pattern coins with the king's head designed by Humphrey Paget and reverses by Kruger Gray (except for the nickel-brass threepence) were produced but none were made available to the public and they are of the highest rarity. These included a 'Scottish' type shilling but not an 'English' shilling nor a half-sovereign.

204 Edward VIII, nickel-brass pattern twelve-sided threepence, 1937

Coins bearing the name and portrait of George V were made and issued throughout 1936 but as he died on 20 January the great majority would have been minted during the reign of Edward VIII. The Maundy coins of 1936 were distributed in person by King Edward but these also bear the name and portrait of his father.

The only coins of Edward VIII issued for general circulation bearing his name or royal cipher, but no portrait, were pennies struck for Fiji and New Guinea, pennies, halfpennies and one-tenth pennies struck for British West Africa and 10 and 5 cents of British East Africa. There are also coins of the Indian princely states of Jodhpur and Kutch which bear Edward's name as well as that of the local ruler.

GEORGE VI 1936–52

From a numismatic viewpoint this reign is of particular interest for several reasons: the replacement of silver coinage by cupro-nickel, the relinquishment of the imperial title, the resumption of minting gold, the issue of two types of shilling each year and the issue of two commemorative crowns. The king's portrait was modelled by Humphrey Paget and faces to the left as did those of his brother and father before him. Gold five- and two-pound pieces, sovereigns and half-sovereigns were struck for the proof sets issued in 1937 but were not issued for general circulation. These all have Pistrucci's St George reverse.

The 'silver' coins can be divided into three different issues: the first being of .500 silver, the second made entirely of cupro-nickel and the last which omits the title Emperor of India. The silver coinage consisted of the crown, half-crown, florin, 'English' shilling, 'Scottish' shilling, sixpence, three-pence and Maundy coins. The silver coronation crown (**205**), only issued in 1937, has a milled edge and on the reverse it has the royal arms with lion and unicorn supporters and with a crown above and the royal motto below. The half-crown is a modified version of the last George V type but the shield is suspended from a ring above and it is not a jousting shield. The florin departs from the cruciform shields type; it has a crowned rose flanked by a smaller thistle and shamrock. The 'English' shilling closely copies the George V type, but has the date in the field instead of in the legend (**206**); the 'Scottish' shilling (**207**), introduced as a compliment to the ancestry of the Queen, formerly Elizabeth Bowes-Lyon, daughter of the Earl of Strathmore and Kinghorne, depicts the seated Scottish lion on a Scottish

205 George VI, Æ crown, coronation commemorative, 1937

206 Æ shilling, 1941, first coinage (.500 silver) 'English' reverse

207 Cupro-nickel shilling, 1948, second coinage 'Scottish' reverse

crown, holding a sword and sceptre with the arms of St Andrew on the left and a thistle on the right. The sixpences of the first and second issues have the imperial cipher G R I (*Georgius rex imperator*) and the silver threepence, which was not minted after 1945, has a rose with a shield bearing the cross of St George.

After the Second World War Britain had to pay back to the United States large amounts of silver borrowed under the 'Lend-Lease' agreement during the war, and it was decided that this could best be done by withdrawing all the silver coin in circulation and replacing it with a base metal coinage of comparatively little intrinsic value. Accordingly, a new coinage was issued in 1947 made of cupro-nickel, an alloy of 75% copper and 25% nickel. The new coinage retained the designs of the old and as the new metal did not look unlike silver, except that it was slightly colder in tone, many people found it difficult to distinguish between the two issues. In fact, there was finer graining on the edge of the new coins. The final abandonment of a silver coinage, though a break with a tradition that was more than a thousand years old, was really only a logical outcome of the step taken in 1816 to make the silver coinage a token currency. The Maundy money was not reduced to cupro-nickel in 1947 but, contrariwise, was restored to the old sterling standard of 0.925 silver.

The issue of a twelve-sided base metal threepenny piece was made as a substitute for the small silver threepence which was inconvenient on account of its size and which was usually relegated to hoards of similar coins saved up in jam jars and piggy-banks. The two coins were issued concurrently for some years but once the larger coin had gained the favour of the public the issue of the silver threepence was discontinued. The large threepence was made of nickel-brass, an alloy of 79% copper, 20% zinc and 1% nickel, and it was given twelve sides so that it could be distinguished easily by touch from other coins (**208**). The reverse design of a clump of thrift was a modification of Madge Kitchener's design for the Edward VIII pattern.

208 Nickel-brass threepence, 1937

It had been customary for the smaller copper and bronze coins to have the same designs as the penny but the bronze coins of George VI have different reverse types. A seated Britannia was retained for the penny but was slightly modified from the reverse design and the Eddystone lighthouse was replaced after having been absent since 1895. The halfpenny was redesigned by Humphrey Paget with a representation of Sir Francis Drake's *Golden Hind*, the first English ship to circumnavigate the globe (**209**). The farthing, designed by Wilson Parker, now had for its reverse type a dainty little wren, one of Britain's smallest birds – a very suitable subject for the smallest British bronze coin.

209 Æ halfpenny, 1937

210 Cupro–nickel sixpence, 1951, third coinage, G VI R

In 1942 Japan was threatening Britain's tin supplies, mostly obtained from Malaya, so in April of that year the amount of tin in the bronze coinage was cut from 3% to 0.5%, the other constituents being 97% copper and 2.5% zinc. This emergency metal was identical in appearance to the normal alloy which was restored in 1945. Pennies struck in the year 1946 were treated with 'hypo' after minting and were thus given a dull brown tone instead of the usual bright finish. This was done to discourage the hoarding of new pennies.

In 1947 India achieved independence and became a republic and consequently King George relinquished the title 'Emperor of India'. A change was made on all denominations of coins issued in 1949 when the IND IMP was omitted from the king's titles. This necessitated the re-spacing of the king's titles and the substitution of G VI R for G R I on the sixpence (**210**), the other reverse designs remaining the same.

In 1951 the Festival of Britain was held in London and other centres and was generally celebrated throughout the country with great enthusiasm, coming as it did after the dark days of war and the years of austerity. It marked the centenary of the Great Exhibition of 1851 and, like that exhibition, it provided a shop window for Britain. The year 1951 was also the four hundredth anniversary of the first English silver crown and a special Festival of Britain commemorative crown was issued. This has the value FIVE SHILLINGS below the king's head and Pistrucci's St George is used as the reverse design, the edge having an incuse inscription: MDCCCLI CIVIUM INDUSTRIA FLORET CIVITAS MCMLI (1851 By the industry of its people the state flourishes 1951). The coins were struck in cupro-nickel and issued in cardboard boxes at a price of 5s.6d. The Royal Mint had a coining press installed at the exhibition site on the South Bank near Waterloo station, now occupied by the Festival Hall, and the Festival crowns were struck there and at the mint at Tower Hill. Proof sets were also issued in 1951 containing the Festival crown. These were in cardboard cases as were sets issued in 1950 which did not contain a crown.

In 1949, 1951 and 1952, small quantities of gold sovereigns were struck at the Mint in order to keep alive the technical skills required for the minting of gold coins. These coins were struck from dies dated 1925 and they had the head of George V. They were not intended for general release in Britain as it was then government policy to discourage hoarding of gold by British citizens, the theory being that gold was a part of the nation's reserves and should be under close control. Some years later some of these '1925' coins were released through the bullion markets.

ELIZABETH II, ACCEDED 1952

The first coins of the present reign were issued in 1953. No specimen gold coins were made available for collectors though a very few proof coins were made for the main national collections. A crown was issued to commemorate the coronation (**211**) and this depicts the Queen in the uniform of Colonel-in-Chief of the Grenadier Guards riding Winston, the horse on which she took the salute at the Trooping of the Colour. The reverse has a central crown around which are the royal arms on four shields and the four national emblems: a rose, shamrock, leek and thistle. The lettered edge reads FAITH AND TRUTH I WILL BEAR UNTO YOU, which comes from the Oath of Homage in the coronation service. The smaller coins had a laureate head of the Queen designed by Mary Gillick, somewhat reminiscent of Leonard Wyon's 'bun' head portrait of Queen Victoria. The half-crown bears the royal arms, the florin bears a large English rose encircled by thistle, shamrock and leek emblems and the sixpence also has the four emblems interwoven. Two different shillings continued to be minted, one with crowned arms bearing the three lions of England and the other with the Scottish lion rampant. On the twelve-sided threepence the earlier thrift design was replaced by a crowned portcullis, the badge of the

Palace of Westminster, but the bronze denominations retained the types of the previous reign. The coins of 1953 used the royal style BRITT: OMN: REGINA (Queen of all the Britains), but in the following year BRITT: OMN: was omitted in view of the changing nature of the Commonwealth which now included several countries with a republican constitution.

In 1960 a second crown was issued with the Gillick head of the Queen but with a reverse similar to the coronation crown, and pieces struck from polished dies were made for sale at the British Trade Exhibition held in New York in that year. A third commemorative crown was issued in 1965 as a memorial to Sir Winston Churchill (**212**). It had an unusual but striking portrait by the sculptor Oscar Nemon and was the first regal coin to bear the image of a commoner.

211 Elizabeth II, crown, 1953, coronation commemorative

212 Crown, 1965, Sir Winston Churchill memorial issue

Between 1957 and 1968 the coinage of gold sovereigns was resumed. Although the sovereign was still legal tender for one pound only, the intrinsic value of the gold content was a little under three pounds in 1957. One reason for the production of the new coins was the need to reinforce the legal argument that the sovereign was still legal tender and could thus be protected in the face of the increasing manufacture of false sovereigns by foreign counterfeiters. Legal actions had been instituted in a number of countries by the Treasury in an effort to stamp out this traffic, some being successful, some not. Another reason for their issue was the profit that could accrue to the Mint from the sale of gold sovereigns in the international bullion market as the coin was in demand at a substantial premium over its intrinsic value. However, the greatest number to be minted in a single year was only some 8,700,000.

In 1966, in order to curtail the hoarding of gold by members of the public and to regulate the amount of gold imported from overseas, restrictions were placed on the importation and collecting of any gold coins minted after 1837. Collectors were required to obtain a special Bank of England licence, but as this had the effect of driving gold dealing underground the licensing system was abandoned in 1970.

The Royal Mint at Tower Hill had been in operation for one hundred and fifty years in 1961; it was almost eighty years since its last major reconstruction and modernization was overdue. In the late 1950s and 1960s it was government policy to decentralize departments of the administration, moving various units to the regions, and in 1967 it was decided to construct a new mint at Llantrisant near Cardiff in South Wales. Part of the new Royal Mint was opened in 1968 and almost 300 million coins had been minted there by the end of that year. When the second phase was completed in 1975 all coin production was concentrated at Llantrisant. Later, die production, seal engraving and medal production were also moved from London to Wales. It is the hope of many numismatists that the old Tower Hill building will eventually be used for a Mint exhibition and money museum, and this would provide another tourist attraction in the vicinity of the Tower of London which was the country's principal mint for many centuries.

The new Royal Mint at Llantrisant is situated at the southern end of the Rhondda Valley, some twelve miles from Cardiff (Figure 5). Her Majesty the Queen opened the Mint on 17 December 1968, only ten months after the foundation stone had been laid and sixteen months after the first turf had been cut in the former green fields. Her Majesty personally struck six of the decimal 1 new penny pieces, the Duke of Edinburgh struck six of the $\frac{1}{2}$ new penny coins and the Prince of Wales minted six of the 2 new penny pieces which, appropriately, carry the Prince of Wales's plumes.

Set within a high-security barrier enclosing a 30-acre site, the minting complex was designed to bring the latest technological developments to bear upon the process of coin manufacture. Coin, medal, die and seal production was moved from London to Wales in stages over a period of several years. In the first phase of construction two buildings were erected to house the operations required for annealing and 'pickling' (cleaning) the blanks required for the new bronze decimal coins prior to their automatic

Figure 5 The Royal Mint, Llantrisant: an aerial view (*Royal Mint*)

inspection, minting in the coining presses, bagging and storage. Both Taylor & Challen and Horden Mason & Edwards presses were installed initially, and others have been added since.

The second phase of construction accommodated a number of modern smelting units operating a continuous casting process, with coinage metal being fed into the top of the huge furnaces and red-hot metal strips being slowly passed out at the bottom in continuous fillets (Figure 6). These fillets, which are over half an inch (15 mm.) thick, are cut into long uniform lengths and are then moved on feeders through the rolling mills until they are reduced to the required thickness. They are then passed slowly through annealing furnaces in order to render the metal less hard before they snake through the blank-cutting machines (Figure 7), the excess perforated fillets (scissel) then being returned to the furnaces for reprocessing. The blanks are then bucketted for transfer to further annealing furnaces, pickling vats and the coining presses (Figure 8). At one point cupro-nickel blanks are fed through a 'marking' machine which raises a slight rim around the edge of each blank so as to make it easier to strike this hard metal. The automatic inspection machines, five to each conveyor line, check the diameter and thickness of each blank and reject any mis-shaped or otherwise defective pieces. Individual feed-hoppers loaded by fork-lift trucks enable batches of blanks to be fed into the mass production system to accommodate small batch production when necessary. After being struck a statistical sample of

Figure 6 Fillets of coinage metal emerging from a furnace (*Royal Mint*)

Figure 7 Scissel being coiled after passing through the blank-cutting machine (*Royal Mint*)

Figure 8   A row of coining presses (*Royal Mint*)

coins from each batch are inspected to maintain a quality control and after a final inspection coins are counted into bags by a 'telling' machine.

Other units accommodated on the site are the Assay Office, the gold coinage unit, the medal department, the die production department and the 'proof coin unit' which handles the striking and packaging of proof and specimen coins for collectors. The central building, the administration block, houses the management, reception, visitors' display and, at the time of going to press, the Mint Museum collection. A labour force of around one thousand is employed, some part-time. A number of staff transferred from London to Wales but the majority are local people, many having been employed in the mining industry previously. In 1967–8 a training factory had been operated for a time at Bridgend in order to train local labour in the skills required. Shift working is in operation in many of the manufacturing processes.

Since April 1975 the Royal Mint has been re-organized as a trading corporation set up under the Government Trading Act of 1973, with a public dividend capital of £7 million, ranking as an asset of the Consolidated Fund. The object of the change was to provide the sort of financial accountability which governed the operations of other manufacturing institutions. In addition to its principal role of manufacturing current coin for domestic use and for overseas countries, making seals and various medals and awards, it mints large numbers of proof and specimen coins for sale to collectors and the general public which it distributes through its Royal Mint Coin Club and the medium of the *Royal Mint Coin Club Bulletin*, a direct mailing operation based at Llantrisant (applications to Royal Mint Coin Club, Freepost, P.O. Box 500, Cardiff CF1 1YY).

In the post-war years various steps were taken towards the decimalization of weights and measures, initially in the realms of science and engineering. In 1960 a joint committee of the British Association for the Advancement of Science and of the Association of British Chambers of Commerce had issued a report entitled *Decimal Coinage and the Metric System – Should Britain Change?* Of the British Commonwealth countries Cyprus changed to decimal coinage in 1955, India in 1957, Pakistan and South Africa in 1961, Australia and the Bahamas decimalized in 1966, New Zealand in 1967 and Jamaica in 1969. The government's own committee of enquiry, chaired by the Earl of Halsbury, was set up in 1961 and published their report in 1963, *Report of the Committee of Inquiry on Decimal Currency*, which recommended that the United Kingdom should also change to a decimal coinage. There was a majority recommendation that the pound should be retained as the main unit of account, that there should be one hundred decimal pence to the pound and that the smallest coin should be a decimal half penny. Following parliamentary approval it was decided that the change-over should take place on 14 February 1971. As a transitional step two cupro-nickel decimal coins were introduced in 1968 denominated 10 NEW PENCE and 5 NEW PENCE and these were of the same size and equivalent value of the old florin and shilling which could continue to circulate alongside the new coins for the time being. Half-crowns, sixpences, threepences, pennies and halfpennies were last minted in 1967. The farthing had been discontinued in 1956 as by then it had virtually gone out of use through inflation. As an educational aid to decimalization specimen packs containing the 10 and 5 new pence of 1968 and bronze 2, 1 and $\frac{1}{2}$ decimal new pence were distributed through the banks, though the bronze coins were not to be legalized for circulation until 'D Day' in 1971. The decimal coins are commonly known by the initial 'p'.

In 1969 a half pound coin, 50 new pence, was introduced. It is a seven-sided coin which is ingeniously designed with slightly curved sides to give it a uniform diameter, enabling it to be used without trouble in an automatic machine. The type is a seated Britannia with a lion reclining behind her. In 1973, to commemorate Britain joining the EEC (European Economic Community), a special type of 50 pence was issued for one year only, having the value in the centre of the reverse surrounded by nine linked hands (**213**). It would have been ten but Denmark decided against joining the Community at the last minute.

The earliest decimal coins have a bust of the Queen by Arnold Machin

213 Decimal coinage, proof 50 pence, 1973, accession to the EEC commemorative

which is somewhat youthful in appearance. The reverses are by Christopher Ironside: the 10p having a lion passant guardant, the 5p a crowned thistle, the 2p the Prince of Wales's plumes, the 1p a crowned portcullis and the ½p an arched crown. In 1972 a crown of traditional crown size, now valued at 25 pence, was struck to commemorate the Silver Wedding of the Queen and Prince Philip and this had a crowned E P with a tiny cupid at the centre of the reverse. Another commemorative crown was issued in 1977 in celebration of the Silver Jubilee of the Queen's accession and this depicts the ampula and spoon that were used in the coronation ceremony set within a floral border. A further crown was issued in 1980 on the occasion of the 80th birthday of Queen Elizabeth the Queen Mother and this has her portrait at the centre of the reverse set within a border of bows and rampant lions on a background of ermine, taken from the armorial bearings of the Bowes-Lyon family (**214**). Then, in June 1981, on the occasion of the wedding of the Prince of Wales to Lady Diana Spencer, a crown was issued with their conjoined portraits on the reverse (**215**). Introduced in 1982 was a new denomination, the 20 pence piece (**216**), and this, like the 50p, is a seven-sided coin, but unlike the larger coin, the outer parts of the fields are raised with incuse inscriptions set into them. The coin was designed by William Gardner and its reverse has a neat crowned rose with the numerals

214 Crown, 1980, Queen Elizabeth the Queen Mother, 80th birthday commemorative

20 at the base ingeniously half raised and half countersunk. As on other coins minted in 1982 the word NEW is at last omitted from the stated values.

The issue of sovereigns, interrupted after 1968, was resumed in 1974 and these are similar to the earlier sovereigns of this reign apart from having Machin obverses. The obverse inscriptions begin to the left of the Queen's portrait and continue over the top of her head, the date of the coin being on the reverse as on the earlier gold. A proof sovereign has been issued every year since 1979; both proof and currency half-sovereigns were issued in 1982 with other proof halves in 1980, 1983 and 1984, and proofs of five- and two-pound pieces were also first issued in 1980, the first time that these last two denominations have been minted since 1937. Proof sets of the silver and bronze coinage have been issued each year since 1970, the set of that year containing the last of the £.s.d. currency system. From the mid-1970s ordinary coinage dies were given a buffed chrome-steel finish which produced a smoother, more brilliant surface to new coins.

215 Crown, 1981, Royal Wedding commemorative

216 Twenty pence, 1982

In April 1983 a base metal one-pound coin was introduced made of nickel-brass. It was almost seventy years since a gold pound, the sovereign, had been issued for general circulation and almost five hundred years since the first gold pound had been minted. The reverse of the first nickel-brass pound has the royal arms with the lion and unicorn supporters and, as a security measure, it has the inscription DECUS ET TUTAMEN (a decoration and safeguard) set into the edge graining (**217**). This was followed in 1984 by a

design of Scottish significance, having a flowering thistle plant encircled by
a royal diadem and with the NEMO ME IMPUNE LACESSIT (No one provokes
me with impunity) inscription on the edge. A Welsh pound (**218**) with the
diadem encircling a leek and with the edge inscription PLEIDIOL WYF I'M
GWLAD (True am I to my country), from the Welsh anthem, was issued in
1985. This will be followed by a flax plant design for Northern Ireland and
an oak tree type for England, all these pounds being for circulation
throughout the United Kingdom. Also approved for issue in 1985 was a
new portrait of the Queen, designed by Raphael Maklouf, the Queen's
head being crowned with the royal diadem worn on state occasions. She is
depicted wearing earrings and a necklace and is given more mature features
than on the portrait by Machin. From the end of 1984 the one-pound Bank
of England note ceased to be issued as it was being replaced by the pound
coin which had a considerably longer life. At the same time the decimal
halfpenny was demonetized as inflation had rendered it practically useless.

217 Nickel-brass pound, 1983, royal arms type

218 Nickel-brass pound, 1985, Welsh type, proof

13

IRELAND

⊰❀⊱

THE NORSEMEN OF DUBLIN

Though a small number of Roman coins have been discovered on the east coast of Ireland, the Romans never occupied the country. There have been quite a number of hoards of tenth-century Anglo-Saxon silver pennies discovered, mainly in those areas that were occupied by Viking invaders, but native Irish society was not based upon a money economy and coins were not minted in Ireland until the closing years of the tenth century. The great Viking incursions into Ireland began in the first half of the ninth century, raiding along the rivers into the very heart of Ireland for the treasures of monasteries and for slaves. Later, under such leaders as Turgeis, Olaf the White and Ivar the Boneless, they settled at a number of centres around the coast, such as Waterford, Wexford, Cork, Limerick, Carling-ford and, most important of all, at Dublin. They also appear to have occupied some inland areas in County Dublin and Meath. At Dublin a dynasty of Norse kings flourished with few interruptions for some three hundred years. The greatest of these kings was Anlaf (Olaf) Cuaran, who died in 981 and who did strike coins at York, but it was his son Sihtric Silkenbeard who instituted the first coinage of silver pennies at Dublin about the year 995.

The earliest Dublin pennies closely imitate the CRVX type pennies of the English king Aethelred II (**219**), some even copying Aethelred's name and the names of English mints and moneyers. The commonest of Sihtric's pennies, commencing about 997, imitate Aethelred's Long Cross type but have the inscription SIHTRIC REX DYFLIN (**220**) or more rarely, SIHTRIC CVNVNC (the Old Norse form of 'king'). There are other unattributed pennies of this type with the strange inscriptions DYMN ROE + MNEGNI and

OGSEN HEA MELNEM which have yet to be completely deciphered. The Long Cross type seems to have been particularly popular with the Dubliners and it appears to have been issued concurrently with, and subsequent to, imitations of Helmet and Small Cross pennies of Aethelred II and the initial Quatrefoil type of King Cnut. All these issues occur with the name of Sihtric. Considerable numbers of these Hiberno-Norse coins have been found in Scandinavian hoards.

219 Hiberno-Norse, Sihtric Silkenbeard, Æ penny of Dublin, type of Aethelred II's CRVX issue, *c.* 995–1000, moneyer Fastolf

220 Æ penny of Dublin, type of Aethelred's Long Cross issue, moneyer Faeremin

221 Æ penny of lower weight and cruder style, with 'two hands' reverse

From the second decade of the eleventh century the Long Cross design remained the basic type for forty years or so. The earlier and heavier coins have a small pellet in each angle of the reverse cross. Later, probably about 1030, a hand is placed in one quarter of the cross and this has the *stigma* clearly shown in the centre of the palm, but the hand quickly degenerates into a branch-like object which is hardly recognisable for what it is (**221**). The inscriptions now become increasingly blundered to the point of being quite unintelligible. At the same time the weight of the penny was reduced until it was little more than half the weight of the English penny.

From the 1060s until the end of the century the 'Aethelred' profile left head remained the predominant obverse type though by then it was of very crude style, but there was also the occasional facing head copied from a contemporary English prototype (**222**). There were also a great number of different reverse types, most of which were copied from coins of English kings from Harthacnut to William II, though a few may owe their origin to Scandinavian prototypes.

By the end of the eleventh century the Hiberno-Norse pennies were becoming very thin and many were made of quite base metal. Some coins with a crozier in front of the face must have been issued by an ecclesiastical authority, the head possibly representing a local saint, possibly Patrick (**223**). The last coins of the Dublin 'Ostmen', as the Norse inhabitants came to be called, were crudely made bracteates or semi-bracteates. Bracteates are pieces struck either from one die only, the obverse design appearing on the reverse in intaglio, or from two dies used in two separate strikings so that the design of the opposite side is also visible. Manufacture of Ostman coinage had probably ceased entirely by the middle of the twelfth century though the Irish ports remained important trading centres.

222 Æ penny with facing head, *c.* 1060–65

223 Æ penny with very crude profile bust and crozier, *c* 1095–1110

EARLY ANGLO-IRISH COINAGE

The Norman conquest of Ireland began in 1169 when Strongbow (Richard FitzGilbert Earl of Pembroke) invaded southern Ireland ostensibly in support of Dermot MacMurrough, the exiled king of Leinster, whose daughter Eva he married. Two years later Henry II visited Ireland to secure the homage of his Norman vassals and some of the Irish chiefs, and the following year he appointed his youngest son John to the lordship of Ireland. Henry had issued no Irish coins and it is probable that John's first Irish coinage was not issued until about 1185. This was an issue of silver halfpennies with diademed head in profile and the inscription IOHANNES. Some five years later a new coinage of halfpennies with a facing head was issued at Dublin, Waterford (**224**), Kilkenny and Limerick in the south and at Carrickfergus and Downpatrick in Ulster. Farthings were also issued with a decorated mascle taking the place of John's head and with four letters of the moneyer's name in the angles of the reverse cross, no mint being indicated on this denomination. Halfpennies and farthings were also minted by John de Courcy, an independent lord of Ulster, *c.* 1185–1205, and he also issued some anonymous farthings in the name of St Patrick.

224 Anglo-Irish, John, second coinage, Æ halfpenny of Waterford, moneyer Marc

225 Third coinage, Æ penny of Dublin, moneyer Roberd

Between 1205 and about 1211 a new coinage of pennies, halfpennies and farthings was minted at Dublin, Waterford and Limerick, to the same quality of fineness as John's English pence. All denominations have the king's head set in a triangle, but the reverses differ – the penny has a radiant sun, a crescent moon and three stars (**225**); the halfpenny a cross, moon and stars, and the farthing a radiant sun only. Quantities of the pennies were exported and they appear in a number of English and continental hoards. Dublin pennies of the moneyer Robert, probably Robert de Bedford, are particularly common.

It was not until 1251 that another Irish coinage was instituted and then the Dublin mint was active for less than three years. The dies for this coinage were made in London and the reverse design follows the type of Henry III's Long Cross pennies, though the obverse retains the head-in-triangle type of the previous reign (**226**). No smaller denominations were issued but coins are sometimes found which have been cut into halves or quarters. Some rare pennies exist of similar type but the style of engraving shows them to have been issued early in the reign of Edward I. They still bear the name HENRICVS REX III', but the moneyer's name is RICARD – undoubtedly the Richard Olof who was put in charge of the Dublin mint about 1275.

In 1279 a new Irish coinage of pennies, halfpennies and farthings was instituted at the time of the great English recoinage of Edward I. The head-in-triangle type is retained for the obverse, but the triangle is now inverted with the point at the base. No moneyers' names appear on the reverse, merely the name of the mint, e.g. CIVITAS VATERFOR (**227**). The mints were initially Dublin and Waterford, later Dublin and Cork, and then at the turn of the century Dublin only. The coinage ceased about 1302. No Irish coinage can be attributed to the reign of Edward II, and the only coins known for Edward III are extremely rare halfpennies of Dublin of the period 1339–40 which are contemporary with the debased halfpennies and farthings minted in England, 1335–43. These Edward III halfpennies still have a head-in-triangle obverse but they can be distinguished by a star before the king's name.

226 Henry III, Æ penny of Dublin, moneyer Ricard

227 Edward I, Æ halfpenny of Waterford

FIFTEENTH–CENTURY ISSUES

There were no Irish coinages during the second half of the fourteenth century or the first quarter of the fifteenth century but about 1426 there was a brief issue of Dublin pennies of the same type as Henry VI's English coinage. Very few have survived; they have a star to the right of the king's head and annulets in the reverse inscription.

With the accession of Edward IV in 1460 a new coinage of groats and pennies was ordered for Ireland and it was issued at three-quarters the weight of the equivalent English denominations in an attempt to prevent the export of coin. The first issue was anonymous, with a large crown set in a tressure on the obverse and an English style cross-and-pellets reverse (**228**). In 1463 a similar issue, with the addition of a half-groat, reverted to giving the king's name and titles though continuing the crown device, whilst on the reverse an outer inscription gives the POSVI DEVM ADIVTOREM MEVM legend that appears on the English issue. In 1465, concurrently with the reduction in weight of the silver coins in England, a new Irish coinage was introduced at two-thirds the revised English weights. The obverse has a cross pattée set within a Yorkist rose, with a sun in splendour as the reverse type. Two years later the weights were decreased again to half that of the

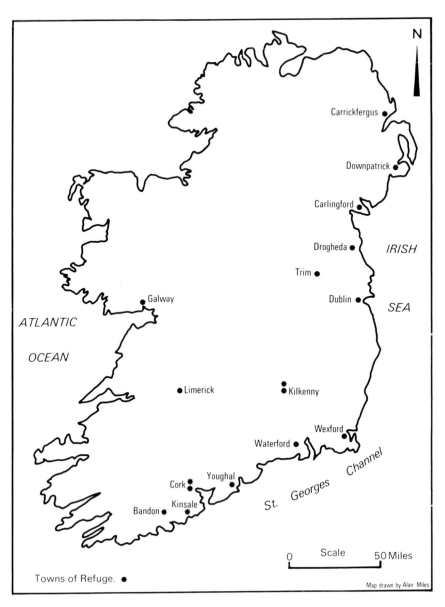

Map 4 Irish mint towns

English coinage and a 'double groat' (8 pence Irish) was introduced at the same weight as the English groat, the Irish penny being the equivalent of the English halfpenny. These have the king's facing head in a tressure, with a rose set in the centre of a radiant sun on the reverse. Mints were opened at Drogheda and Trim in addition to Dublin.

Between 1460 and 1470 there were various issues of base metal farthings and half-farthings. These either have a crown on one side and a cross on the other, some having the name of (*St*) PATRIK, or a mitred head of the saint and the inscription SALVATOR (Saviour) on the reverse, though the latest issue, probably *c.* 1467–70, has a shield bearing three crowns on the obverse and a rose on sun in the centre of a cross.

228 Edward IV, crown coinage, Æ groat of Dublin

229 Light cross and pellets coinage, Æ groat of Drogheda, with G on the king's breast

No Irish coins were minted for Henry VI during his brief restoration in 1470 but during the second half of the reign of Edward IV (1470–83) a coinage of English type was issued from the mints of Dublin, Drogheda (**229**), Limerick, Trim, Waterford and Cork, the earliest being a groat of about 40 grains weight, later reduced to about 32 grains. Many of the groats have the letter G on the king's breast, denoting the mintmaster Germyn Lynch. Some of the pennies of these issues have a voided quatrefoil at the centre of the reverse cross so they appear similar, at first sight, to English pennies of York. The final issue of the reign has suns and stars alternating at the sides of the king's crown and shoulders, and a simple rose is set in the centre of the reverse cross.

The first Irish coinage of Richard III (**230**) follows the pattern of the last (Rose-on-cross) issue of Edward IV. In 1483 a new coinage was instituted which was to continue with some variations until about 1490. It is now known as the 'Three Crowns' coinage from the three crowns set vertically down the reverse cross. The obverse displays the royal arms in place of a regal portrait and the earliest issues have the name RICARD, but after Richard's death and the accession of Henry Tudor in England the divided loyalties of two powerful factions in Ireland are illustrated on the coinage. Waterford, under the Butler family, at first supported Henry and issued groats with his name; but at Dublin Gerald FitzGerald, Earl of Kildare, the justiciar of Ireland, had attained a pre-eminent position of virtual independence and he continued to support the Yorkist cause. The first coins issued under his authority omit the king's name, merely reading REX ANGLIE FRANCIE – DOMINVS HYBERNIE (**231**). Then, in the spring of 1487 the young pretender Lambert Simnel was crowned as 'King Edward VI' in Dublin and for a few weeks Three Crowns groats were issued at Dublin and at Waterford with the name 'EDWARDVS'. In June 1487 England was invaded but the pretender's army was cut to pieces, Lambert Simnel was captured and was relegated to the position of scullion in the royal kitchens.

230 Richard III, Rose-on-cross coinage, Æ groat of Drogheda

231 Henry VII, Three Crowns coinage, Æ half-groat of Dublin

Following Lambert Simnel's defeat Three Crowns groats and halfgroats were minted with a miniature escutcheon charged with the saltire of Kildare set on either side of the royal arms (**232**). The later Three Crowns coins usually have an ♄ below the crowns, some having the king's name though some omitting it. Early Three Crowns coins have triple pellets at the cross-ends but later coins have triple annulets.

In 1494 Sir Edward Poynings was appointed Lord Deputy and with an English army removed Kildare from power. Shortly afterwards a new Tudor coinage of English type was begun, with Dublin the sole mint. Most of the coins were atrociously minted from poorly cut dies with misspelt inscriptions. Some groats have the POSVI DEVM inscription adapted to PROVIDEBO ADIVTORIVM (I will provide assistance); some coins have open crowns (**233**), others have arched crowns; some pennies have a portrait, others have a large crowned h. The coinage ceased some years before Henry's death and for about thirty years the Dublin mint seems to have been inactive.

232 Gerald, Earl of Kildare, Three Crown coinage, Æ groat with Kildare shields by the royal arms

233 Henry VII, late portrait coinage Æ groat of Dublin

THE SIXTEENTH CENTURY

In 1534 Henry VIII had a new coinage for Ireland produced at the London mint but made of a lower quality silver than English coin. The coinage consisted of groats and half groats, with the crowned royal arms on the obverse and a distinctive crowned Irish harp on the reverse. The ciphers of three of Henry's queens appear by the harp: A for Anne Boleyn (**234**), I for Jane Seymour and K for Katherine Howard, all jointly with an H for Henry; later coins, from 1540, have just HR for *Henricus rex*. Silver of varying quality was used and towards the end of the reign it was reduced from two-thirds fineness, to half fineness and eventually to only one quarter fineness. The last and basest 'Harp' coins were minted at Bristol by William Sharrington and these have a WS monogram as a mintmark. From 1544 the groats were tariffed at 6 pence Irish.

Early in the reign of the young Edward VI, the Dublin mint was again re-opened to coin groats, half-groats, pennies and halfpennies tariffed at 6 pence, 3 pence, $1\frac{1}{2}$ pence and 3 farthings respectively. They were made in imitation of Henry VIII's English money, having Henry's name and portrait (**235**) and most were of very base silver. Shillings of English type

234 Henry VIII, first Harp coinage, Æ groat with H and A (for Anne Boleyn) by harp

235 Edward VI, coinage with name and portrait of Henry VIII Æ groat of Dublin

236 Mary, base Æ shilling

with the head of the young King Edward VI were issued in 1552, dated MDLII, with a harp as a mintmark.

Under Mary Tudor a handsome shilling was issued with a charming portrait of the queen on the obverse and the royal cipher beside a large crowned harp surrounded by the legend VERITAS TEMPORIS FILIA (Truth is the daughter of Time) (236). These together with a groat of similar design are dated MDLIII, or more rarely MDLIIII. The half-groat and penny are undated. After Mary's marriage to Philip of Spain in 1553, their two busts are shown face-to-face on a shilling of 1555 and on groats of various dates to 1558. These coins were made of poor quality (.250 fine) silver and are often poorly struck: the inscription is POSVIMVS DEVM ADIVTOREM NOSTRVM (We have made the Lord our Helper).

The first coinage of undated shillings and groats of Elizabeth followed a similar pattern and was equally base, but in 1561 this and earlier base silver was recoined into shillings and groats of $\frac{11}{12}$th (.916) fineness and on these coins an ornate shield on the reverse displays three harps (237). From early on in Elizabeth's reign until the end of the sixteenth century English money appears to have circulated in Ireland. Then in 1601, at the time of the campaigns against the native Irish led by O'Neill in Ulster, a new very base coinage of shillings, sixpences and threepences was issued together with copper pennies and halfpennies. These coins have the royal arms on one side and a crowned harp on the other.

James I had new fine silver 'Irish' shillings (**238**) and sixpences minted in London to replace Elizabeth's base emergency coinage, and these were lighter in weight than the 1561 issue. After 1607 no more silver was minted and English coinage became the standard currency in Ireland.

237   Elizabeth I, 'fine' silver coinage shilling, 1561

238   James I, second coinage Æ shilling, mm. escallop

COINAGE OF THE GREAT REBELLION

Rebellion against English Protestant rule broke out in 1641. To supplement the amount of coin available to finance war against the rebels, the Lord Justices in Dublin and later the Earl of Ormonde, who was made Lieutenant of Ireland in 1643, issued a succession of emergency coinages between 1642 and 1649. The earliest of these issues, sometimes called 'Inchiquin' money, were crudely cut and hammered lumps of metal which were stamped only with their weight (**239**). They ranged from a crown marked '19 dwt. 8 gr. (19 pennyweight 8 grains) to a threepence marked '23 gr.' and some of the smaller denominations were impressed with annulets to mark the number of pence value. The 'Dublin Money' issue of 1643 had the mark of value 'vs' or 'IIs.VID' struck on both sides and the

'Ormonde' coinage of 1643–4 had the value on one side and a C·R surmounted by a large crown on the other (**240**).

A coinage of gold 'weight money' bearing the weights '8 dwtt. 14 gr.' and '4 dwtt. 7 gr.' was issued in 1646 but is now exceedingly rare. These weights were those of the 'pistole' (French *louis d'or*) and its half, coins that were commonly in circulation in Ireland. A final royalist coinage of silver crowns and half-crowns was issued by the Earl of Ormonde in 1649 after the execution of Charles I, naming the young Prince Charles CAR. II. D, G, MAG. BRIT., etc.

239 Charles I, Civil War 'Inchiquin' Æ half-crown with weight of 9 dwt. 16 gr.

240 'Ormonde money' coinage, Æ crown, Vˢ.

Meanwhile the royalist Confederation of Catholics had set up their own administration at Kilkenny in 1642. From here they issued crude halfpennies and farthings copied from the English 'Richmond' farthings; also silver half-crowns made in imitation of the king's English coinage, with a mintmark cross on one side and a mintmark harp on the other, usually known as 'Blacksmith's' half-crowns. Then in 1643–4 the Catholics minted crowns and half-crowns which are sometimes called 'Rebel Money', resembling the 1643 'Dublin' money, but with a large cross on one side.

Finally, there were various emergency coinages issued by Parliamentary garrisons besieged in various ports in Munster: Bandon, Cork, Kinsale and

Youghal. Some emergency farthings were made by stamping initials, such as BB for Bandon Bridge, or various devices, such as a bird and T on pieces for Youghal town, upon crudely cut flans. Other halfpennies and farthings were made by countermarking Confederate Catholic copper or even by using foreign copper coins. At Cork some crude shillings and sixpences (**241**) bearing the name of the city and the date 1647 were minted. The shortage of coin, especially of small change, was partly remedied by the extensive issues of private merchants' penny and halfpenny tokens during the years 1653–79.

241 Parliamentary forces besieged at Cork, Æ sixpence, 1647

FROM THE RESTORATION TO GEORGE IV

In 1660 Charles II granted a licence to Sir Thomas Armstrong for minting farthings, his coins being very similar in design to the coins which had been produced privately under licence in England before the Commonwealth. However, the Irish authorities were opposed to their circulation; relatively few were minted and the issues of merchants' tokens continued unabated. Probably about the year 1674 an issue of halfpennies and farthings, known as the 'St Patrick's money', was made in Dublin though little is known of the circumstances of the coinage or its legal status. The coins depict King David kneeling, playing a harp; the halfpenny has St Patrick holding a cross and crozier, preaching to a multitude, and the farthing shows the saint driving away snakes and other creatures (**242**). Most of the coins have a plug or spot of brass impressed into the flans to inhibit counterfeiting. It seems likely that this was a private issue which may have been circulated without the opposition of the authorities in Dublin, but the coins were withdrawn and the issues of merchants' tokens were suppressed when a regal coinage of halfpennies bearing the king's bust was issued in 1680 under a licence granted to Sir Thomas Armstong and Col. George Legg (**243**). In 1685 this licence was transferred by James II to Sir John Knox, the Lord Mayor of Dublin.

After King James was forced to leave England in 1689 he first went to France but later landed in Ireland to continue the struggle for the throne. Being short of funds an emergency coinage of half-crowns, shillings and sixpences was minted in base metal from old cannon, church bells and other

242 Charles II, St Patrick coinage, Æ farthing with brass plug on obverse

243 Regal coinage, Æ halfpenny, 1681

scrap and these became known as 'Gunmoney' coins. They are unusual in that they were inscribed with the month as well as the year of issue (**244**), the intention being to stagger their eventual redemption over a period of time. The first sixpences were dated 'June 1689', and the first half-crowns and shillings 'July 1689'. In April 1690 the size of the coins was reduced and many of the heavier half-crowns were re-stamped into crown pieces which depict the king on horseback (**245**). Besides the gunmoney denominations pennies and halfpennies were minted in pewter with a copper plug through the centre of the flans. The last dates of the gunmoney were September and October 1690. After William III entered Dublin the coins were reduced to the value of their metal content and in 1691 they were demonetized. At Limerick, which held out for James II until 1691, the large shillings were re-minted into halfpennies and small shillings into farthings (**246**) depicting a seated figure of Hibernia holding a harp and a cross.

Regular issues of halfpennies were made at Dublin with the conjoined heads of William and Mary, 1692–4, and with the head of William III alone in 1696, but after that no more specifically Irish coins were minted for a further 25 years. Then, in 1721, William Wood, a London merchant, was granted a patent to mint a new coinage of Irish halfpennies (**247**) and farthings. These were made at his Bristol foundry but they were widely criticized in Ireland, especially by Dean Swift in his 'Drapier's Letters', on the grounds that they were a fraud on the Irish people. Having difficulty in getting them into circulation in Ireland, Wood eventually shipped quantities of them over to the colonies in America where there was a

244 James II, Gunmoney coinage, Æ halfcrown, large size dated May 1690

245 Æ crown (restruck large halfcrown) 1690

246 Siege of Limerick, Æ farthing (restruck Gunmoney shilling), 1691

247 George I, William Wood's coinage Æ halfpenny, 1723

perennial shortage of coin– the same fate that befell the called–in 'St Patrick's' coinage in the previous century.

A new Irish regal copper coinage of halfpennies and farthings with the head of George II was undertaken by the London mint between 1736 and 1755 and again in 1760 in response to various token issues which had begun to reappear in Ireland, and these were a considerable improvement on the late seventeenth-century issues. Perhaps because the 1760 issue was delayed, a considerable quantity of imitation halfpennies, and some scarcer farthings, were coined locally in 1760. These are known as the 'Voce Populi' coins from the proletarian inscription which replaced the name of the monarch (**248**).

Further issues of Irish halfpennies were produced at the Tower Mint in London at various dates between 1766 and 1782. Silver coinage, however, was in very short supply in Ireland and what did exist was mostly very worn by the end of the century. Thin discs of metal purporting to be shillings or sixpences circulated locally, counterstamped with initials by traders who issued them. In 1804 the Bank of Ireland contracted with Matthew Boulton, of the Soho mint near Birmingham, for the supply of a quantity of six-shilling bank tokens which were restruck from Spanish or Spanish-American 8 *real* pieces. These were the same size as the English five-shilling bank tokens of the same year, there being a 20% difference between the two currencies. The London mint struck 10 and 5 pence silver bank tokens in 1805–6, 30 pence tokens in 1808 (**249**) and a further issue of 10 pence in 1813. These were the last Anglo-Irish silver coins to be minted.

248 George III, 'Voce Populi' token Æ halfpenny, 1760

249 Bank of Ireland token Æ halfcrown, 1808

A new copper coinage of pennies, halfpennies and farthings was minted by Matthew Boulton in 1805–6. Though there was a formal union between Great Britain and Ireland in 1800, the two Exchequers were not merged until 1817 and the two currencies were not standardized with equivalent values until 1821. The last regal coins made specifically for Ireland were a coinage of George IV pennies (**250**) and halfpennies of

1822–3. These were withdrawn in 1826 and for the next hundred years United Kingdom coinage was the only currency in Ireland.

There is shortly to be issued a new United Kingdon nickel-brass one pound coin which will have a design of Northern Ireland significance, a flax plant encircled by a diadem, a reference to the Irish linen industry. In the six counties of Northern Ireland, which remain an integral part of the United Kingdom of Great Britain and Northern Ireland, the UK coinage is the legal currency and it also circulates widely in southern Ireland as well.

250 George IV, Æ penny, 1822

IRISH FREE STATE AND REPUBLIC

With the setting up of the Irish Free State in 1920, following years of agitation for Home Rule, a separate Irish coinage was planned and finally instituted in 1928. Percy Metcalfe, the English engraver, won an international competition to provide designs for the new coinage with his fine compositions of horse, salmon, bull, wolfhound, chicken and chicks, pig and piglets, woodcock and hare (**251**). In 1939 the name *Saorstat Eireann*

251 Irish Free State, coinage of 1928, Æ halfcrown to Æ farthing

was replaced by the simpler *Eire*, a name which indicated the whole of Ireland though the northern counties were now separated. Eire had been declared a republic in 1949 but no further change was made to the coinage as a result. The half-crown, florin and shilling were minted in silver and the sixpence and threepence in nickel. However, owing to the rise in the value of silver all these denominations were made in cupro-nickel from 1951.

A ten-shilling piece was issued in 1966 to commemorate the 1916 Easter Rising, the obverse having a bust of the nationalist leader Patrick Pearse and the reverse depicting the mythical Irish hero Cuchulainn. Irish decimal coinage was instituted in 1971 at the same time that the UK adopted a decimal coinage, though, as a preliminary stage, a 10 pence and 5 pence had been issued in 1969, these coins being of equal value to the florin and shilling. On the decimal coins, which retain a harp on the obverse, the seven-sided 50 pence has a woodcock reverse, the 10 pence and the 5 pence retain the salmon and bull, while the new bronze 2p, 1p and ½p have interlaced bird motifs taken from early Irish manuscripts.

14

SCOTLAND

=⟩ ⟨⟨⟩⟨⟩ ⟨=

THE HOUSE OF MALCOLM CANMORE

Coinage in Scotland began even later than in Ireland, though numerous Roman coins have been recovered from those parts of the country that were under Roman military occupation and various hoards of Anglo-Saxon and Viking coins have been found in areas of Scandinavian settlement along the west coast and in the Western and Northern Isles. It was not until the reign of David I (1124–53), a son of Malcolm Canmore, that the Scottish mints of Edinburgh, St Andrews, Roxburgh, Berwick and Carlisle began minting silver pennies, Cumbria and Northumbria being claimed by the Scottish king at this period. David's son Henry Earl of Northumberland also minted pennies at Carlisle, Corbridge and possibly Bamborough. All the coins of David and Henry have an obverse portrait copied from King Stephen's first type and the earliest have a reverse of this type, that is, a cross moline with a fleur-de-lis in each angle (**252**). Their later coins have a cross pattée with pellets, annulets or crescents in the angles, their last issues having a cross fleury reverse and one type of Earl Henry having a cross-crosslet with small crosses in the angles (**253**). As on English silver pennies of the period the names of the moneyer and mint appear on the reverse.

Malcolm IV (1153–65) continued the Cross Fleury type with a profile bust (**254**), but on some rare coins he is shown with a facing bust and a cross-headed sceptre over one shoulder and a lis-headed sceptre over the other. Malcolm was succeeded by his brother William 'the Lion' (1165–1214). His early coins are extremely rare, but around 1174 he issued a new coinage, the Crescent-and-pellet type, which has a pellet and crescent in each angle of a cross pattée. Those coins with the king's sceptre having a cross pattée at the

252 David I, Æ penny of Edinburgh, Cross Moline type, moneyer Erebald

253 Henry, Earl of Northumberland, Æ penny of Bamburgh (?), moneyer Willem

254 Malcom IV, Æ penny of Roxburgh (?), type IV

top (**255**) correspond to the English 'Tealby' coinage (1158–80) and those with a cross of pellets at the top of the sceptre correspond to the Short Cross coinage commencing in 1180. Perth and 'Dun'(*fermline*) appear as mints for the first time. In 1195 the coinage was redesigned with a head more like that on the English Short Cross coins, though in profile, not full-face, and with stars in the angles of the voided short cross on the reverse (**256**). For some two hundred years it seems to have been a convention that, while English coins had a facing head, the regal head on Scottish coins was always depicted in profile. William's latest coins omit the name of the mint as the Edinburgh moneyers, first Hue and later Adam, issued coins jointly with Walter of Perth. They also have the Norman-French form 'Le rei Wilam' instead of the Latin *Willelmus rex*. Coins in William's name continued to be issued for a number of years into the reign of Alexander II (1214–49) while coins of Alexander in his own name are quite rare.

Shortly after Alexander III (1249–86) succeeded his father a new 'Long Cross' coinage was issued closely matching the English Long Cross reverse, except that the coins continued to have stars in the angles, not pellets (**257**). A number of new mints now appear: Aberdeen, Ayr, Forfar, 'Fres' (Forres?), Glasgow, Inverness, Kinghorn, Lanark, Montrose, Renfrew and Stirling. Then, about 1280, closely following Edward I's reform of the

255 William the Lion, Æ penny of Perth, Crescent-and-Pellet coinage, moneyer Folpolt

256 Æ penny, Short Cross and Stars coinage, joint moneyers Hue and Walter

257 Alexander III, first coinage, Æ penny of Edinburgh, moneyer Alisander

English coinage, a new neat Scots penny was issued (**258**), together with a round halfpenny and farthing, having the inscription ALEXANDER DEI GRA (etc.) and with the title REX SCOTORVM or ESCOSSIE REX on the reverse instead of the moneyer and the mint. The mints were indicated by a variation of privy marks consisting of mullets and stars each with five, six or seven points, giving nine possible combinations. It is probable that coins with four mullets of five points were minted at Edinburgh and that those with four stars of six points (the commonest) were minted at Berwick, but the mint of origin of coins with other totals of points is somewhat uncertain.

Alexander's heiress was his three-year-old granddaughter Margaret, a daughter of Eric II of Norway, known to the Scots as the 'Maid of Norway'. She did not survive the journey to Scotland in 1290, and Edward I was called upon to act as arbiter between the thirteen 'competitors' who had some claim to the succession. He chose John Baliol, a descendant of David I. John's coins follow a similar pattern to those of Alexander III, his earliest issue being of somewhat coarser style. His only coins to bear a mint name are pennies and halfpennies of St Andrews – CIVITAS SANDRE. There was strong opposition to John who finally abdicated in 1296, and after a further ten years of struggle Robert Bruce, another descendant of David I, was crowned king in 1306. His pennies (**259**), which

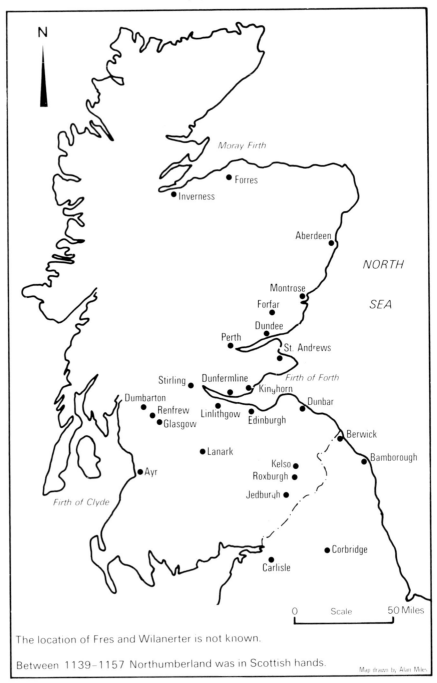

N

Moray Firth

● Forres
● Inverness

Aberdeen ●

NORTH

SEA

Montrose ●
Forfar
● Dundee
Perth ●
St. Andrews ●

Stirling ● Dunfermline ● *Firth of Forth*
Kinghorn ●
Dumbarton ● Dunbar ●
● Renfrew Linlithgow ●
● Glasgow Edinburgh ●

Berwick ●

● Lanark Bamborough ●

Kelso ●
● Ayr Roxburgh ●

Firth of Clyde Jedburgh ●

● Corbridge

Carlisle ●

0   Scale   50 Miles

The location of Fres and Wilanerter is not known.

Between 1139–1157 Northumberland was in Scottish hands.

Map drawn by Alan Miles

Map 5   Scottish mint towns

follow the design of the two previous reigns, are scarce, his halfpennies are rare and his farthings are extremely rare. He was succeeded by his young son David II (1329–71), who was crowned in 1331. David's reign was interrupted by Edward Baliol, John Baliol's son, who siezed the throne in 1332, was expelled in 1334 but restored by Edward III before retiring to England in 1338. No coins of Edward Baliol are known.

258 Alexander III second coinage, Æ penny, with ESCOSSIE REX on reverse

259 Robert Bruce, Æ penny

260 David II, first coinage, Æ penny

David, who was married at the age of four to a daughter of Edward III, spent most of the first ten years of his reign in France. His earliest coinage consists of an issue of halfpennies and farthings only, possibly contemporary with Edward III's coinage of 1335–43 also of halfpennies and farthings only. One of David's early halfpennies is inscribed MONETA REGIS D/AVID SCOTOR (Money of David King of the Scots). David's next issue consisted of pennies and halfpennies of similar design but of distinctive style (**260**), and with the weight of the penny now reduced from $21\frac{1}{2}$ grains to 18 grains, the same weight as Edward III's 'Florin' coinage of 1344–51.

David, who had been captured at the Battle of Neville's Cross in 1346, remained a prisoner at the court of Edward III until 1357 when he was released on the promise of a substantial ransom, and it was probably at this time that the first brief issue of Scottish gold coins was minted. They are close copies of Edward's gold nobles, with the king depicted standing in a ship and holding a sword and shield, but the shield being charged with the rampant lion of Scotland within a fleury border (**261**). At the same time a coinage of groats (4 pence) (**262**), half-groats and pennies was minted at Edinburgh and Aberdeen, commencing with quite an attractive portrait of the king which became uglier over the years. The groats and half-groats have the inscription DNS P(*ro*)TECTOR M(*eu*)S & LIBERATOR M(*eu*)S (The Lord *is* my protector and my liberator), seemingly a thanksgiving for David's release from captivity. In 1367 there was a reduction in weight of the silver coins, the penny being reduced to 14.3 grains and the coins being distinguished by a star set behind the king's head or at the base of the sceptre.

261 *N* noble or half-mark, as type of Edward III

262 Second coinage, *R* groat of Edinburgh

THE EARLY STEWARTS

Robert II (1371–90), the first of the Stewart line, was the son of Walter, the hereditary High Steward of Scotland, and of Marjorie, the daughter of Robert Bruce. He issued no gold coins but continued a silver coinage of similar type to that of his predecessor. This was minted at Edinburgh, Perth and Dundee, and some coins have the initial B of the mintmaster Bonagius inserted behind the king's crown.

The coins of Robert III (1390–1406) can be divided into heavy and light coinages. A regular gold coinage was now introduced consisting of a lion, valued at 5 shillings (**263**), and a half lion; the former having crowned arms on the obverse, with a crucified St Andrew on a saltire cross on the reverse, and the latter having an uncrowned shield and a plain saltire cross flanked by fleurs-de-lis. The reverse inscription on the lion, abbreviated on the half, is XPC REGNAT XPC VINCIT XPC IMPERAT (Christ reigns, Christ conquers, Christ commands). The silver coinage now changes to the English pattern with a facing head and, on the reverse, three pellets in the angles of the cross. About 1403 the weight of the gold lion was reduced by roughly one third and the groat was reduced from 46 to about 28 grains (**264**). Pennies and halfpennies were now minted in debased silver.

263 Robert III, heavy coinage, Æ/ lion, St Andrew on reverse

264 Light coinage, Æ groat of Perth

Under James I (1406–37), who was held as a hostage in England until 1424, a new gold coin called the 'demy' (**265**) was introduced, together with its half. The demy was valued at 9 shillings, and at 54 grains weight it was the equivalent of the continental ducat. It had the Scottish arms set on a lozenge-shaped shield, with a St Andrew's cross set in a lis-decorated panel on the reverse. The groats of James I have a fleur-de-lis in two angles of the reverse cross and are increased in weight to about 36 grains. Base pennies and halfpennies continued to be minted.

James II (1437–60) continued the issue of the gold demy until 1451 when he reverted to minting lions and half-lions, the lion being issued at the same weight as the old demy but now valued at 10 shillings. They repeat the St Andrew design of Robert III except for having small crowns in the field. Groats were initially valued at 6 pence Scots, but in 1451 the weight of the groat was increased to 59 grains and the value raised to 12 pence, the coins being distinguished by having crowns set in two angles of the reverse in place of the two lis. The early base pennies of about 16 grains weight were reduced in 1451 to little more than 10 grains (**266**) and the halfpenny was discontinued.

The reign of James III (1460–88) is notable numismatically for the first debasement of the gold coinage, the introduction of a realistic portrait of the king and the introduction of a copper farthing. The first issue of 12 penny groats and halves began about 1467 and these have a pierced mullet in two angles of the reverse cross, some having a TL (the initials of the mintmasters Todd and Livingston) by the king's neck. Then in 1471 a base silver 6 penny groat was introduced which has a neat three-quarter facing bust of the king with a portrait of typical Renaissance style, the reverse having mullets and thistle heads in alternate angles of the cross. In 1475 a new gold coin was issued, the 'rider' of 23 shillings Scots (**267**), with its half and quarter, showing the king on a galloping horse, flourishing a sword. The 'cavalier' type, the *franc à cheval*, had been introduced by Jean le Bon in France more than a hundred years previously and had then been copied by the Dukes of Brittany, Burgundy and Brabant and by the Counts of Hainault, Holland and Flanders and others, so it was a type well known in international commerce. A light-weight 12 penny silver groat and its half, together with a 'penny' valued at 3 pence, were also introduced in 1475.

265 James I, *N* demy (of 9 shillings)

266 James II, billon penny, saltires by king's neck

267 James III, *N* rider (of 23 shillings)

In 1484 James issued a new gold coin, the unicorn valued at 18 shillings Scots, but instead of being in the traditional 'fine' gold (23½ carat fine at this period), the coins were struck in 21 carat gold (**268**). The obverse has a heraldic unicorn with a chained crown around its neck and one foreleg supporting the royal arms, and on the reverse is a radiant sun at the centre of an ornate cross. It is unusual in the omission of the king's name and titles, having the EXVRGAT DEVS ET DISSIPENTVR INIMICI EIVS (Let God arise and let His enemies be scattered, *Psalms 68,1*) legend on both sides. In the same year there was introduced a 14 penny groat (**269**) and its half with a half-left crowned bust and with crowns and triple pellets in the angles of the reverse cross.

268 *N* unicorn (of 18 shillings)

269 *R* fourteen-penny groat of Edinburgh, with half-left bust

Replacing the old 4 penny denomination James issued a base silver coin of .500 fineness (6oz fine), the plack and its half, having the crowned arms on the obverse and a cross fourchée on the reverse with a saltire at the centre and crowns in the angles. Besides billon pence and halfpence, James also issued copper or brass farthings, commonly known as 'Black Money', with a crown or crowned IR on one side and a saltire on the other, or with three lis in a trefoil on the obverse and a cross with crowns and mullets in the angles of the reverse. Some of these have the inscription MONE PAVP or MO PAVPER (the poor's money). Other copper pennies with an orb on one side and a Latin cross on the other are believed to have been issued by James Kennedy, Bishop of St Andrews (**270**). They used to be known as 'Crossraguel' pennies on account of the large hoard of them discovered at the abbey there.

James IV (1488–1513) continued the issue of unicorns and halves but with his name and title. The lion or crown was reintroduced, though of baser gold than the lions of James II, the weight being slightly reduced but the value increased from 10 shillings to 13s. 4d., i.e. 160 pence or a merk (mark). At first the 14 penny groat and its half were continued, having two crowns or a crown and a lis alternating with pellets in the angles of the reverse cross, but about 1496 the weight of the groat was reduced by a fifth and the new coins were valued at 12 pence. Some of the gold and silver coins have a 4, IIII or Q, QT or QRA (for *quartus*) at the end of the obverse inscription. Billon placks (**271**), half placks and pennies were also issued.

270 Æ penny of St Andrews, Bishop Kennedy (?)

271 James IV billon plack (4 pence)

During the minority of James V (1513–42) unicorns and halves similar to those of James IV were minted, though the unicorn was now valued at 20 shillings. Some are found countermarked with a cinquefoil device, a family badge of James, Earl of Arran. In 1526, the year that Henry VIII introduced a gold crown in England, a gold crown was issued for James V and valued at 20s. Scots. It is closer in style to the *écu d'or au soleil* of Francis I of France than to the English crown, and it has the crowned royal arms on the obverse flanked by St Andrews crosses, with a radiant sun above, and a cross fleury on the reverse with thistle heads in each angle (**272**). At the same time a groat (**273**) and one-third groat were issued, valued at 18 pence and 6 pence Scots respectively, and having a crowned head in profile to right, as did Henry VIII's groats and halves on the English coinage of 1526. James's billon placks have a design similar to that of his predecessor except that they have a mullet at the centre of the reverse cross and crowns and saltires in the angles. In 1538 there was a new coinage of billon bawbees (**274**) valued at 6 pence Scots, with halves and quarters: they have a large crowned thistle head flanked by 1 5 and, on the reverse, a saltire within a crown. James's last

272 James V, second coinage, *A*/ crown (of 20 shillings)

273 *R* eighteen penny groat

274 Third coinage, base *R* bawbee (6 pence)

275 *A*/ two-thirds ducat or 'bonnet' piece, 1540

gold coinage, issued 1539–40, was of ducats of 40 shillings and two-thirds ducats (**275**). The coins are known as 'bonnet pieces' from the flat hat topped by a diadem worn by the king.

Mary (1542–67), the only surviving child of James V by his second wife Marie of Lorraine, was only a week old when she succeeded to the throne. Her coinage can be divided into five periods: those issued before her first marriage, during her marriage to the Dauphin of France, during her first widowhood, during her marriage to Henry Stewart Lord Darnley and, finally, during her second widowhood. The first of Mary's gold crowns, valued at 22 shillings, closely followed the pattern of those of her father except for cinquefoils by the royal arms in place of saltires. A smaller 20 shilling piece of 1543 has a crowned MR monogram on the reverse. In 1553 a lighter crown of 22 shillings and its double of 44 shillings have a crowned monogram of MARIA and MARIA REGINA respectively, and they have the letters IG flanking the royal arms on the obverse, i.e., for *Iacobus gubernator* (James, Earl of Arran, the Regent of Scotland). In the same year a silver testoon, valued at 4 shillings Scots, carried a profile portrait of the young queen. In 1555 a three pound portrait gold piece (**276**) and its half were issued together with a new heavier testoon of 5 shillings having a crowned M on the obverse flanked by crowned thistle heads. These were replaced the following year by a lighter coin having M R by a crowned royal arms and a cross potent with small crosses in the reverse (**277**). Billon bawbees, half bawbees and placks were issued at this period, together with a billon lion or 'hardhead' valued at 1½d. Scots with a crowned M on the obverse and a rampant lion on the reverse. There were also billon pennies with a crowned facing bust (**278**) and pennies of 1556 with the inscription VICIT VERITAS (Truth has conquered) in two lines across the field.

276 Mary, *A⁄* three pounds 1555

277 *Æ* testoon (5 shillings), 1556

278 Billon penny, portrait issue, infant head

A gold ducat of 1558, valued at 60 shillings Scots, with the heads of Francis and Mary face-to-face is one of the classic rarities of the Scottish gold series, but the non-portrait silver testoons and half-testoons of the period of Mary's first marriage, though scarce, are not unduly rare. Those dated 1558–9, issued while Francis was still Dauphin, have a shield with the arms of the Dauphin impaled with the arms of Scotland and an obverse inscription ending D D VIEN (*Delfinus et delfina Viennae*, Dauphin and Dauphine of Vienne), the reverse having crosses of Lorraine by the royal F M monogram. Those dated 1560–1 (**279**), when Francis had become King of France, have the arms of France impaled with those of Scotland and their titles R R FRANCO SCOTORQ (King and Queen of France and Scotland). The reverse inscription on the earlier coins is FECIT VTRAQVE VNVM (He hath made both one), and on the later coins VICIT LEO DE TRIBV IVDA, (The Lion of the tribe of Judah hath prevailed, *Revelations* 5,5). Billon groats of 12d. Scots, dated 1558–9, have a heraldic dolphin (for Dauphiné) and a thistle head at the sides of the crowned F M monogram on the obverse and the inscription IAM NON SVNT DVO SED VNA CARO (They are no more twain but one flesh) in four lines on the reverse. The base $1\frac{1}{2}$d. 'hardheads' have crowned dolphins by the royal monogram.

After the death of Francis, Mary issued a gold crown which has the Scottish arms impaled with the demi-arms of France. Only one example has survived. There are, however, testoons (**280**) and half testoons of 1561–2 which have an attractive portrait of the queen in a widow's bonnet, wearing a costume with a high neck and lace ruff.

279   Mary and Francis, Æ testoon, after accession to French throne, 1560

280   Mary, first widowhood, Æ testoon, 1561

During the period of Mary's marriage to Lord Darnley (1565–7) there were minted large silver ryals, valued at 30s. Scots, with the names MARIA & HENRIC' and crowned arms, and on the reverse a tortoise climbing a crowned palm tree with a scroll inscribed DAT GLORIA VIRES (Glory gives strength). Two-thirds (**281**) and one-third ryals were also minted, but testoons, only known of 1565, are extremely rare. Ryals and fractions minted during her second widowhood omit Henry's name.

281 Mary and Lord Henry Darnley, Æ two-thirds ryal (20 shillings), undated

THE LATER STEWARTS

James VI (1567–1625) was only one year old when Mary abdicated and his long reign provides the most varied and interesting coinages of all the Scottish monarchs. Not only did he take a personal interest in the coinage, but his eldest son Henry, Prince of Wales, began the formation of a major royal coin collection. A silver ryal, sometimes known as a 'sword dollar' (**282**), and its two-third and one-third fractions were struck in 1567–71, having crowned arms on the obverse and a sword, point upward, surmounted by a crown and dividing a hand (the Hand of Providence) from the value XXX, XX or X, the inscription being PRO ME SI MEREOR ME (For me, but against me if I deserve it).

James's second coinage, 1572–80, consisted of silver half merks of 6s. 8d. Scots, together with quarter merks, the values 6–8 and 3–4 flanking the royal arms, and thistle heads and crowns set in the angles of the reverse cross. Two more denominations, the merk and two-merks or 'thistle dollar', were added later, a large thistle on the reverse dividing the letters I R. Also minted in 1575 and 1576 was a twenty-pound gold coin (**283**), a most handsome piece with an attractive half-length figure of the young king in armour holding a sword in one hand and an olive branch in the other, the legend in a panel below being IN VTRVNQVE PARATVS (prepared for either, i.e. war or peace). In 1578 various earlier coins were called up in value and genuine pieces stamped with a crowned thistle head countermark, Mary's testoons being raised to 7s. 4d. and Mary's and James's ryals to 36s. 9d., the fractions being adjusted in proportion.

A third coinage, 1580–1, consisted of a ducat of 80 shillings, with a bare-headed bust of the young king in a cuirass and ruff, and silver 16, 8, 4 and 2 shilling pieces of similar design to the second coinage but with a crown added above the thistle on the reverse. The fourth coinage, 1581–7, comprised gold lion nobles, valued at 75 shillings, and two-thirds and one-third nobles which depict a seated facing lion holding a sword and sceptre, and silver 40, 30 (**284**), 20 and 10 shilling pieces which have a crowned and armoured half-length figure of the king holding a sword. The large 40 shilling piece is particularly rare.

In 1588 a gold thistle noble was issued valued at 14s. 8d., or 11 merks, having the crowned arms superimposed upon the Ship of State and, on the reverse, a thistle arranged as a central cross with sceptres in the angles and the inscription FLORENT SCEPT PIIS REGNA HIS IOVA DAT NVMERATQE (Sceptres flourish with the pious, Jehovah gives them kingdoms and numbers them).

282 James VI, first coinage, Æ ryal or 'sword dollar', 1570, with countermark of 1578 revaluing at 36s. 9d.

283 Second coinage, Æ twenty pounds, 1575

284 Third coinage, Æ thirty shillings, 1582

285 Æ 'balance' quarter merk, 1591

286 Seventh coinage, Æ ten shillings, 1594

That this design and inscription should be chosen in the year that the great Spanish Armada was harried and dispersed may not be entirely coincidental.

James's sixth coinage, 1591–3, included a gold 80 shilling coin called a 'hat piece' as it depicted the king in a tall hat with rounded top, the reverse having a crowned lion receiving a sceptre from the heavens, with the word 'Jehovah' in Hebrew characters above the clouds and with the inscription TE SOLVM VEREOR (Thee alone do I fear). The silver consisted of 'balance' half and quarter merks (**285**) which have a sword and scales of Justice on the reverse and the inscription HIS DIFFERT REGE TYRANNVS (In these a tyrant differs from a king).

The seventh coinage, 1593–1601, comprised gold riders and halves, silver 10 and 5 shillings and 30 and 12 pence. The gold rider of 100 shillings depicts the king in armour on a horse galloping to right and the issue coincided with the resurrection of the rider type on the 'cavaliers' of the Dutch United Provinces. The silver pieces have a bare-headed bust of the king in armour (**286**) and, on the reverse, a thistle with three flowers and the legend NEMO ME IMPVNE LACESSIT, (No one shall hurt me with impunity). The eighth coinage, 1601–4, consisted of gold sword-and-sceptre pieces of 120 shilling value (**287**) and their halves and silver thistle merks, halves, quarters and eighths. The gold has the inscription SALVS POPVLI SVPREMA LEX (The safety of the people is the supreme law) and the silver has a large crowned thistle and the inscription REGEM IOVA PROTEGIT (Jehovah protects the kingdom).

287 Eighth coinage, *N* sword-and-scéptre piece (6 pounds), 1601

288 *R* six shillings, 1605

As heir to his kinswoman Elizabeth I (he was a great-great-grandson of Henry VII) James VI succeeded to the throne of England in 1603 and immediate steps were taken to secure the uniformity of weight and fineness of Scottish and English denominations and also a similarity of design, though the current ratio of £1 sterling to £12 Scots was still maintained. A Scottish unit of £12 Scots was thus equivalent to the English unite and the 60 shillings Scots equalled the English crown. The Scottish gold denominations were the unit, double crown, Britain crown, half-crown (30s. Scots) and thistle crown (48s. Scots), and the silver denominations were the 60, 30, 12, 6, 2 and 1 shilling Scots. The 60 and 30 shillings had the king on horseback and the 12 and 6 shillings (**288**) had a portrait. The initial issue had the English arms in the first and fourth quarters of the royal arms, with Scotland in the second and Ireland in the third quarter, but in 1610 the arrangement was changed on the Scottish coinage with the rampant lion of

Scotland transferred to the first and fourth quarters. The thistle crown was similar to the same English denomination valued at 4s., and the 2 and 1 shilling Scot were similar to the English half-groat and penny. The Scottish denominations can be distinguished by the Scottish crown which has a fleur-de-lis decoration at the centre and sides, with crosses between, as distinct from the English crown which has crosses at the centre and sides and fleurs-de-lis between.

James's smaller denominations consisted of billon 8d. placks and half placks of .250 fineness; 2d. hardheads and half-hardheads introduced in 1588 of only one-twenty-fourth silver; 4d. saltire placks issued in 1594 of the same alloy; and then copper portrait 'turners' (2d. named after the French *double tournois*) and pennies with three thistle heads on the reverse. At the time of the 1575 revaluation of earlier silver coins, genuine placks and hardheads of Mary were countermarked with a star within a heart, a device of the Earl of Morton, the Regent (**289**). After his English accession James issued new turners and pennies with triple thistles on the obverse and a lion rampant on the reverse, with one or two pellets behind to indicate the value.

289 Æ 'hardhead' of Mary, with 1575 star-in-heart countermark of the regent, the Earl of Morton

290 Charles I, A/ unit (12 pounds) Briot's coinage

Charles I (1625–49) continued the Scottish coinage unaltered for ten years apart from the change of name, even Charles's portrait looking much like that of his father, though the gold thistle crown and half-crown were discontinued. In 1636 new half merks, 40 pence and 20 pence were minted, all portrait pieces, the first having vi 8 behind the king's head (6s. 8d.), the second xl and the last xx. In 1635 Nicholas Briot, the French engraver responsible for the fine machine-made English coinage of Charles I, was appointed master of the Edinburgh mint and produced some beautifully engraved gold and silver coins signed with his initial 'B' (**290, 291**). He was joined by his son-in-law John Falconer, who signed his dies with the letter 'F', and who succeeded him as mintmaster in 1646.

291 Æ half-mark, Briot's coinage

In 1642 a new coinage of 3 and 2 shilling pieces replaced the half merk and its fractions, and these new coins have a thistle head and a II respectively behind the king's head. A coinage of copper turners and pennies had been minted in 1629 of similar type to those of James I, but in 1632–9 a coinage of very light-weight turners was extensively counterfeited, these coins having a crowned C II R on the obverse. They were replaced in 1642 by a new issue of heavy weight turners having a crowned C R, an issue which continued into the reign of Charles II.

Charles II was proclaimed king in Scotland within a month of his father's execution and his Scottish coronation took place at Scone in January 1651. The Edinburgh mint, however, did not reopen until 1664 when a coinage of silver 4, 2, 1 (**292**) and ½ merks was produced from puncheons prepared in London by Thomas Simon. Dies were made in Edinburgh by Falconer, his initial 'F' appearing on some of the later coins. The rather fine bust of the king facing right is laureate, draped and cuirassed, and the values LIII/4 (53s. 4d.), xxvi/8, xiii/4 and vi/8 appear at the centre of four shields arranged cross-wise on the reverse. In 1675 there was a change of type with a left-facing bust of the king designed by the Roettiers at London but minted from Edinburgh-produced dies and manufactured by improved machinery. The denominations of the new issue are usually known as the dollar and its half, quarter, eighth and sixteenth, this last being a 40d. piece. In 1680 the values were called up, the merk or quarter-dollar being revalued at 14s. Scots and the sixteenth dollar at 42d. Scots. A large copper bawbee, 6d. Scots (**293**), was issued 1677–9, together with a turner or 'bodle', this latter having a crowned sword and sceptre instead of a royal head.

Under James II (VII), 1685–9, silver 40 and 10 shilling pieces were minted in 1687–8, both with a laureate bust and the value below. The former has crowned arms on the reverse and an edge inscribed NEMO ME IMPVNE LACESSIT ANNO REGNI TERTIO (or QVARTO), and the latter has a St Andrews cross with royal emblems separating the shields on the reverse, the edge being plain. Dies for a 60 shilling piece were prepared, the shield on the reverse being set within the Collar of the Order of the Thistle, but no coins were struck from them until 1828 when Matthew Young, the London coin dealer, had some strikings made for collectors in gold and silver.

292 Charles II, first coinage, Æ merk, 1669

293 Æ bawbee, 1677

William and Mary (1689–94) issued 60 shilling pieces in 1691–2 with their conjoined busts, a crowned shield on the reverse and the edge inscription PROTEGIT ET ORNAT (It protects and adorns) ANNO REGNI TERTIO. Forty shilling pieces of similar type were issued 1689–94 (**294**), and 20 and 10 shilling pieces were also issued but without edge inscriptions. The 5 shillings had a crowned WM on the reverse with a small v below on the 1691 coin and a v below the busts on the 1694 issue. Copper bawbees follow the pattern of the Charles II coins and turners or 'bodles' have a crowned monogram on the obverse (**295**).

After Mary's death 40, 20, 10 and 5 shilling pieces were minted with William's head, the 40 shillings having an inscribed edge and regnal year. His bawbees follow the pattern of earlier years but the bodles revert to the crowned sword and sceptre obverse last used by Charles II.

In 1701 gold pieces of £12 and £6 Scots were minted from gold imported by the Darien Company, more properly entitled 'The Company of Scotland trading to Africa and the Indies'. Like the African Company in

London, it made representations to have its bade included in the design of the coins. This was agreed and the badge, the sun setting on the sea, was placed below the king's head (**296**). The Company's abortive expeditions sent in 1699 to found a trading settlement in the Darien isthmus, a country it proposed to call 'New Caledonia', had been miserable failures due to lack of adequate provisions, sickness and the active opposition of the Spaniards. The coins, now rare, are commonly, though erroneously, called 'pistoles' and 'half pistoles'.

294 William and Mary, Æ 40 shillings, 1691

295 Æ turner (2 pence), 1691

In 1705–6 Scots 10 and 5 shilling pieces were minted with the bust of Queen Anne, the former having crowned arms on the reverse (**297**) and the smaller coin having a crowned thistle. No Scottish copper was minted in this reign. The Act of Union of 1707 provided for coinage of the same standard and values in both countries and crowns, half-crowns, shillings and sixpences of 'English' type were struck at the Edinburgh mint between 1707 and 1709. These have an E or E★ below the queen's bust (**298**). The Edinburgh mint was now closed and thereafter all coinage for Scotland was provided by the Royal Mint.

In the early years of the nineteenth century Spanish dollars circulated in Scotland countermarked by different banks and private companies, such as Lanark Mills (**299**), for values between 4s. 6d. and 5s. 6d. In 1937 a 'Scottish' shilling or, more correctly, a UK shilling of Scottish type, was minted in addition to the 'English' shilling as a compliment to the Scottish ancestry of Queen Elizabeth, now the Queen Mother. This had a Scottish crown surmounted by a seated facing lion holding a sword and sceptre (as on the

296 William III, *N* twelve pounds (or 'pistole'), 1701, with Darien company emblem

297 Anne, Æ 10 shillings, 1705

298 Post-Union Æ shilling, Edinburgh mint, E★ below bust

299 Spanish Æ 8 reals, 1791, countermarked for use at Robert Owen's mills at New Lanark, value 5 shillings

lion noble of James VI) and flanked by a shield bearing a St Andrews cross and by a thistle head. Until decimalization in the present reign a 'Scottish' shilling had the arms of Scotland surmounted by a Scottish crown. On the present UK decimal coinage a crowned thistle design appears as a Scottish emblem on the 5p piece. On the commemorative 25 pence issued on the Queen Mother's 80th birthday the Scottish lion and three bows on a field of ermine are set as a recurring border motif around her portrait, these being the charges on the Bowes-Lyon arms. In 1984 a new UK nickel-brass one pound coin was introduced, one of a series of four with national emblems, having a Scottish flowering thistle encircled by a royal diadem.

15

THE ISLANDS OF MAN,
LUNDY, WIGHT
AND THE CHANNEL ISLANDS

⇥❦❧⇤

The first coins to be struck in Man (Celtic, *Manau*; Manx, *Ellan Vannin*) were crude imitations of the silver pennies struck by the Hiberno-Norse kings of Dublin (**300**). The Dublin pennies were themselves imitations of the Long Cross pennies of Aethelred II of England. These Manx pennies were issued around AD 1020–30, but from this period onwards it was English, Irish and some Scottish and foreign coins that were used on the island until the first copper coins were struck for Man in 1709. Man had its own dynasty of local kings between the eleventh and thirteenth centuries who owed nominal allegiance to the kings of Norway, but they did not issue their own coins. Magnus of Norway ceded Man to Alexander III of Scotland in 1266 but shortly afterwards sovereignty was claimed by Edward I of England. In 1406 Henry IV granted the island to Sir John Stanley whose descendants became Earls of Derby and who ruled as 'kings' of Man until 1505. Man was inherited by James Murray, second Duke of Atholl, in 1736, but certain of his rights were purchased by the Crown under the Revestment Act of 1765. Man has retained internal self-government with its own parliament, the Tynwald.

During the second half of the seventeenth century John Murray of Douglas issued a halfpenny token bearing the legs of Man, the Manx symbol, and certain Irish tokens were authorized for circulation on the island.

Cast copper pennies and halfpennies (**301**) were made for James, the tenth Earl of Derby, in 1709. They have the Stanley crest, an eagle and child, with the family motto SANS CHANGER on the obverse, and the Manx triune, three conjoined legs, with the legend QVOCVNQVE GESSERIS STABIT

(Wherever you throw it, it will stand) on the reverse. Copper or bronze pence and halfpence of similar type were struck 1721–33, having the Earl's I D cipher with a 'I' or '½' between the legs. In 1758 a coinage of pence and halfpence was issued by James, Duke of Atholl, having a crowned A D monogram on the obverse and a triune on the reverse (**302**). A regal coinage of pence and halfpence was issued in 1786 and 1813, the latter being minted by Matthew Boulton at his Soho foundry.

300 Hiberno-Manx, Æ penny in imitation of Hiberno-Norse penny of Dublin, *c*. 1025

301 Lord of Man, James Earl of Derby, cast Æ halfpenny, 1709, with Stanley crest and the legs of Man

302 James, Duke of Atholl, Æ penny 1758

Between 1811 and 1831 a number of local tokens were issued by bankers and merchants in Douglas, Castletown and Ramsey. These include a five shilling piece and other values with a view of Peel Castle, issued by the Douglas Bank, and pence and halfpence depicting Atlas carrying the world on his shoulders issued by bankers who were also agents of the Atlas Fire Insurance Co. During the eighteenth and early nineteenth centuries there had been fourteen pence to the shilling, but in 1839 a new coinage of Victorian pennies, halfpennies and farthings was produced at the Royal Mint, London, and issued at only twelve pence to the shilling. These were the same size as the British copper coins, with the same head of the queen but with the legs of Man on the reverse. However, there was considerable opposition to this coinage on account of the change in value, so the issue was discontinued and from September 1840 all previous local coinage was demonetized and replaced by United Kingdom coinage.

During the Second World War brass 6d., 1d. and ½d. tokens were issued for use in the internment camps which were set up on the island. In 1965 a privately produced set of gold £5, £1 and £½ non-legal tender coins was issued to commemorate the bicentenary of the Crown's 'revestment' of Man. In 1970, just prior to decimalization, the Manx authorities issued a cupro-nickel crown with the tailless Manx cat depicted on the reverse (**303**). On decimalization in 1971 a new coinage of the size, shape and value of the UK coinage was issued with a Viking ship on the 50 pence (**304**), and on the other denominations, the legs of Man, the Tower of Refuge, Peregrine falcons, an interlaced cross and a ragwort plant. In 1972 a Queen Elizabeth II Silver Wedding crown was also issued. Since then multitudinous official commemorative pieces struck in gold, silver, platinum and other metals by the Pobjoy Mint have been issued for the tourist trade, collectors and for 'investment' purposes. The first base metal one-pound piece to be issued in the British Isles was minted for the Isle of Man in 1978 (**305**) and in 1983 the first of a series of four one-pound coins featuring the towns of the island depicted the castle of Peel.

303 Elizabeth II, cupro-nickel crown, 1970, Manx cat

304 Decimal 50 new pence, 1971, Viking ship

305 Manx virenium one pound, 1981, legs on map

LUNDY ISLAND

Lundy Island, situated in the Bristol Channel 12 miles from the Devon coast, was at one time thought to have been the site of a mint during the Civil War but this claim has not been substantiated. In 1925 the owner of the island, Martin Coles Harman, who was known locally as 'king' of Lundy, issued pennies (**306**) and halfpennies called Puffins and half Puffins. They have his portrait on the obverse and the reverses illustrate the singular seabird for which Lundy is famous. In a celebrated court case Harman's claim that Lundy was outside British jurisdiction was overruled and the coins were declared illegal under the 1870 Coinage Act, a nominal £5 fine being imposed. Similar coins dated 1965 are modern reproductions of little numismatic value.

306 Lundy Island, Martin Harman, Æ 'puffin', 1929

ISLE OF WIGHT

No coins have been issued for the Isle of Wight, but some seventeenth-century halfpenny and farthing tokens were struck for local tradesmen and there are also eighteenth-century halfpenny tokens.

THE CHANNEL ISLANDS

The Channel Islands of Guernsey, Jersey, Alderney, Sark and Herm are that part of the medieval dukedom of Normandy that still remains to the British Crown. French coinage was in common use in the islands and French denominations of account were in legal use in Jersey until 1834 and in Guernsey until 1921. It is believed that local coins may have been minted in the islands in the sixteenth and seventeenth centuries, but if so they do not appear to have survived.

Five shilling tokens were issued in 1809 by the Bank of Guernsey, run by Bishop de Jersey & Co., but their circulation was soon banned and the bank failed in 1811. In 1830 the Guernsey authorities issued copper 4 (**307**) and 1 doubles, the double being a French denomination derived from the *double tournois*. An 8 double was added in 1834, being the equivalent of the British penny, and a 2 double (or farthing) in 1858. These coins have the arms of Guernsey, three lions passant-guardant, the old arms of England/Normandy, with a sprig of laurel issuing from the top of the shield, and on the reverse the value and date across the field.

In 1848–50 and 1870–1921 British currency was made legal tender jointly with French currency, after which sterling was the sole legal tender. Until 1921 there were 21 Guernsey shillings (2016 doubles) to the British pound, thereafter 20 Guernsey shillings (1920 doubles) to the pound. In 1864 smaller coins were minted in bronze of identical design to the copper coinage, the type being unchanged through the reigns of Victoria, Edward VII, George V and George VI as no monarch's head or name appears on the coins. In some years minting was contracted out to Heaton's of Birmingham and these coins have a small letter H at the bottom of the reverse.

307 Guernsey, Æ 4 doubles, 1830

In 1956 a new coinage of 8 doubles and a scalloped cupro-nickel 3 pence was issued, the obverse design being copied from the old seal of Guernsey with the inscription s(*igillum*) BALLIVIE INSVLE DE GERNEREVE (Seal of the Balliwick of the Island of Guernsey) and with a Guernsey lily on the reverse of the 8 doubles and a cow on the 3 pence (**308**). In 1966 on the 900th anniversary of the Norman dynasty of England a square cupro-nickel 10 shillings was minted with the head of Queen Elizabeth II on one side and a representation of William I on the other (**309**).

With decimalization the 'double' denominations were superseded by a coinage of 100 pence to the pound. In 1968 cupro-nickel 10 and 5 new pence were issued, followed by a 50p. in 1969 and by bronze coins of 2, 1 and $\frac{1}{2}$ new pence in 1971. In 1977 the word NEW was dropped and in 1981 a square 1 pound was issued in copper-nickel-zinc. All these coins have the Guernsey seal obverse. The £1 has a floral reverse, the 50p. a ducal cap with an ermine brim (**310**), 10p. a cow, 5p. a lily, 2p. a windmill, 1p. a seabird and $\frac{1}{2}$p. just the value. Commemorative crowns (25 pence) were issued in 1972 for the Queen's Silver Wedding, in 1977 for the Silver Jubilee, in 1978 for the royal visit to Guernsey, in 1980 for the 80th birthday of the Queen Mother and in 1981 for the wedding of Prince Charles and Lady Diana Spencer.

308 Cupro-nickel threepence, 1956, Guernsey cow

309 Cupro-nickel ten shillings, 1966, William I commemorative

310 Decimal cupro-nickel 50 new pence, 1969, ducal cap

JERSEY

Several hoards of gold and billon Gaulish Armorican coins have been found on the island but they probably all originate from the French mainland and were brought over by refugees from Caesar's Gallic wars.

In 1813 an issue of 3 shilling and 18 pence silver tokens was made by the States of Jersey (the Jersey government) being minted by the Royal Mint, London, from Spanish dollar silver (.892 fineness). These have the inscription STATES OF JERSEY around the island's arms – three lions passant-guardant. Some copper penny and halfpenny tokens were also minted privately in 1813. At the time French currency was the legal tender, but in 1834 it was decided to change to a sterling currency. As the French *livre* contained 20 *sous*, a sou being equivalent to a halfpenny, and there were 26 livres to the pound, the sterling shilling contained 26 sous, i.e., there were 13 Jersey pence to the shilling. The first Jersey copper coins minted in 1841 were denominated 1/13 OF A SHILLING (**311**) 1/26 OF A SHILLING and 1/52 OF A SHILLING, equivalent to a British penny, halfpenny and farthing. Unlike the coins of Guernsey, this and succeeding coinages all bear the monarch's head.

311 Jersey, Victoria, Æ $\frac{1}{13}$th shilling, 1851

In 1866 there was a change to an issue of bronze $\frac{1}{13}$ and $\frac{1}{26}$ shillings, the queen now shown wearing a coronet decorated with oak leaves in place of the earlier ornamented fillet. Another change to the currency was made in 1877 with the shilling now containing 12 pence, thus bringing the island's coinage into conformity with UK currency. The coins of that year were minted by Heaton and Son and it was the only year in which a $\frac{1}{48}$ shilling was issued. The pattern of the George V coins was changed twice: in 1923 the reverse arms were redesigned and the inscriptions set on two scrolls, and in 1931 the scrolls were removed (**312**). In the years 1949–52 $\frac{1}{12}$th shillings were issued with the inscription STATES OF JERSEY changed to ISLAND OF JERSEY and the words LIBERATED 1945 were added. In 1954 coins with the Queen's head were issued with the same legend and date, but in 1957 the island's name was changed to BAILIWICK OF JERSEY. A nickel-brass one-fourth shilling (3 pence) was introduced in 1957 and in 1964 this was changed to a twelve-sided coin to make it of uniform size to the UK threepence. On the tercentenary of the Restoration $\frac{1}{12}$ shillings were issued with C II R 1660–1960 E II R below the arms, and the $\frac{\star}{12}$ths of 1966 have the dates 1066–1966 by the shield to commemorate the conquest of England by William of Normandy (**313**), a cupro-nickel 5 shilling piece also being issued on the same occasion.

Decimal 10 and 5 cupro-nickel new pence were introduced in 1968 (**314**), with a seven-sided 50 pence added in 1969 and bronze 2, 1 and $\frac{1}{2}$ new pence in 1971. The NEW was dropped in 1981 and a square copper-nickel 1 pound was issued in the same year commemorating the Battle of Jersey

312 George V, Æ $\frac{1}{12}$th shilling, 1933

313 Elizabeth II, cupro-nickel crown, 1966, Battle of Hastings commemorative

314 Cupro-nickel 10 new pence, 1968

of 1791 when a French invasion of the island was repulsed. Other commemorative coins have been issued for the Silver Wedding of Queen
Elizabeth II and the Duke of Edinburgh (1972), the Queen's Silver Jubilee
(1977) and for the wedding of the Prince of Wales and Lady Diana Spencer
(1981).

SUGGESTIONS FOR
FURTHER READING

꒭ ꗈ ꗈ ꒫

The books and articles listed below are only a small selection from the total literature on British numismatics, but they will provide a starting point for a more detailed study of the coinage. The selection of articles from the *British Numismatic Journal* (*BNJ*) and the *Numismatic Chronicle* (*NC*) covers only a minute fraction of the research available in the 53 volumes of the former and the 143 volumes of the latter. Many other articles of interest will be found in the 91 years of Spink's *Numismatic Circular* (*NCirc*), the 39 years of *Seaby's Coin and Medal Bulletin* (*SCMB*) and in *Coin & Medal News* (and in its predecessor, *Coins and Medals*). Of particular importance for the specialist are the volumes of the *Sylloge of Coins of the British Isles* (*SCBI*).

INTRODUCTION (GENERAL)

G. C. Brooke, *English Coins* (3rd ed., London 1955)
I. D. Brown & M. Dolley, *A Bibliography of Coin Hoards of Great Britain and Ireland 1500–1967* (London 1971)
R. A. G. Carson (ed.), *Mints, Dies and Currency: essays dedicated to the memory of Albert Baldwin* (London 1971)
Sir John Craig, *The Mint* (Cambridge 1953)
M. J. Freeman, *The Bronze Coinage of Great Britain* (Motherwell 1970)
P. Grierson, *Bibliographie numismatique* (2nd ed., Bruxelles 1979)
— *Numismatics* (London 1975)
H. A. Grueber, *Handbook of the Coins of Great Britain and Ireland* (revised ed., London 1970)
C. R. Josset, *Money in Britain* (London 1962)
R. Ll. Kenyon, *Gold Coins of England* (London 1884)
H. W. A. Linecar, *British Coin Designs and Designers* (London 1977)

H. Linecar & A. G. Stone, *English Proof and Pattern Crown-size Pieces 1568–1960* (London 1968)

J. Mackay, *A History of Modern English Coinage: Henry VII to Elizabeth II* (London 1984)

M. A. Marsh, *The Gold Sovereign* (Cambridge 1980)

— *The Gold Half Sovereign* (Cambridge 1984)

J. O'D. Mays, *The Splendid Shilling* (Burley 1982)

S. Mitchell (ed), *Standard Catalogue of British Coins: 1, Coins of England and the United Kingdom* (London 1985)

J. J. North, *English Hammered Coins* (2 vols., London, 1 revised 1980, 2 1960)

Sir Charles Oman, *The Coinage of England* (London 1931)

C. W. Peck, *English Copper, Tin and Bronze Coins in the British Museum 1558–1958* (London 1960)

J. Porteous, *Coins in History* (London 1969)

B. Robinson, *The Royal Maundy* (London 1977)

R. Ruding, *Annals of the Coinage of Great Britain and its Dependencies* (3 vols., 3rd ed., London 1840). Still valuable for documentary material

H. A. Seaby & P. A. Rayner, *The English Silver Coinage from 1649* (4th ed., London 1974)

C. H. V. Sutherland, *English Coinage 600–1900* (London 1973)

J. D. A. Thompson, *Inventory of British Coin Hoards AD 600–1500* (London 1956)

J. D. A. Whiting, *Trade Tokens: a social and economic history* (London 1971)

I CELTIC BRITAIN

D. Allen, 'The Belgic dynasties of Britain and their coins', *Archaelogia* 90 (1944)

— 'The origins of coinage in Britain: a reappraisal', *Problems of the Iron Age in Southern Britain* (ed. S. S. Frere, London 1961)

— *An Introduction to Celtic Coins* (London 1978)

B. Cunliffe (ed.), *Coinage and Society in Britain and Gaul: some current problems* (C. B. A. Research Report no. 38, 1981)

R. P. Mack, *The Coinage of Ancient Britain* (London 1975). The standard reference

2 ROMAN BRITAIN

G. Askew, *The Coinage of Roman Britain* (2nd ed., London 1981)

R. A. G. Carson, *The Principal Coins of the Romans* (3 vols, London 1978–81)

R. A. G. Carson, P. V. Hill & J. P. C. Kent, *Late Roman Bronze Coinage* (London 1960)

P. J. Casey, *Roman Coinage in Britain* (Princes Risborough 1980)

J. P. C. Kent, *Roman Coins* (London 1979)

H. Mattingly, *Roman Coins from the Earliest Times to the Fall of the Roman Empire* (reprint London 1967)

H. Mattingly & others, *Coins of the Roman Empire in the British Museum* (6 vols, London 1923–76, most reprinted). An important reference

H. Mattingly, E. A. Sydenham & others, *The Roman Imperial Coinage* (10 vols, London 1923–81, most reprinted). The standard reference

H. A. Seaby, *Roman Silver Coinage* (4 vols, new ed. London 1978–82)
D. R. Sear, *Roman Coins and their Values* (3rd ed., London 1981)
S. W. Stevenson & others, *A Dictionary of Roman Coins* (reprint London 1982)

3 ANGLO-SAXON ENGLAND

C. E. Blunt, 'The coinage of Athelstan, king of England 924–939', *BNJ* 42 (1974)
C. E. Blunt, C. S. S. Lyon & B. H. I. H. Stewart, 'The coinage of southern England 796–840', *BNJ* 32 (1963)
M. Dolley, *Anglo-Saxon Pennies* (London 1966)
R. H. Dolley, 'Coinage', *Medieval England* (ed. A. L. Poole, London 1958)
R. H. M. Dolley, *Viking Coins in the Danelaw and Dublin* (London 1965)
R. H. M. Dolley (ed.), *Anglo-Saxon Coins: studies presented to Sir Frank Stenton on his 80th birthday* (London 1961)
G. Galster, *The Royal Danish Collection, Copenhagen, Parts I–V*, *SCBI* 4, 7, 13–15, 18 & 22 (1964–75). Particularly valuable for later Anglo-Saxon, Hiberno-Norse and Anglo-Norman coins
F. C. Keary & H. A. Grueber, *Catalogue of the English Coins in the British Museum: Anglo-Saxon Series* (2 vols, reprint London 1970). The standard reference
H. R. Mossop, *The Lincoln Mint c. 890–1279* (Newcastle upon Tyne 1970)
E. J. E. Pirie, *Catalogue of the Early Northumbrian Coins in the Mueseum of Antiquities, Newcastle upon Tyne* (Newcastle upon Tyne 1981)
C. H. V. Sutherland, *Anglo-Saxon Gold in relation to the Crondall Find* (Oxford 1948)
The above listing barely touches on the numerous works in *NC* and *BNJ*. A useful reference to this material is given by Dr E. J. Harris in *SCMB* 1963 (Mar. & Nov.)

4 THE NORMANS

W. J. Andrew, 'Numismatic history of the reign of Henry I', *NC* 1900
G. C. Brooke, *A Catalogue of English Coins in the British Museum: The Norman Kings* (2 vols, London 1916). The standard reference
P. W. P. Carlyon-Britton, 'A numismatic history of William I and II', *BNJ* 2 (1905)
R. H. M. Dolley, *The Norman Conquest and the Norman Coinage* (London 1966)
R. P. Mack, 'Stephen and the Anarchy 1135–1154', *BNJ* 35 (1966)

5 THE EARLY PLANTAGENETS

D. F. Allen, *A Catalogue of English Coins in the British Museum: The Cross-and-Crosslets ('Tealby') Type of Henry II* (London 1951). The standard reference
H. B. E. & J. S. S. Fox, 'Numismatic history of the reigns of Edward I, II and III', *BNJ* 6–10 (1909–13)
L. A. Lawrence, 'The Short Cross coinage', *BNJ* 11 (1914)
— 'The Long Cross coinage of Henry III and Edward I', *BNJ* 9–11 (1912–14)
— 'The coinage of Edward III from 1351', *NC* 1926, 1929 & 1932
W. J. W. Potter, 'The gold coinages of Edward III', *NC* 1963

6 THE LATER PLANTAGENETS

C. E. Blunt & C. A. Whitton, 'The coinage of Edward IV and Henry VI (restored)', *BNJ* 25 (1945–7)

G. C. Brooke, 'Privy marks in the reign of Henry V', *NC* 1930

W. J. Potter, 'The silver coinages of Richard II, Henry IV and Henry V', *BNJ* 29–30 (1959–60)

P. F. Purvey, 'The pence, halfpence and farthings of Richard II, of the mints of London York and Durham', *BNJ* 31 (1962)

J. D. A. Thompson, 'Continental imitations of the rose nobles of Edward IV', *BNJ* 25 (1945–8)

C. A. Whitton, 'The heavy coinage of Henry VI', *BNJ* 23–24 (1938–44)

E. J. Winstanley, 'Angels and groats of Richard III', *BNJ* 24 (1941–4)

7 THE TUDORS

D. G. Borden & I. D. Brown, 'The milled coinage of Elizabeth I', *BNJ* 53 (1983)

I. D. Brown, 'Some notes on the coinage of Elizabeth I with special reference to her hammered silver', *BNJ* 28 (1955–7)

R. Carlyon–Britton, 'The last coinage of Henry VII', *BNJ* 18 (1925–26)

C. E. Challis, *Tudor Coinage* (Manchester 1978)

D. M. Metcalf, *Coins of Henry VII, Ashmolean Museum, Oxford, SCBI* 23 (London 1976)

W. J. Potter & E. J. Winstanley, 'The coinage of Henry VII', *BNJ* 30 (1961)

H. Symonds, 'The coinage of Queen Mary Tudor, 1553–8', *BNJ* 8 (1911)

C. A. Whitton, 'The coinages of Henry VIII and Edward VI in Henry's name', *BNJ* 26 (1949–51)

8 JACOBEAN TO COMMONWEALTH ENGLAND

D. F. Allen, 'The coinage of Cromwell and its imitations', *BNJ* 24 (1941–4)

G. C. Boon, *Cardiganshire Silver and the Aberystwyth Mint in Peace and War* (Cardiff 1981)

G. R. Francis, 'Silver coins of the Tower mint of Charles I', *BNJ* 12–15 (1916–20)

M. Lessen, 'A summary of Cromwell coinage', *BNJ* 35 (1966)

R. C. Lockett, 'Notes on the mints of Exeter and Truro under Charles I' *BNJ* 22(1934–7)

H. W. Morrieson, 'The coinages of Thomas Bushel', *BNJ* 10–20 (1913–30)

P. Nelson, 'The obsidional money of the Great Rebellion, 1642–1649', *BNJ* 2 (1905)

J. J. North & P. J. Preston–Morley, *The John Brooker Collection of Coins of Charles I* (London 1984)

H. Schneider, 'The Tower gold of Charles I', *BNJ* 28–30 (1956–61)

H. A. Seaby, 'Silver coins of James I', *Notes on English Silver Coins 1066–1648* (London 1948)

— 'Charles I–Tower silver coins', *Notes on English Silver Coins 1066–1648*

A. E. Weightman, 'The royal farthing tokens', *BNJ* 3 (1906)

G. C. Williamson, *Trade Tokens issued in the Seventeenth Century* (3 vols, reprinted London 1967)

9 THE RESTORATION TO THE GREAT RECOINAGE

T. B. H. Graham, 'Charles II's hammered silver coinage', *NC* 1911
— 'The recoinage of 1696–97', *NC* 1906
H. W. Morrieson, 'A review of the coinage of Charles II' *BNJ* 15 (1919–20)
P. Nelson, 'Notes on the Great Recoinage of William III', *BNJ* 3 (1906)
H. Schneider, 'The hammered gold coins of Charles II', *BNJ* 36 (1967)

10 THE EIGHTEENTH CENTURY

H. Apling, 'The "Lima" coinage of George II', *SCMB* March 1970
J. Atkins, *The Tradesmen's Tokens of the Eighteenth Century* (London 1892), for the
    listing of 'Imitation of the Regal Coinage', pp. 385–395
R. Dalton & S. H. Hamer, *The Provincial Token-Coinage of the 18th Century* (reprint
    London 1967)

11 THE NINETEENTH CENTURY

Annual Report of the Deputy-Master and Comptroller of the Royal Mint (London
    1870–1900)
R. C. Bell, *Copper Commercial Coins, 1811–1819* (Newcastle upon Tyne 1964)
— *Unofficial Farthings 1820–1870* (London 1975)
R. Dalton, *The Silver Token Coinage 1811–12* (London 1922)
W. J. Davis, *The Nineteenth Century Token Coinage* (reprint London 1969)
M. J. Freeman, *The Victorian Bronze Penny (1860–1901)* (n.d.)
H. Garside, *British Imperial Copper and Bronze Coinage* (London 1920, supplement
    1925)
W. J. Hocking, *Catalogue of the Coins, Tokens, Medals, Dies and Seals in the Museum
    of the Royal Mint* (2 vols, London 1906)
E. M. Kelly, *Spanish Dollars and Silver Tokens* (London 1976)
M. Phillips, *The Token Money of the Bank of England* (London 1976)
J. O. Sweeny, *A Numismatic History of the Birmingham Mint* (Birmingham 1981)

12 THE TWENTIETH CENTURY

Annual Report of the Deputy-Master and Comptroller of the Royal Mint
    (London 1901–1975)
G. P. Dyer, *The Proposed Coinage of King Edward VIII* (London 1973)
Report of the Committee of Inquiry on Decimal Currency (London 1963)

13 IRELAND

G. Coffey, *Guide to the Collection of Irish Antiquities (Royal Irish Academy
    Collection): Anglo-Irish Coins* (2nd ed., Dublin 1911)
M. Dolley, *Medieval Anglo-Irish Coins* (London 1972)
R. H. M. Dolley, *The Hiberno-Norse Coins in the British Museum*, *SCBI* 8 (London
    1966)
A. Dowle & P. Finn, *A Guide Book to the Coinage of Ireland* (London 1969)

J. Lindsay, *A View of the Coinage of Ireland* (Cork 1839)

P. Nelson, 'The coinage of Ireland in copper, tin and pewter', *BNJ* (reprint London 1905)

W. O'Sullivan, *The Earliest Anglo-Irish Coinage* (2nd ed., Dublin 1964)

P. Seaby & P. F. Purvey, *Standard Catalogue of British Coins: 2, Coins of Scotland Ireland and the Islands* (London 1984). With a select bibliography

W. A. Seaby, *Hiberno-Norse Coins, Ulster Museum, Belfast*, SCBI 32 (London 1984)

— *Anglo-Irish Coins: John-Edward III, Ulster Museum, Belfast*, SCBI 10 (London 1968)

W. B. Yeats & others, *The Coinage of the Saorstat Eireann* (Dublin 1928)

D. Young, *Coin Catalogue of Ireland 1722–1968* (Dublin 1969)

14 SCOTLAND

E. Burns, *The Coinage of Scotland* (3 vols, Edinburgh 1887)

R. W. Cochran-Patrick, *Records of the Scottish Coinage* (Edinburgh 1876)

H. L. Dakers, 'The first issue of David II', *BNJ* 32 (1941)

D. M. Metcalf (ed.), *Coinage in Medieval Scotland, 1100–1600* (B. A. R. Reports 45, 1977)

Mrs. J. E. L. Murray, 'The early unicorns and heavy groats of James III & IV', *BNJ* 40 (1971)

— 'The first gold coinage of Mary Queen of Scots', *BNJ* 49 (1979)

J. K. R. Murray, 'The Scottish silver coinage of Charles II', *BNJ* 38 (1969)

— 'The Scottish gold and silver coinage of Charles I', *BNJ* 39 (1970)

J. K. R. Murray & B. H. I. H. Stewart, 'The Scottish copper coinages 1642–1697', *BNJ* 41 (1972)

I. H. Stewart, *The Scottish Coinage* (2nd ed, London 1967)

— 'Scottish Mints', *Mints, Dies and Currency* (ed. R. A. G. Carson, London 1971)

P. Seaby & P. F. Purvey, *Standard Catalogue of British Coins: 2, Coins of Scotland, Ireland and the Islands* (London 1984)

15 MAN, LUNDY, WIGHT AND THE CHANNEL ISLANDS

C. Clay, 'On the brass, copper, and other currency of the Isle of Man', *Proc. Manchester Num Soc*, I–V (1864–7)

M. Dolley, 'A Hiberno-Manx coinage of the eleventh century', *NC* 1976

J. A. Mackay, *Isle of Man Coins and Tokens* (Sutton 1977)

W. Marshall-Fraser, 'The Coinages of the Channel Islands' *La Société Guernesiaise* Vol. 14 (1949)

A. L. T. McCammon, *Currencies of the Anglo-Norman Isles* (London 1984)

P. Nelson, 'Coinage of the Isle of Man', *NC* 1899

F. Pridmore, *The Coins of the British Commonwealth of Nations: 1, European Territories* (London 1960)

P. Seaby & P. F. Purvey, *Standard Catalogue of British Coins: 2, Scotland, Ireland and the Islands* (London 1984)

INDEX

With a few exceptions, types (designs) of coins are omitted from the index. The following abbreviations are used:

archb.	archbishop	emp.	emperor
bp.	bishop	k.	king
d.	duke, duchess	pr.	prince, princess
e.	earl	q.	queen

Art R